Indians in Color

This book is a product of my ethnographic imagination. Names, characters, places, events, and incidents are used fictitiously. Any resemblance to actual events, or locales, or persons, living or dead, is at least partially coincidental. The dialogue contained herein is intended as a stage play and should not be quoted or considered to be the actual words of the speakers unless a reference citation is given.

To be an Indian in modern American society, to see yourself in Hollywood films or in paintings by Western artists or in Wild West shows is in a very real sense to be unreal and ahistorical ... it is to be one of the vanquished, to be a person who has vanished, no longer visible.

Vine Deloria J (1969/1988, p. 2, paraphrase)

Indians in Color
Native Art, Identity, and Performance in the New West

Norman K. Denzin

LONDON AND NEW YORK

First published 2015 by Left Coast Press, Inc.

Published 2016 by Routledge
4 Park Square, Milton Park, Abingdon, Oxon OX14 4RN
605 Third Avenue, New York, NY 10017

Routledge is an imprint of the Taylor & Francis Group, an informa business

Copyright © 2015 Taylor & Francis

All rights reserved. No part of this book may be reprinted or reproduced or utilised in any form or by any electronic, mechanical, or other means, now known or hereafter invented, including photocopying and recording, or in any information storage or retrieval system, without permission in writing from the publishers.

Notice:
Product or corporate names may be trademarks or registered trademarks, and are used only for identification and explanation without intent to infringe.

Library of Congress Cataloging-in-Publication Data

Denzin, Norman K.
  Indians in color : native art, identity, and performance in the new West / Norman K. Denzin.
    pages cm
  Includes bibliographical references and index.
  ISBN 978-1-62958-278-8 (hardback : alk. paper)—ISBN 978-1-62958-280-1 (institutional eBook)—ISBN 978-1-62958-281-8 (consumer eBook)
  1. Indians in art. 2. Ethnicity in art. 3. Indians in popular culture—United States. 4. Indian art—20th century. 5. Indian art—21st century. 6. Taos Society of Artists. 7. Institute of American Indian Arts. I. Title.
  NX652.I53D46 2015
  704.03'97—dc23
                      2015015468

  ISBN-13: 978-1-62958-278-8 (hbk)
  ISBN-13: 978-1-62958-279-5 (pbk)

Contents

List of Plates		6
Acknowledgments		7
Dramatis Personae		9
Chapter 1	Native Art, Identity and Performance in the Postmodern West	15
Chapter 2	Disneyland Indians, Paris, circa 2014	37
Chapter 3	Copper-colored Primitives	65
Chapter 4	Taos Indians on Canvas	99
Chapter 5	Postmodern Indians on Canvas	125
Chapter 6	Indian Painters, Patrons, and Wild West Shows: A New Imaginary	151
Coda	Back to the Future	181
Appendix A	Time Line: Staging and Marketing American Indians, and Federal Indian Policy	185
Appendix B	The Taos Society of Artists and Their Descendants	193
Notes		195
References		211
Index		221
About the Author		229

Color plates appear after page 124.

List of Plates

1 Ernest L. Blumenschein, *Star Road and White Sun* (1920)

2 T. C. Cannon, *Mamma and Poppa Have the Going Home Shiprock Blues* (*circa* 1976)

3 T. C. Cannon, *Collector # 5* (1975)

4 Eanger Irving Couse, *Elk-Foot of the Taos Tribe* (1909)

5 Albert Lujan, untitled, *Taos Pueblo* (*circa* 1940)

6 Kevin Red Star, *Crow Indian Parade Rider* (1982)

7 Fritz Scholder, *Indian with Tomahawk* (1970)

Acknowledgments

For their contributions to this project I thank Mitch Allen, Katherine Ryan, Paul Atkinson, Sara Delamont, Johnny Saldana, Robert Rinehart, Larry Zimmerman, Sharon Irish, Shantel Martinez; Mary Robinson, Housel Director, and Sean Campbell, Image Rights and Reproductions, McCracken Research Library, Buffalo Bill Historical Center; and the curators and staff at the Eiteljorg Museum of American Indians and Western Art. All that is good in this book is due to Mitch Allen.

I thank Hannah Jennings for book design and production skills, Michael Jennings for copy editing and proofreading, and Ray Nader for the production of the index. I am most grateful to Kevin Dolan, James Salvo, and Nathalie Tiberghien for their patience and meticulous assistance with copyediting, layout, proofing and with the final production of the text. I also thank the students at the University of Illinois who patiently sat through formal and informal seminars, listening to earlier versions of my arguments about art, the politics of representation, Native Americans, the postmodern West, performance ethnography, cultural studies, politics and pedagogy. Finally, I gratefully acknowledge the moral, intellectual and financial support given this project by the past and current directors of the Institute of Communications Research, Clifford Christians, Paula Treichler, Angharad N. Valdivia, and William Berry.

Dramatis Personæ

These characters appear throughout the plays in this book.

Adams, Kenneth Miller—artist

Alexie, Sherman—contemporary American Indian writer from Spokane/Coeur d' Alene

Allen, Mitch—cultural archaeologist and publisher

Baca, Elmo—New Mexico State Historic Preservation Officer

Benjamin, Walter (1892–1940)—German philosopher and cultural critic

Berninghaus, Oscar E.— artist

Blumenschein, Ernest—artist

Brass, Ferlyn—Native performer (Key First Nation, Saskatchewan)[1] in Disneyland Paris

Brenneman, Jina—curator, Harwood Museum

Brindza, Christina C.—curator, Whitney Gallery of Western Art

Brody, J. J.—art historian

Brooka, Van Wyck (1866–1963)—American literary critic

Brooks, Mel—actor, director

Bruised Head, Tom—Native performer (Peigan Nation and Blood Nation, Alberta) in Disneyland Paris

Buffalo Bill, aka William Cody (1846–1917)—performer extraordinaire

Carson, Kit (1809–1868)—American frontiersman and Indian fighter

Couse, Eanger Irving—artist

Mr. Coyote—Navajo trickster

Ms. Coyote—Navajo trickster

de Jesus, Juan—carpenter, model

Deloria, Philip—historian, author of *Playing Indian* (1998) and *Indians in Unexpected Places* (2004)

Deloria, Vine, Jr. (Dakota Sioux)—American Indian activist, author of *Custer Died for Your Sins* (1969/1988)

Denzin, Norman K., aka author

Depp, Johnny—Native performer

Durand-Ruel, Auguste—good friend of Buffalo Bill and announcer in Paris Disney Wild West shows

Dust, Kevin (Kave)—Native performer (Alexis First Nation)[1] in Disneyland Paris

Eaton, Marjorie (1901–1986)—American actress, painter and Juan Mirabal's partner

Eiteljorg, Harrison—carpenter, model

Fassnacht, Annette—art critic, Santa Fe New Mexican

Fried, Stephen—cultural historian, author of book on Fred Harvey

Giroux, Henry—American and Canadian scholar and cultural critic, and one of the founding theorists of critical pedagogy in the United States

Gorman. R. C. (1931–2005)—Navajo artist

Gover, Kevin (Pawnee/Comanche)—Director, National Museum of the American Indian

Graburn, Nelson, H. H.—anthropologist of art

Graves, Jen—author of "Maybe Don't Wear a Warbonnet to the First-ever All-Native Art Exhibit at Bumbershoot, and Don't Trip Over Custer"

⚏ Dramatis Personæ

Greene, Graham—Native Canadian (Oneida) actor whose film credits include *Thunderheart* (1992), *Maverick* (1994), *Winter's Tale* (2014)

Harrison, Carter—Native performer

Hassrick, Peter—art historian

Hennings, E. Martin—artist

Hewett, Edgar L. (1865–1946)—anthropologist, archaeologist, founder and first director of the Museum of New Mexico

Higgins, W. Victor—artist

Highwater, Jamake—art critic

Hogue, Alexander—Sante Fe Museum director

Hombre—Hollywood Indian

Jung, C. C.—psychoanalyst

Kovach, Margaret—scholar

Kramer, Kevin—employee of Disneyland Little Beaver

Lawrence, D. H.—novelist

Looking Elk (Martinez), Albert (1888–1940)—Native Taos artist

Luhan, Mabel Dodge—art patron

Lujan, Albert (1892–1948)—Native Taos artist

Lujan, Vernon G.—museum exhibition consultant, Native Taos artist

McBride, Henry—modernist art critic

McNenly, Linda Scarangella—anthropologist

Mickey and Minnie Mouse, Disney characters—for copyright purposes for this text, aka William and Alice Red Cloud

Minnehaha—fictional Native American woman documented in Henry Wadsworth Longfellow's 1855 epic poem, "The Song of Hiawatha"

Mirabal, Eva (Eah-Ha-Wa)—artist

Mirabal, Juan (1903–1970)—Native Taos artist

Mustus, Kevin (Wiley)— Native performer (Alexis First Nation) in Disneyland Paris[1]

New, Lloyd Kiva (1916–2002)—Cherokee, artist, designer, co-founder (1982) of Institute of American Indian Arts

Oakley, Annie (1860–1926)—performer in Buffalo Bill's Wild West Show

O'Keefe, Georgia (1887–1986)—artist

Parks, Stephen (1944–2013)—owner of Parks Gallery, Taos

Parsons, Elsie (1875-1941) anthropologist

Phillips, Bert—artist

Phillips, Ruth, Director of Museum Anthropology and Professor of Fine Art and Anthropology, University of British Columbia

Pocahontas (1595–1617)—Powhatan, aka, Amonute; later married an English Settler and was renamed Rebbecca Rolfe; became a princess in 1995 Disney film

Raheja, Michelle H.—author, *Reservation Reelism: Redfacing, Visual Sovereignty and Representations of Native Americans in Film* (2010); English professor

Rangel, Ernest—Navajo recruiter and performer for Disneyland Paris[1]

Red Cloud, Anthony—fictional performer in Euro-Disney Wild West Show

Red Cloud, William and Alice—see Mickey and Minnie Mouse

Red Star, Kevin (1943–)—Crow artist

Red Star, Wendy—Crow Indian cultural archivist and performance artist who explores the experience of being a Crow Indian in contemporary society

Reeves, Tom—Euro-Disney consultant

Said, Edward (1935–2003), literary theorist

Schimmel, Julie—art historian

Scholder, Fritz (1937–2005)—Native American (one-quarter Luiseño) painter

Seventh Generation Performers (SGP), from the seventh generation principle (Iroquois)—the decisions we make today should be assessed in terms of their effects seven generations into the future

⊞ Dramatis Personæ

Sharp, Joseph Henry—artist

Sitting Bull (aka Tatanka-Iyotanka)—Lakota chief who led the defeat of Custer

Ghost of Sitting Bull

Secagawea (1788–?)—Lemhi Shoshone woman who accompanied the Lewis and Clark Expedition

Silverheels, Mark (1912–1980)—Mohawk, Disney performer, fictional son of Jay, who was well known for playing Tonto in the Lone Ranger radio and television series

Simpson, William H.—advertising director for the Atchison Topeka and Santa Fe Railway

Smith, Paul Chaat—curator, Smithsonian National Museum of the American Indian

Suspaman, aka Christian Parish Takes the Gun—flute player, drummer, powwow dancer, hiphop artist from Crow Agency

Taylor, Bradley F.—art historian and collector

Tonto—fictional American Indian sidekick of Lone Ranger

Turner, Pauline Strong—professor of anthropology and gender studies

Ufer, Walter—artist

Vizenor, Gerald (Minnesota Chippewa)—professor, Native American writer

Wasserberger, Leslie—art historian/critic and artist

Watson, Samuel E., III.—historian of Native American art

Welch, James (1940–2003)—award-winning Native American author (Blackfoot/Gros Venre) of *Killing Custer* (1994), *Winter in the Blood* (1974), and *The Heartsong of Charging Elk* (2000)

Wheelwright, Mary Cabot (1878–1958)—heiress, wealthy art patron who supported Albert Looking Elk Martinez's work

White Deer, Waylon Gary (Choctaw Nation)—professor of Choctaw Studies at Bacone College, Oklahoma; internationally known painter

Witt, David L—curator, expert on the three Taos Pueblo painters

Yellowbird, Carter—Native recruiter for Disneyland Paris[1]

Yashi, Demian Dine—artist, performer

CHAPTER ONE
Native Art, Identity and Performance in the Postmodern West

Historically, the role of the Indian artist has been primarily that of a performer, working from a script written by whites (Brody, 1971, p. 179, slight paraphrase).

It was primarily through the work of a group of 12 painters known as the Taos Society of Artists (TSA) that America began its 20th-century romance with the Southwest and its Indians (Peters, 1988, p. 1; see also Taggett and Schwarz, 1990, p. 3).[1] This romance built on an infatuation that had been established in the 19th century with the paintings of Native Americans done by George Catlin, Charles Bird King, Alfred Jacob Miller, Karl Bodmer, and John Mix Stanley.

Indians in Color: Native Art, Identity, and Performance in the New West by Norman K. Denzin, 15–36. © 2015 Taylor & Francis. All rights reserved.

INDIANS IN COLOR

Carter Henry Harrison (1860–1953): five-term Chicago mayor (1897–1905, 1911–1915), art patron to TSA artists, letter to Walter Ufer, member of the Taos Society of Artists:

> Walter, I can take a couple of your paintings this year. I want one of either the Santa Cruz or the Ranches of Taos Church. I would like an Indian on horseback crossing the sage brush with either mountains or a pueblo building showing in the background and painted towards dusk—no color except a suggestion of red in the horizon & turquoise blue in the upper sky.
>
> Walter, Please paint your Indians a little darker—the Chicago public does not know that the Pueblo Indians are not as dark colored as the ordinary Red Man and consequently think you off in your color. Another thing, paint in color that shows better under artificial light. Your yellows are beautiful by day, but look off at night in electric light. (Bickerstaff, 1955a, p. 142)

I've told this story before. Since an early age I have been a cultural tourist in the postmodern West. In the 1950s my brother Mark and I spent our summers, until we were young teenagers, with our grandparents on their farm south of Iowa City, Iowa. Saturday nights were special. Grandpa loved those "Cowboy and Indian" movies, and so did I. Every Saturday Grandma fixed an early supper. After supper, Grandpa and I, wearing going-to-town-clothes, drove to Iowa City to catch the first movie of a double-feature at the Strand Theatre starring John Wayne, or Glen Ford, or Henry Fonda, or Jimmy Stewart. It was a grand movie palace, Italian Renaissance style; a large canopy with yellow and red striped awnings extended from the building to the curb. Rich draperies and colorful movie posters adorned the lobby. The ceiling dome was finished in gold and silver leaf. Huge chandeliers hung from the ceiling. Grandpa and I always tried to get one of the box seats, the best seat in the house he said.

We'd time our arrival to town to allow for a stroll up and down Clinton and College Avenues, always seeing this neighbor or that

Chapter I ⁘ Native Art, Identity and Performance in the Postmodern West

neighbor, catching up on gossip, talk about rain, crops, the market price of beef or pork, whether corn would be shoulder high by the 4th. Then we'd hurry to get in line to buy our tickets to the movie.

Today, I dream myself back into those soft summer nights in cool darkness, nighttime dreams of cowboys, Indians, the cavalry, six-guns, stage coaches, barroom ladies, and school marms, and blonde-haired little boys running after a lonely rider on a horse. "Shane, Shane, Shane, come back." I still remember the names of the movies: *Stage Coach, Broken Arrow, Colt 45, She Wore a Yellow Ribbon, Winchester '73, High Noon, Naked Spur, Searchers, Far Country, Bend of the River,* and *Shane,* the only film I ever watched with my father. We'd leave by 6:00 and often not get back until after 11:00, especially if we stayed for the double feature. The house would be quiet when we got back home; Grandma and Mark would be in bed. And we'd whisper and tiptoe as we came up the stairs, so as not to awaken anyone.

It was always the same movie, bad Indians, good cowboys, dead Indians, dead cowboys. The Indians always looked the same: dark brown skin, bare chests, straight black hair, bows, arrows, bareback riders on swift horses, buckskin clothing, fancy headdresses, tom toms beating in the background, tipis, woman called squaws, happy little children playing along the river bank, barking dogs in the village. Always the same movie. Always the same Indians.

I wanted to be a cowboy when I grew up. So did Mark, I think. I don't know about Grandpa. He could be anybody he wanted to be. On Saturday mornings, while Grandma made hot doughnuts for us in the new deep-fat fryer in her big country kitchen, we watched "Cowboy and Indian" television shows: "The Lone Ranger," "Red Rider and Little Beaver," "Roy Rogers and Dale Evans," "Sky King." Mark and I had cowboy outfits—wide-brimmed hats, leather vests, chaps, spurs, little pistols, and gun belts. Grandpa bought us a horse. There is a picture of Mark and me in our cowboy outfits on the back of sway-backed Sonny, the horse who was deaf in the right ear. In fourth grade I was Squanto in the Thanksgiving play about the Pilgrims. When we played cowboys and Indians, sometimes I was an Indian—Tonto, or Little Beaver.[2] Sometimes I was the Lone Ranger or Red Rider. I could be anyone

I wanted to be. And this is the point, as Philip Deloria reminds us; I could be a hobby Indian, a white boy playing Indian (1998, pp. 128–129). I had that right. I could be Squanto, or Little Beaver, or Tonto, or Red Rider, or the Lone Ranger. At a moment's notice I could appropriate an Indian identity for myself.

In 1987 my wife and I spent three weeks vacationing in Red Lodge, Montana. We've returned every year, and in 1994 bought a small cabin 60 miles from Cody, Wyoming, and the Buffalo Bill Historical Center (BBHC). The BBHC became a research site in 1995 when I started focusing on the paintings of Native artists, including Fritz Scholder (Luiseno), Kevin Red Star (Crow), R. C. Gorman (Navajo), and T. C. Cannon (Kiowa, Choctaw) in the Whitney Gallery of Western Art. At the same time I was examining the exhibits devoted to Buffalo Bill, his Wild West Show and the presence of Lakota and Oglala Sioux in his show, including Sitting Bull.

In 2011 the Indianapolis Eiteljorg Museum of American Indians and Western Art in Indianapolis became a second research site because of the attention it gave to early 20th-century Southwestern Anglo Art, especially the paintings of Indians made by the Taos Society of Artists (see Appendix B). Of special interest were the ways in which these two museums located Western Art, Anglo painters, Native Americans, and the American West on a global stage. As I looked at many of the paintings of Indians in those two museums I saw versions of the same Indians I had watched as a young child in the Strand Theatre in Iowa City. It was as if I was back in my childhood. Time stood still. Indians everywhere.

This book, part performance text, part historical ethnodrama, part autoethnography, comes out of the intersection of these childhood memories with these repeated visits to the BBHC, and the Eiteljorg.[3] Hours spent looking at Indians and cowboys. How do I name these feelings; guilt, sadness, longing? Henhawk (2013, p. 519) cuts to the chase. He says these feelings represent another one of the ironies of white privilege and white guilt. Here I am, writing my way out of a past

Chapter 1 ⚙ Native Art, Identity and Performance in the Postmodern West

that was handed to me by the media, Hollywood, post-World War Two American culture, my grandfather, his dreams, his fantasies, and my own life as a critic of the West. But this life has taken me to the contemporary Postmodern West and its great regional museums where Indians and their identities still live. I linger here in these spaces of memory, Wild West Shows, and museums, performing my way out of a West I do not want to be part of.

This Project: Redfacing and Three Aesthetic Moments

So I write another chapter in an undoing of the past. *Indians in Color: Native Art,*[4] *Identity and Performance in the Postmodern West* continues my critique of the treatment of Native Americans[5] in art, museums, and Wild West shows in the contemporary West. It extends the project started in my 2013 book, *Indians on Display: Global Commodification of Native Americans in Performance, Art and Museums,* namely the examination of the commodification through performance and art of Native Americans in the colonial and postcolonial west. *Indians in Color* is a study in the politics of memory, art, race and performance.

Specifically, I examine the representations of Native Americans produced in three historical moments, by three groups of artists: the European-trained Taos Society of Artists (1898–1927); the 'tourist' paintings of three Indigenous Taos Pueblo Painters, who modeled for TSA painters (1920–1950); and the so-called Chapter Three Artists[6] (1960–): Fritz Scholder, R. C. Gorman, Kevin Red Star. The Chapter Three Artists taught in, or were trained in, the Institute of American Indian Art, Santa Fe (see Appendix B). The Chapter Three painters produced a radical postmodern artistic aesthetic that challenged the romantic Noble Savage created by the TSA. I co-mingle these moments and their images with scenes from the cowboy and Indian movies of my childhood.

These three artistic formations—modern, pre-modern, postmodern[7]— offer competing versions of America's 20th- and 21st-century Native American. It is necessary to revisit the history and politics behind these three discourses. Doing so permits a critical appraisal of how Native Americans should be represented today.

Reading Race

A complex argument organizes my reading of these three artistic movements.[8] The artistic representations of Native Americans have always been about colonial privilege, about race, about dark-skinned bodies, about how white and Native artists represent the bodies of persons of color—red, dark skin, brown, black, tan. It has always been about the uses of racialized visual languages grounded in popular culture and its codes and discourses, including film, music, literature, ethnography, paintings, Wild West minstrel shows, and Indianist reenactments (Kalshoven, 2015). This is what Raheja calls "redfacing," that is, the politics of creating and preserving images of a vanishing dark-skinned Indian and Noble Savage for a white audience, a form of privileged ethnic spectatorship (2010, p. xiii). Through the middle of the 20th century this visual language of color was used by Native and non-native artists alike. The same Indian, two sets of creators (see Dunn, 1968, pp. 362–368; Hoffman, 1986).

Indeed, until the emergence of the Institute of American Indian Art (IAIA)[9] in Santa Fe in 1962, modern Indian art was art primarily produced by Native Americans for white patrons using artistic techniques taught by white instructors (Brody, 1971; Eldredge, Schimmel, and Truettner, 1986; Sims, 2008a). After 1962 a new aesthetic emerged, a post-modern, postindian[10] Indian art, a radical art that celebrated Indian identity, even as it depicted Indians as victims of an oppressive white culture (Gibson and Leaken, 2014). This new art was consumed by a new generation of celebrity patrons,[11] elevating Native artists like R. C. Gorman and Fritz Scholder to the status of pop icons, Indigenous Andy Warhols.[12]

Production Sites

This Native art, its history, production and subject-matter, is anchored in Taos, the Taos Pueblo,[13] and Santa Fe, New Mexico, the home of IAIA. It must be read through the politics operating in these sites. The interpretation of this new art must also be written through the culture and rituals of the Taos Indians. They fiercely protected their sacred rituals, and did not allow the practice of their rituals to be witnessed

Chapter 1 ⚏ Native Art, Identity and Performance in the Postmodern West

by Anglo artists or anthropologists (Parsons, 1936, p. 4; 1962, pp. 1–2). Hence, an idealized Taos Indian was produced by Anglo painters, an Indian who would be un-done by the new generation of Native painters trained in Santa Fe at IAIA.

The subject of this new art is explicitly political. It is radically subjective. It raises key questions:

Whose racialized Indian is being painted?

Can white artists any longer claim any right at all, contested or not, to paint Native Americans?

Can the legacies of this art, which are now not so new, serve to advance an agenda of empowerment: can they function as an aesthetic pedagogy of liberation (Friere, 1992)?

These are the central questions I examine in this book.

Disneyland, Wild West Shows and Paintings of Indians

My narrative unfolds in five interconnected chapters plus this chapter.

The following quote from Ernest Blumenschein (1898), founding member of TSA, provides a segue to Chapter Two. Blumenschein's short article appeared in *Harper's Weekly* on April 30, 1898. He had attended a Buffalo Bill Wild West Show at Madison Square Garden. Before the show he mingled back stage with Indian performers. After the show he wrote:

> Bedouins are whirling and tumbling through the dust and sunshine; scene-painters are retouching the marvelous blue mountains; Mexicans and Cubans and Cowboys lazily willing away the early morning hours. A young Indian writes a letter ... directed to Miss Alice Lone Bear, Pine Ridge Agency, South Dakota ... I enter a large room. Several ugly-looking bucks push me around while a few old men arrange feathers in a new war bonnet ... All connected with the show eat in a great room on the ground floor. Here in their working-clothes, or in the picturesque attire of their homes (for Cossack, Mexican and Indian refuse civilized costume) ... After dinner is over preparations for the evening performance begin.

With pigments, a good Indian type is made hideous in a short interval—bodies and limbs are painted half white, half green, or with circles, and crescents, and stars. The feathers come off the wall, sleigh bells jingle and tinkle, the squaws 'ti-ti' in their high shrill voices. A blast from a bugle starts them off to saddle their ponies on which they are soon mounted for the grand entry. The cowboy band starts up 'Hail, Columbia,' the bugle sounds again, the great canvas curtain is drawn, and the howling warriors dash wildly into the pubic gaze.[14]

Blumenschein would soon gravitate from writing short articles about Wild West shows to illustrating Indian stories by Stephen Crane and Hamlin Garland for *McClure's Magazine* and *Harper's Weekly* (Cunningham, 2008, pp. 26–27).[15] Sadly, the Buffalo Bill Wild West Show he described in 1898 is still going on in Paris in 2014.

Blumenschein's observations of Native Americans in Buffalo Bill's Wild West Show perfectly illustrates Raheja's (2010) arguments concerning "redfacing" and the intersection of art and performance in 20th- and 21st-century America:

Stemming from a long tradition of staged performances such as The Wild West shows that were themselves informed by American Literature's obsession with Native American plots and subplots, film and visual culture [art] have provided the primary representational field on which Native American images have been displayed to dominant culture audiences in the twentieth and twenty-first centuries. These representations have also been key to formulating Indigenous people's own self images.[16]

From the 19th century forward, the Wild West show, with its alignments with visual culture—advertising, art and painting, film—was the cultural engine that reproduced redfacing for American popular culture.

Chapter Two, "Disneyland Indians, Paris, circa 2014," starts with Graham Greene on a YouTube video reading the call for Native performers to audition for the Disneyland Buffalo Bill Wild West Show in Paris. Scenes of poverty from the Pine Ridge Reservation appear on the screen. It seems that when we talk about Native Americans, art,

Chapter 1 ⚏ Native Art, Identity and Performance in the Postmodern West

painters, and the West, we can never get too far from Buffalo Bill and his minstrel show. Disneyland lurks in the background (see Giroux and Pollock, 2010). Like in this recent advertisement.

Disneyland Paris Seeks New Recruits for Wild West Show, April 2014

Disneyland Paris is auditioning locally for Cowboys and Indians with exceptional horsemanship skills for the facility's new musical extravaganza, Buffalo Bill's Wild West Show ... with Mickey[17] and Friends. The western-themed spectacle, which still features Buffalo Bill, Sitting Bull, Annie Oakley, and a multitude of Cowboys and Indians, replaced the long running original production on April 4th last year at the grand premiere in Paris, France. This time around, Sheriff Mickey and a cast of Disney's beloved characters have joined the adventure.[18]

Wendy Red Star, Crow Indian cultural activist and performance artist, offers an alternative view, focusing on performances and artworks that contest images of the vanishing dark-skinned Indian.

I've created my own version of a Wild West Show. I call it *Wendy Star's Wild West & Congress of Rough Riders of the World*.[19] It will be held in the Fisher Pavilion, Seattle, August 30–September 1, 2014. My show combines performance, and art. I have Indian artists, painters, fancy dancers. I tell the story of the West from the Indian's point of view. We re-enact the Battle of Little Big Horn. Our show and artists challenge the representations of the west currently being staged by Wild West Paris Disneyland. It's time to stop this Disneyland travesty, even if Disney does hire Native Americans as performers.

This four-act historical ethnodrama critiques Paris Disneyland, the Buffalo Bill Wild West Show and its use of Native Americans as re-enactors of a Wild West that never was.[20] Drawing on Pirandello's *Six Characters in Search of an Author* (1921/1998a), the play uses the voices of Native Americans drawn from popular culture—Tonto, Pocahontas, Little Beaver, Minnehaha, Secagawea, Hombre. These characters are Indigenous activists, and they are asking for an author who will write a play that deals with real Indians and their plight. The activists, along with avatars, disrupt the performances that occur in the Disneyland Wild West Show. As the curtain comes down Count Basie's "April in Paris" (from the movie, *Blazing Saddles*, 1974) plays over the sound system. The Seventh Generation Performers join hands with the Indian activists and slowly dance around the stage. The theatre goes dark. The audience breaks out in cheers.

The play asks if new stories of the West can be performed, and if so, how. While the critique in this chapter is situated in Paris Disneyland, it could as easily be located in Disney Parks in Tokyo, London, or Rust, Baden-Wurttemberg, Germany. These global Wild West shows, with audience participation, enact recurring fantasies of colonial domination over Native Americans. By performing its own reflexive critique, my play is intended to mimic the Paris Wild West Show and expose this ideology. The criticisms are also intended to apply to Anglo paintings of Native Americans and mainstream Hollywood movies that represent Indians (see Hearne, 2012 a, b; Howe, 2013a).

Chapter Three, "Copper-Colored Primitives," contests the paintings of the twelve artists who were founding members of the Taos Society of Artists. This group produced a body of work (more than 400 paintings) that is popular and important to the present day (see Broder, 1980, pp. 312–321; Goodman and Dawson, 2008; Hassrick, 2008, 2009a, b; Lujan, 2003; Witt, 2003a, b). The TSA paintings of Taos Indians were presented to the public as accurate representations of an ancient, but dying culture. These paintings presented a unified Indian subject who was in danger of disappearing. The TAS painters helped turned Taos into a tourist site where their art and the material artifacts of Pueblo culture could be bought and sold.

Step back in time. Broder, the historian of art and the American West, locates the TSA project in its historical moment:

> After the final defeat of the Indians at the Battle of Wounded Knee and the surrender of Sitting Bull in 1890, Indians no longer had to be feared.[21] Throughout the West they were confined to reservations. Many artists sentimentalized a defeated race and became interested in scenes of the ceremonial and daily life of aboriginals

Chapter 1 ⚉ Native Art, Identity and Performance in the Postmodern West

who lived peacefully with nature ... Several of the early Taos artists were romantics who wished to celebrate the idealized West of the past ... the idyllic life of the noble Indian living in harmony with nature. (1980, pp. 6–8, 215, paraphrase)

Walter Ufer, a member of the Taos Society of Artists, extends Broder and inserts a bitter irony into the situation:

The Society of Taos Artists refused to paint the Taos Indians as a people who had been defeated and Americanized and turned into passive, dejected people, second-class citizens living on the edges in the white man's world. Instead they romanticized the Taos Indian, creating a Noble savage at home in a western landscape. Ironically the Indians they turned into noble savages were in fact poor laborers, and servants working as models for TSA artists. (Walter Ufer, in Broder, 1980, p. 215, paraphrase)

The Atchison, Topeka and Santa Fe Railroad commissioned artwork by the TSA painters. They wanted Indians painted in a certain way. They turned these paintings into advertisements promoting tourism in the Southwest. The play sets up a critical dialogue between the TSA painters, who wanted to be recognized as true artists, approved by Anglo art critics, and members of the Taos Pueblo who served as models for the TSA artists and their commercial artwork and challenged the value of Western critics approving of TSA art.

Taos Pueblo Indians and Indigenous painters contest the way Taos Indians and Taos culture were represented by the TSA and by Elsie Parsons, a Columbia trained anthropologist. They critique Parsons, who criticized them for being too modern. Georgia O'Keeffe mediates an imaginary verbal dispute between Elsie and Albert Looking Elk Martinez. The play culminates in a play within a play, "A Protest on San Geronimo Feast Day, " performed by the Seventh Generation Performers (SGP),[22] Coyote, Ms. Coyote, the Forgotten Taos Painters, Carl Jung, and the San Geronimo Clowns. The fictional performance takes place in the Taos Pueblo on San Geronimo Feast Day, September 30, 2015.[23]

The work of the Taos Society of Artists is alive and well today. Their paintings hang in the Indianapolis Eiteljorg Museum of American

Indians and Western Art.[24] Indeed, the Eiteljorg has an entire room devoted to the work of the Taos Society of Artists, including paintings by Joseph Sharp, Bert Phillips, Ernest Blumenschein, E. I. Couse, Oscar Berninghaus, and Herbert "Buck" Dunton (see www.harwood-museum. org/collections/taos-society).[25]

The history of art in Taos, up until the present, has been written almost entirely through the eyes and works of white artists. The history inevitably starts with the stories of the founding members of the Taos Society of Artists, then moves to Georgia O'Keeffe and the post-war Taos Moderns, then to the work of contemporary Anglo artists, including Peter Parks, Agnes Martin, Jen Price, and Larry Bell (see Shipley and Weller, 1969; Weller, Donavan, et al. 1948–1963; Witt, 1992; also www.harwoodmuseum.org/collections/contemporary).[26]

Chapter Four, "Taos Indians on Canvas," challenges this official history by taking up three Indigenous Taos artists, Albert Lujan, Albert Looking Elk Martinez and Juan Mirabal, who until recently were not included in the story of Taos art scene. While they started out as models for TSA painters, they soon became artists in their own right. But their art was dismissed as the work of untrained primitives. The two Alberts and Juan responded by successfully marketing their own art. Their paintings challenged the work of the TSA painters and were an authentic Indigenous expression of the Pueblo and its values.[27]

In 2003 the Harwood Museum of Art of the University of New Mexico in Taos organized a three month exhibition of the work of three Indigenous Taos Pueblo painters: Albert Looking Elk Martinez, Albert Lujan, and Juan Mirabal (see Witt, 2003a, b). These three painters were anomalies in the history of Santa Fe and Taos art. They were excluded, until 2003, from the history of Southwest Indian painting. Their work was defined as unschooled and derivative and not worthy of white patronage or gallery sponsorship (see www.tfaoi.com/aa/3aa/3aa495. htm). Today, it is respected and collected for its naturalistic realistic style (see Baca, 2003; Lujan, 2003; Witt, 2003b).

Chapter Five, "Postmodern Indians on Canvas," focuses on the Institute of American Indian Art and the radical art of Fritz Scholder, R. C. Gorman, and Kevin Red Star, aka Third Chapter Artists. It re-visits the founding moment of the TSA, when Ernest Blumenschein, fresh from his experiences with the Buffalo Bill Wild West Show in New York City, made his way down the mountain to Taos after his wagon broke down. Here, he discovers his dark skinned subject in Taos, launching a history that is still alive today.

The Institute of American Indian Art, under the leadership of Lloyd Kiva New, created a space for a new art to emerge, what Gerald Vizenor (1999, 2008) would call "postindian"—a new radical Indian free of colonial trappings. This new art was framed in part by the energy of the anti-Vietnam war protests and the growth of the American Indian Movement. Fritz Scholder re-visited the tragedy of Wounded Knee and Custer's Last Stand and painted drunk Indians and vampires. Kevin Red Star worked with images from the pre- and post-reservation period, including tipis, warriors on horses, reservation policemen, fancy dancers wearing beaded leggings seen on pairs of Levi-Strauss blue jeans. He transformed these images and symbols into decorative postmodern collages of elegant, somber and joyous Indians outside time (Hoffman, 1986, p. 266).

T. C. Cannon's "Collector # 5 or Osage with Van Gogh" (woodblock print on rice paper) shows an elegantly dressed Osage in his wicker chair between a Navajo rug and Van Gogh's painting, "Wheatfield," which is hanging on the wall behind him (Hoffman, 1986, p. 267). Here two art worlds exist side-by-side—high modernist art and postmodern Native art. Cannon's painting says modern Indians make their own art and are comfortable moving through different art worlds (Hoffman, 1986, p. 267).

In April 2013 the Harwood Museum of Art celebrated the Third Chapter of the Taos Art Colony, honoring the work of Native artists Fritz Scholder, R. C. Gorman, and Woody Crumbo, and Anglo painter Jim Wagner (see www.harwood museum.org/news/view/4 5). This group of Native artists took control of the representation of Indians; they created a new postmodern Indian.

In 2008 an exhibition titled "Fritz Scholder: Indian/not Indian" was held concurrently at the Smithsonian Institution's National Museum of the American Indian and the George Gustav Heye Center in

New York City. A volume of the same name was published the same year (Sims, 2008). Scholder's Indian paintings could be interpreted as a direct challenge to the romantic Indian of the Taos Society of Artists. (See nmai.si.edu/exhibitions/scholder/biography.html.)

Chapter Five culminates in a one-act play, "Native Artists Attempt to Take Back the Day." The Seventh Generation Performers, along with the San Geronimo Clowns, praise the work of the Third Chapter artists. Supaman, a contemporary Crow nation musician, fancy dances across the stage. The play culminates in a dialogue about the exhibits of TSA art in the Eiteljorg Museum. R. C. Gorman, Fritz Scholder and Kevin Red Star lead a protest, calling for a new art that has yet to be imagined.

This art will no longer require, as art once did, the death of one kind of Indian painting and the death of one kind of Indian painter and the birth of a new painter who happens to be Indian (Highwater, 1986, p. 241). It requires only a commitment to the tradition already established by Scholder, Red Star, Cannon, Gorman and their heirs.

My themes all come back together in Chapter Six, "Indian Painters, Patrons, and Wild West Shows: A New Imaginary." The chapter begins with a dialogue over what is Indian Art and who has the authority to paint an Indian, and examines the three questions raised earlier in this chapter:

Whose racialized Indian is being painted?

Can white artists any longer claim the uncontested right to paint Native Americans?

Can the legacies of this art, which is now not so new, serve to advance an agenda of empowerment; can it function as a pedagogy of liberation?

The play unfolds as a series of imaginary dialogues between the Disney characters Mickey and Minnie, the Seventh Generation Performers, Buffalo Bill, Tonto, Johnny Depp, Coyote, Ms. Coyote, Ernest Blumenschein, Elsie Parsons, the two Alberts and Juan, Fritz, R. C., Kevin, Gerrald Vizenor, and contemporary Native artist, Wendy Red Star.[28] The characters review the ways in which 20th- and 21st-century

Chapter I ⊞ Native Art, Identity and Performance in the Postmodern West

painters and traveling Wild West minstrel shows turned Native Americans into commodities and sold them to a global audience.

Earlier themes are revisited: performance, colonialism, museums, Wild West shows, co-mingled fantasies, Mickey and Minnie Mouse, Buffalo Bill, Sitting Bull, global capital paying artists to paint only a certain kind of Indian. The TSA artists sold the West, or rather the Southwest, by painting a particular kind of Indian (Taggett and Schwartz, 1990). The Taos Indian was a marketable commodity. Ernest Blumenschein and his fellow artists hired Indians to pose as models and staged them in Western landscapes. Indeed, through their paintings the TSA school supplied the necessary imagery for the establishment of Taos and Santa Fe as national tourist sites.

They said they were doing more than railroad art. They said they were following in the footprints of Gauguin and Van Gogh; the Taos Indian was their primitive. But were they really anything more than railroad artists selling images of Indians to the highest bidder? Doesn't their Taos Indian get folded into new performative spaces, into new sites of consumption—advertisements for the AT&SF railroad, art galleries, art shows, museums, even Wild West shows where AT&SF railroad calendars and postcards were sold?

Vine Deloria, Jr., discusses the implications of representations such as these for how whites approach the lives of real Indians:

> Understanding Indians is not an esoteric art. All it takes is a trip through Arizona or New Mexico, watching a documentary on TV, having known *one* in the service, or having read a popular book on them.... Rarely is physical contact required. There is no subject on earth so easily understood as that of the American Indian. (1969/1988, p. 5, italics in original)

Chapter Six brings the work of contemporary aboriginal re-enactment artists up against these lingering colonial cultural formations. It seeks to chart a new beginning, a new way of thinking about how the West might have been painted, and hence won. I want to do more than found a new museum, one where whites are on exhibit and Native Americans are the tourists. I want to discover a wild Native art that finally breaks free of five hundred years of colonial oppression. I want a Native art that imagines its way into utopian spaces that have yet to be (Graves, 2014; Strong, 2013). The play ends with a new anthem, "Bury My Art at Wounded Knee"[29] (see www.tumblr.com/search/Radical Indigenous Survivance & Empowerment).[30]

A Coda, "Back to the Future," questions my place in this narrative while celebrating the concept of survivance (Vizenor, 2008) embodied in the work of the Forgotten Taos Pueblo Painters and the Chapter Three artists.

It's all here in these five chapters and coda: art worlds (Becker, 1982), performance, colonialism, museums, Native art, whites painting Indians, tourist consumption, Wild West shows, global capital constructing and selling 19th-century images of Indianness, Indians as hostile, blood thirsty savages, co-mingling fantasies, Mickey Mouse, Buffalo Bill, Sitting Bull, Wendy Red Star and her contested views of the Wild West.

Memory and Identity: Whose Indian?

There are tensions at work in these chapters. There is a tension between those Native Americans who perform in Wild West shows and those Wild West Paris Disney operators who keep the racist 19th-century minstrel representations of Indians alive (Graves, 2014; McNenly, 2012). There is a tension between the work of contemporary Native artists like Wendy Red Star, who wants to empower the Native American through art, and global corporations like Wild West Paris who continue to sell 19th-century images of Native Americans. There is a tension between the 20th-century Society of Taos Artists who painted a 19th-century pastoral Indian, fit for assimilation, and the Taos Three who modeled for these painters while painting their own images of Taos and its residents. There is a tension between the Society of Taos painters and the Chapter Three painters who resisted assimilation and inspired a new (Seventh) generation of scholars and activists who insist on honoring, managing and creating their own Indigenous cultural heritage (see Benally, 2013; also Aleiss, 2005; Allen, 2012; Nicholas, 2013).[31]

These tensions create a space for dialogue, a conversation about memory, identity, art, race and the West. But history repeats itself. What is the reader to make of the announcement earlier in this chapter concerning Disneyland Paris, 2014? In 1891 William Cody employed Lakota Sioux who were survivors of the Battle of Wounded Knee (located on the Pine Ridge Reservation) in his European Wild West Show (Denzin, 2013). In 2015 the great grandchildren of those survivors are still performing in a Wild West show. There is agency here, but what does it mean for a larger politics of representation? How do we untangle politics, performance, representation, intention, and meaning? Whose history? History for whom? Whose Indian? Whose West? Whose memory?

Performing History

I suture my texts into these contested historical spaces. Biegert calls this *committed documentation*, that is, the commitment to ground the narrative in the available historical record (see Biegert 1976, quoted in Peyer, 1989, p. 553; also Benjamin, 1983). However, the record is read through a 21st-century lens. I refuse to regard the representations of Native Americans by 20th-century artists (TSA) apart from my critical views on race, Native Americans and postmodern society. Of course this is a form of historical presentism (Fischer, 1970; Skinner, 2002), applying the standards of the present to the past. On this I follow Benjamin's advice about writing history under a white colonial regime. Benjamin's histories rip the present out of its present context, connecting it to its historical past and its ideological contradictions (Benjamin, 1983, p. 24; 1968, pp. 255–266). This is history turned inside out, meant to be read aloud, history that disturbs and moves back and forth across the seamless boundaries connecting the past, the present, and the future (Benjamin, 1983, p. 24).

In interpreting these performances and paintings, and the work of these painters, I am less interested in figuring out what each one means, or what each artist intended. I am more interested in figuring out my responses to them, and the consequences of these responses for further interpretations of the painting itself. A painting, a painter reaches you with a painting. His or her Indian looks you in the eye. You may try to forget the painting, but it won't let you; its imagery haunts you. So it is for me with the paintings and artists that I discuss in the chapters that follow. I cannot get them out of my head.

An artist of course is a performer who stages and creates a painting. A painting is a performance, a performance the painter performs for an imaginary audience. When I interpret a painting, my interpretation is a performance. The paintings I discuss are performances, dramas, stories of the white gaze, brown bodies turned into art, stories of conflict, and violence. To understand what they mean, I must again, following Benjamin, do more than locate them in their historical moment. I must read myself into them, as if I were looking in a mirror. With the exception of the paintings by the Forgotten Taos Three and the Third Chapter Native artists what I see in the TAS paintings are people—Taos Indians, Sioux, Navajo, Cheyenne, Crow, men, women, children—who are not free. They are trapped in an imaginary pastoral present, an imaginary landscape, players in a violent story they can't get out of. They could be part of a scene in *Broken Arrow, Stage Coach, Hombre, Little Big Man, Dances with Wolves*.

I have attempted to write myself into a shared space with the painters, and with you. If we can share this space long enough, perhaps we can imagine how this tragic piece of late 19th- and early 20th-century history could have been done differently. And if so, maybe, just maybe, such events will never happen again. That is my goal.

My thesis is simple: The TSA paintings and the Disney Wild West Shows function as paradigmatic images of First Nations people and their place in Western history. They represent 19th- and 20th-century Western American art in the service of official governmental history. As cultural documents, they reproduce prevailing racist views of Native Americans and their place in U.S. history and contemporary popular Western culture. In contrast, the paintings of the Indigenous Taos Pueblo painters and the Chapter Three artists offered a new politics of representation, a new Native American.

Chapter 1 ⚏ Native Art, Identity and Performance in the Postmodern West

How Wild West Shows (and the Taos Society of Artists) Sold Out the West:
Performing the Text

Except for this chapter, the chapters the chapters in this book are plays intended to be performed—that is, read aloud. A "Dramatis Personae" listing all the characters and their historical identities preceded this chapter. These characters appear throughout the text. Recurring characters are the Navajo tricksters, Mr. Coyote and Ms. Coyote (on Coyote see Valdez and Elsbree, 2005), the Seventh Generation Performers (SGP) (Benally, 2013), and Tonto, the fictional Indian sidekick to the Lone Ranger in the long-running television series.[32] The voices of Coyote, Ms. Coyote, Seventh Generation Performers and Tonto are meant to be disruptive.[33]

Borrowing from Anna Deavere Smith (2000, 2004), Kaufman et al. (2001, 2014), and Saldana (2011), I use the craft and techniques of theatre, performance autoethnography, and critical historical analysis.[34] I call this historical autoethnography. In each chapter I offer a performance text, a staged ethnodrama that is part myth, part critique, an experiment in [auto]ethnographic montage. These staged events are intended to bring the reader into a critical moral discourse. I organize citations, YouTube video clips, links to museum exhibits of specific art works, speeches, and other entries in ways that highlight critical, reflexive associations. My goal is to undo official history and to create a space for marginalized voices, alternative histories, new ways of writing the past so new futures can be imagined. Each play imagines a politics of resistance, a new politics of possibility, new ways of re-imagining the future and the past. Madison, after Dolan (2005), calls these utopian performatives. They are akin to Freire's pedagogies of hope (Dolan, 2005, p. 5; Freire, 1992; Madison, 2010, p. 26; 2012, p.182).

Each play revolves around specific acts of resistance and activism. These acts of resistance use performance as the vehicle for contesting official art history and the status quo. A double reflexivity is at work. The performance text as a play uses performativity as a method for making a slice of contested reality visible. The performance potentially brings the audience into a state of critical reflexivity concerning the events under discussion—somehow the world *can* be a better place (Dolan,

2005, p. 5). The act of witnessing a utopian performative is itself a performative, interpretive act. The coyote trickster leads us into this new space (Bhabha, 1994, pp. 46–49; Conquergood, 2013, p. 27; Haraway, 1991, p. 201). The intent is to create a counter-memory, an alternative history of the present.

Each play is based on imaginary and actual historical documents, interviews, reports. Each play constructs its own scenes of memory. I rearrange these scenes, suppressing, distorting, even inventing scenes, foregoing claims to exact truth or factual accuracy, searching instead for emotional truth, for deep meaning (see Blew, 1999, p. 7; Stegner, 1990, p. iv).

Each chapter contains the essential dramatic elements of a play: plot, storyline, script, dialogue and monologues, dramatic structure (acts, scenes, units), time line, characters, stage, and dramatic arc—beginning, middle, end, turning points (Saldana, 2005, p. 15). I arrange the speech of certain characters (Coyote, Ms. Coyote) in a poetic-like structure, attempting to convey a specific sense of character with this form (see Smith, 2000, p. 53). Each play is part mystory and part autoethnographic ethnodrama (Saldana, 2005, pp. 1–2, 15, 2011; Ulmer, 1989, p. 210).[35]

While there are often elaborate stage instructions in this text, costumes, stage sets, and props "can be as minimal or as ornate as one imagines" (Smith, 2004, p. 6). Actors can play several parts. "Gender and race do not need to match those of the characters played" (Smith, 2004, p. 7). Stage directions and props can be suggested, including the use of masks. If audio visual equipment is available, images and the text of some of the documents in the plays, such as timelines and letters, may be projected. While I use acts and scenes to mark movement through the play, I have been informed by Smith's notion of the frame as a way of marking a scene within an act (2004, p. 5) and Kaufman's concept of moment, to mark a unit of theatrical time, a play being a series of interconnected frames and moments (Kaufman et al., 2001, p. xiv; 2014, p. 102).

The act of reading aloud in a group, or co-performing, creates a shared emotional experience that brings the narrative alive in ways that

Chapter 1 Native Art, Identity and Performance in the Postmodern West

silent reading cannot. The parts can be spoken going around in a circle of any number of readers or by two speakers. To simplify, I have identified each part as Speaker One or Speaker Two. Each speaker names his or her character before reading the character's lines. In writing the monologues and dialogues that appear in each play, I was guided by Walter Benjamin's argument (1969) that a critical text consists of a series of quotations, documents, excerpts, and texts placed side by side. This narrative strategy produces a de-centered narrative, a multi-voiced text with voices and speakers speaking back and forth, often past one another.

Unless indicated in quotations marks, quotations—words attributed to a speaker—are paraphrases of an original text that is cited. These are not the character's words but my interpretations of what they might say if they were persuaded to participate in this performance. This is especially true of those characters in the play who are currently alive; these are my hypothetical interpretations of their thoughts and not their own words. The caveat that appears on the copyright page of this book operates at all times:

> *This book is a product of my ethnographic imagination. Names, characters, places, events, and incidents are used fictitiously. Any resemblance to actual events, or locales or persons, living or dead is at least partially coincidental. The dialogue contained therein is intended as a stage play and should not be quoted or considered to be the actual words of the speakers unless a reference citation is given.*

In challenging these racist myths and cultural representations, I follow Hall (1997) and Smith (1997) who argue that it is not enough to replace negative representations with positive representations. The positive-negative debate essentializes racial identity, and denies its "dynamic relation to constructions of class, gender, sexuality [and] region" (Smith, 1997, p. 4). It takes two parties to do racial minstrelsy. Race is performative, contextual, and historical. Stereotypes of whiteness are tangled up in racial myth, in minstrel shows that re-play the Wild West, leading whites to look Western and Native Americans to look Indian (Dorst, 1999).

By unraveling these myths, and their meanings and origins, I point to the diversity and complexity of racial representations and racial performances in American popular Western culture. I seek to replace old stereotypes with new understandings. I want to show how historical discourse can in fact turn back on itself, revise its stance toward the past, and perform new, progressive representations of cultural difference.

I advance a critical performative pedagogy which hopefully allows us to dream our way into a militant democratic utopian space, into a space which also exposes and criticizes the racist politics buried deep inside the American democratic imagination. The challenge is to take up again Kittridge's (1996) and Limerick's (2001) charge to rethink Western history and mythology by starting out at the ground level, starting all over again. In bringing the past into the present, I insert myself into the past and create the conditions for rewriting and hence re-experiencing it. I want to invent a new version of the past, a new history. I want to create a chorus of discordant voices, memories, and images concerning art as a representational form. In so doing I contest current images of Western and Native artists, and the place of Wild West shows in our collective imagination.

This book completes a four-part series about Native Americans, art, painters, Wild West shows and the postmodern West. This book is about finding our way into these new performative spaces. I turn in Chapter Two to Native Americans performing in Buffalo Bill's Wild West Show in Paris, circa 2014. Imagine Wendy Red Star in the audience, sharing her critique of Buffalo Bill and Disney with anyone who will listen.

Chapter 2
Disneyland Indians, Paris, circa 2014[1]

ACT ONE
Prologue

If you belonged to me, I would not let them have you perform in a show like this. (Queen Victoria to Black Elk, a member of Buffalo Bill's Wild West Show, 1892)

The American Imagination demands the real thing and, to attain it, must fabricate the absolute fake. Ever since Indigenous communities were first portrayed in literature, and visual culture, Europeans and Euro-Americans have projected their fantasies on the 'New world' canvas and created the 'absolute fake' Indian who never existed off the page [or stage], sometimes compelling Native Americans to

---

Indians in Color: Native Art, Identity, and Performance in the New West by Norman K. Denzin, 37–63. © 2015 Taylor & Francis. All rights reserved.

play these roles as well. This practice was particularly evident on the nineteenth and twentieth century with the advent of new performative contexts such as Wild West Shows, world's fairs, and western films [and art] that situates Native Americans in a barbaric past, useful as icons only in museums. (Raheja, 2010, p. 137)

Clearly they wanted a particular kind of fake Indian, one who looked and acted like the stereotype, that is, a copper-skinned Noble Savage. (Ms. Coyote)

The lights go down. A YouTube video is projected on the giant drop down screen in the center of the arena.

Graham Greene reads the text[2] below from the Lakota Country Times, as scenes from Paris Disneyland Buffalo Bill's Wild West Show[3] and the Pine Ridge Indian Reservation[4] appear on the screen.[5] An audience of Anglo-European tourists in Col. Cody's Saloon and in grandstand bleachers sits quietly viewing the YouTube video:

Speaker One: **Graham Greene**

> **Dateline: April 27, 2014**: *Personnel from Disneyland will be auditioning recruits for its Wild West Show in Paris. Since 1992, Cowboys and Native North Americans have been a part of the Disneyland Paris Wild West production. Next month casting consultant Tom Reeves will help Disney procure talent from the Cheyenne River and Pine Ridge Indian Reservations, as well the Browning, Montana, area.*
>
> *Mr. Reeves said, "They must be eighteen years of age, be able to ride bareback and go through some obstacle courses and have the ability to work in a team environment." There is a housing allowance, airfare to and from France, bonus premiums, and a contract for two shows, five days a week. Candidates will be interviewed by Kevin Kramer of Euro-Disney.*

Chapter 2 ❖ Disneyland Indians, Paris, circa 2014

ACT ONE, SCENE ONE
The New Recruits Arrive

(The stage is bare, no scenery, no props, just a folding table and two chairs. On the table are various items, including bows, arrows, tomahawks, spears, Indian headdresses, beaded moccasins, buckskin shirts, lariats, buffalo skulls. Western music can be heard. A stage-hand comes on stage and begins organizing the items on the table. The stage manager stops him.)

Speaker One: **Stage Manager**

Stop, it is time for rehearsal.

The director and six Native American actors (Lakota Sioux), the new recruits selected by Kevin Kramer and Tom Reeves, step on stage. They begin rehearsing for the new cowboy and Indian musical "Buffalo Bill's Wild West Show… with Mickey and Friends." The actors begin picking up various clothing items, rehearsing lines, going over stage directions, striking poses, stretching, and limbering up. Off-stage, horses can be heard snorting and stomping their feet. The Western music stops.

Speaker Two: **Native American Actors** (new recruits) in unison

This is a terrible script. It says here we have to play Indian for Disneyland characters. Nobody brought this up during auditions.

Speaker One: **Director**

Not true, the call for auditions said this was a new musical involving Mickey and his friends. But I agree with you, pretty dumb. You can't get ahold of good Wild West scripts anymore; everybody is doing the same old same old: blood thirsty savages, attacks on the Deadwood Stage Coach, cowboy and Indian horse races, buffalo herds, and Annie Oakley sharpshooters. Nothin' new, folks been doin' this stuff since before Buffalo Bill even got the idea of a Wild West show.[6]

Speaker Two: **Actors** (new recruits) in unison

Who but Disney executives would think that adding Disney characters would make for a good script?

39

Speaker One: **Director**

These days, if you wanna do Wild West in Paris, you gotta do Disney.

❖ ❖ ❖

ACT ONE, SCENE TWO
Six Indians in Search of an Identity[7]

Before the rehearsal can even begin, six more American Indian actors walk onto the stage. They look lost and perplexed. They are wearing nametags, masks, buckskins, headdresses, and are initially identified only as Imaginary Indian One (Father), Imaginary Indian Two (mother), Imaginary Indian Three (daughter), Imaginary Indian Four (son), Imaginary Indian Five (grandfather), Imaginary Indian Six (grandmother). Their masks are meant to reveal an inner emotion specific to each character, such as remorse, revenge, disdain, grief, loss, fear.[8] The six imaginary Indians walk up to the director.

Speaker One: **Imaginary Indians** in unison

We're here in search of an author who will write a play that will express our true identities (Pirandello, 1921/1998a, p. 10). We need somebody who can write a play for us, or write parts for us in this play. We're from Pine Ridge, not a pretty place, a poor reservation. We are Lakota Sioux, also from the Ogala tribe. We caught the last flight to Paris last night. We are professional actors, and come from a long line of acclaimed Indian performers. We need work, but we also have a story to tell and need someone who can help us tell it.

Speaker Two: **Director**

Get off my stage. I have no time for crazy people.

Speaker One: **Imaginary Indians** in unison

We mean no harm. We just want someone who can help us finish our story. It is a sad story. We have experienced a lot of pain, but we are hopeful. The original author got a better gig and split. We need a new author, but having a new director may work, too.

Speaker Two: **Six original actors** (new recruits, who are not wearing masks) in unison

Hey, Mr. Director, what' going on? This is our play. We worked hard to get here. Not only do you have us playing with imaginary Disney mice—Mickey and Minnie—but now there are six new characters we may have to work with.

Speaker One: **Director**

Everybody calm down. There is plenty of work for everybody. Give me a little time to figure this out. I may need some help.

Speaker Two: **Imaginary Indians** in unison

We want an author who understands real Indians. Granted we are professional actors, but we are also Indigenous rights activists. We are always thinking ahead to the *seventh generation*.[9]

Speaker One: **Imaginary Indian # 2**

We want stories that protect our cultural traditions and promote cultural survival (Portalewska, 2013, p. 18). This is the story we want to tell.

Speaker Two: **Mitch Allen** (cultural archaeologist and publisher) soto voice

There are many other people thinking about these problems. Have you heard of IPinCH (see Nicholas, 2013)?

Speaker One: **Imaginary Indians** in unison

We believe in being disruptive. We oppose the use of Indigenous images for commercial purposes, from Wild West shows, to Crazy Horse Malt Liquor to Johnny Depp playing Tonto, to Anglo painters, like those Taos Society artists, painting red-skinned Indians for railroad advertisements.

Speaker Two: **Imaginary Indian # 4**

This Disneyland Wild West Show is just one more example of the marketing Native culture for white entertainment.

INDIANS IN COLOR

Speaker One: **Imaginary Indian # 6**

We want somebody like Jim Welch with his sad story, *The Heartsong of Charging Elk* (2000). This is a historical novel about a Sioux Indian who as a child witnessed the battle of Little Bighorn and as a young adult performed in Buffalo Bill's Wild West Show when it toured Europe. Charging Elk was left behind in France recovering from an injury. He struggled to make his way in an alien culture. Or give us a sad Louise Erdrich story like *Shadow Tag* (2010), or Sherman Alexie with his funny painful stories in *Lone Ranger and Tonto Fist Fight in Heaven* (1993), or LeAnne Howe with her travel stories in *Choctalking on Other Realities* (2013a). Give us a Native American who can write stories about real Indians and their life problems.

Speaker Two: **Imaginary Indian # 1**

We've had too much experience playing pretend Indians for white folks.

Speaker One: **Imaginary Indians** in unison

This is redfacing, just bein' another old black sambo for the whiteman (Raheja, 2010, p. 21).

ACT ONE, SCENE THREE
Introductions

Speaker One: **Imaginary Indians** (each actor wears a mask that fits his or her character) in unison

If we are going to ask for a new play, we need to introduce ourselves.

Speaker Two: **Imaginary Indian # 1** (father: remorse)

I often play the part of Tonto.

Speaker One: **Imaginary Indian # 2** (mother: grief)

I play the part of Minnehaha.[10]

Chapter 2 ⬛ Disneyland Indians, Paris, circa 2014

Speaker Two: **Imaginary Indian # 3** (daughter: loss)
I was always Pocahontas.

Speaker One: **Imaginary Indian # 4** (son: fear)
I was always Little Beaver.[11]

Speaker Two: **Imaginary Indian # 5** (grandfather: revenge)
I play half-breeds; they often call me Hombre.[12]

Speaker One: **Imaginary Indian # 6** (grandmother: distain)
I play Secagawea, or sometimes just a squaw.

Speaker Two: **Imaginary Indian # 1**
Playing these made-up characters was OK—it was work, and it paid—but it felt kind of crazy, like looking at ourselves through a veil.

Speaker One: **Original Actors** in unison
Isn't it all illusion, anyway?

Speaker Two: **Imaginary Indians** in unison, LOUDLY
Illusion is one thing. Reality is something else. As for us, Six Indians in Search of an Identity, we want new story lines. We're trapped. But unless you give us some lines we won't even exist outside of this little play.

Speaker Two: **Director**
Who are you kidding? You can always go back to the rez.

ACT ONE, SCENE FOUR
Imaginary Indians, Part Two

Speaker One: **Imaginary Indians** in unison
Not so quick Mr. Director: How'd you like to go back and pretend to be Minnehaha, or Little Beaver, or Tonto, or Hombre, or some other Indian character played by Paul Newman or Johnny Depp?

Speaker Two: **Tonto, aka Imaginary Indian # 1, aka Jay Silverheels**

We came to this theater because we wanted a new beginning.

Speaker One: **Little Beaver, aka Imaginary Indian # 4**

How are we going to drag our Indian bodies back to the rez if we only exist inside this play?

Speaker Two   **Hombre, aka Imaginary Indian # 5**

Hey, I'm Navajo—no, I'm Lakota Sioux. Wait, I'm no half-breed. I gotta life outside these pretend Indian parts.

Speaker One: **Minnehaha, aka Imaginary Indian # 2**

Go figure. There is even a real person playing Mickey Mouse. Remember Mickey and Minnie are also known as William and Alice Red Cloud.[13]

Speaker Two: **Imaginary Indians**

It gets complicated when you talk about playing an imaginary Indian in Disneyland. What's real and what's an illusion?

Speaker One: **Director**

It's all illusion. They call this metatheatre—plays about plays. Why would you be here if you didn't understand this?

Speaker Two: **All Indians,** real and imaginary

Yeah, but, Mr. Director, not all of can get off this stage. We are going to search for another author. It feels like you have us running in circles.

Speaker One: **Little Beaver, aka Imaginary Indian # 4**

Here's our biggest fear, whiteman. Our faces may grow to fit these masks we've been given to wear. We could become every Indian's worst fear—that is, a real live make-believe Indian who is dressed up to look like a real life make-believe Indian. Who wants to run around for the rest of their life being Tonto, Little Beaver, or Minnehaha?

Chapter 2   Disneyland Indians, Paris, circa 2014

Speaker Two: **Director**

> Stop. Stop. Take a break. I gotta get these Indian boys from South Dakota ready for the show tonight. I'll get back to you. I got a call into three of those new Indian writers, but nobody's callin' back. I know you want an honest play, and I do, too.

Speaker One: **Imaginary Indians** exit the stage in silence

Lights dim, curtain comes down.

ACT TWO, SCENE ONE
Rehearsing

Curtain rises, lights dim.

Stage Right: Spotlight shines on the dressing room, backstage at the Paris Disney Wild West Show. The new group of recruits from the reservation are about to give their first live performance. They have been in daily rehearsals since they arrived eight weeks ago.

Speaker One: **Kevin Kramer**

> Be calm. You will do just fine. Remember you have been training for this moment. You were selected because you demonstrated outstanding skills.

Speaker One: **Carter Yellowbird**

> I've been doing these shows for ten years. Listen you youngsters, you are just like me. Performing is in our blood. We all have parents, grandparents, aunts and uncles, nieces and nephews who have been performing for decades in Native ceremonies and reenactments. Your grandparents may have even worked in Hollywood.[14]

Speaker Two: **Ghost of Sitting Bull**

> Carter is right. Some of your grandparent's parents performed in Europe with Buffalo Bill. I did, too. Before Buffalo Bill there

was George Catlin's Traveling Indian Gallery. My aunt posed for paintings by Catlin, and he hung them in his gallery.

Speaker One: **Ms. Coyote**

My great grandmother and my grandmother made a little money sewing fancy costumes for Hollywood directors who hired Native and non-Native performers to play Indians.

Speaker Two: **Kevin Kramer**

Here at Disneyland Paris we just want to give the tourists a good old-fashioned western-themed spectacle, with real cowboys and Indians. I don't care what you may want to call it—staged reenactments, revisionist role-playing—whatever, just give a good show!

ACT TWO, SCENE TWO
What Is Real?

Speaker One: **Sheriff William Red Cloud (aka Mickey Mouse)** to new recruits[15]

We've never seen a real Indian before. Just kidding!

Speaker One: **Ms. Coyote**

I've never seen a talking mouse in a costume before.

Speaker One: **Mark Silverheels**

My father played the part of a dumb Indian for a fictional lawman, who wore a mask and rode a white horse. How made-up and pretend can you get, Kemosabe?[16]

Speaker Two: **Ms. Coyote**

I don't know, boys. Your grandparents performed with a made up character called Buffalo Bill. I know he was a real human being. But his show was almost entirely fantasy and make-believe. How is that different from performing with Mickey and Minnie Mouse who are cartoon characters? Who is real and who is pretend anyway?

Chapter 2 ⚑ Disneyland Indians, Paris, circa 2014

Speaker One: **Imaginary Indians** in unison

Hey, we didn't come to Paris to be in a show where they kill Indians. We coulda stayed on the reservation and been in that show.

Center Stage: Spotlight on theatrical release poster for Blazing Saddles *(see en.wikipedia.org/wiki/Blazing_Saddles).*

Speaker Two: **Imaginary Indians** and **New Recruits** as a Greek chorus

How about a part in that Mel Brooks movie, *Blazing Saddles*. [17] That is serious Hollywood, maybe even better then Disneyland. It had a black sheriff in Rock Ridge, an all-white frontier town where everybody had the last name of Johnson, and an army of thugs consisting of Indian agents, Mexican bandits, muggers, con men, vipers and dim-wits. Mel played a Yiddish-speaking Indian chief. Dressed in ornate plains *schmattes* (including war bonnet), and riding a paint pony, Mel and his warriors come upon a prairie schooner carrying an African-American family. "Chief" Brooks looks at the little group as they huddle together in terror, and then turns to his closest companion, who is raising his tomahawk to strike.

Speaker One: **Chief Mel Brooks**

No, no, zayt nisht meshuge! Loz im geyn! Abi gezint! Take off! Hosti gezen in dayne lebn? [Don't be crazy! Let him go. As long as you're healthy! Take off! Have you ever seen such a thing?] Let the family go in peace. They darker than us!

Speaker Two: **Imaginary Indians** and **New Recruits**

This is offensive. Are we sure we want to be in a movie like this. Seems more than a little racist.

Speaker One: **Imaginary Indians and New Recruits as a Greek chorus** cont'd

Still, we could use a little jazz music here. Everybody loved "April in Paris" in that last scene in *Blazing Saddles*. Anyway, aren't we in Paris, and it is April.

47

ACT TWO, SCENE THREE
Who's Writing Our Story?

Speaker One: **Imaginary Indians** to director

Are you writing a play for us, or not? Do you have someone in mind? Do you even know what writing our story might mean? You are a non-Indian. You can't write our story. Look at what happened with the Mel Brooks *Blazing Saddle* movie. He wrote himself into the script, and he then played an Indian Chief.

Speaker Two: **Director**

Of course I can. What are you talking about? Buffalo Bill didn't have Indian writers for his shows. Anybody can write an Indian story. Don't criticize Mel Brooks; that movie was a great put-down of western movies.

Speaker One: **Imaginary Indians**

Brooks's movie proves our point. Not just anybody can do Indian movies today. Not anymore they can't. Times have changed. We write our own stories now, and they aren't called Indian stories.

Speaker Two: **Director**

So what is an Indian story or play?

Speaker One: **Imaginary Indian**

Simple. Like W. E. B. Du Bois said about a black story (1926), a Native American story is a story written by a Native American for Native Americans about Native American problems. A non-Indian can't write this story. Period.

Speaker Two: **Director**

Can a non-Indian direct a Native American play?

Speaker One: **Imaginary Indian**

What do you think?

Speaker Two: **Ms. Coyote**
Where do we go from here?

Speaker One: **Stage Manager**
Back to work. We got a show to put on.

ACT THREE, SCENE ONE
Colonel Cody's Saloon

Stage Right: Spotlight shines on billboard outside the entrance to the Paris Disney Wild West Show. Col. Cody's Saloon is just inside the entrance. Tables, chairs and bleachers face the performance arena.

Stage Directions: The audience enters the open-air saloon, which faces the stage in the center of the large arena. Upon entrance, each audience member is asked to put on a cowboy hat with a red, green, blue or gold colored ribbon. Members are directed to sit at one of four groups of tables, corresponding to the color of the ribbon on their hat and the name of the ranch that they will represent: Gold Star, Red River, Blue Moon, Green Mountain.
** A country western band plays softly.

** A diorama of an Indian village is projected on the giant drop down screen in the center of the arena.

** The arena darkens, a backdrop curtain rises "to reveal cliffs and a sunrise" (McNenly, 2012, p. 146).

** Indian flute music plays softly.

House lights dim. On stage a spot light shines on the announcer, William and Alice Red Coud, Annie Oakley, Goofy, Buffalo Bill, and Chief Sitting Bull. The audience cheers. A spotlight sweeps the stage. The flute music continues. The voice of Auguste Durand-Ruel (announcer, friend of Buffalo Bill) reverberates through the theatre.

Speaker One: **Auguste Durand-Ruel**

GOOFY ... ANNIE ... SITTING BULL ...
BUFFALO BILL...

Waiters, dressed as cowboys and cowgirls, take meal orders and deliver food and drinks to the tables. The audience starts eating while settling in for the performance.

ACT THREE, SCENE TWO
The Program

House lights dim. Curtain comes up.

Speaker One: **Auguste Durand-Ruel**

Let the show begin—Give a big cheer for Sitting Bull and the Native performers from the reservation, ladies, gentlemen, and children. Welcome. All of our performers are here. Enjoy your Texas BBQ meal, put on a cowboy hat, or an Indian headdress, if you prefer. You will get to meet Buffalo Bill, Annie Oakley, Chief Sitting Bull, and the Wild West Riders. You will relive the real Wild West alongside real Lakota Sioux Indians from South Dakota. You will get to interact with Disneyland stars. As the competitions get going be sure to wave your cowboy hats in support of the team that defends the honor of your ranch.[18]

Stage Left: Spotlight shines on program for 2014 Paris Wild West Show.

PROGRAM

Speaker One: **Auguste Durand-Ruel** *reading from the program that each audience member has been given. The program is also projected on a large screen, as in a Powerpoint presentation.*

This shows honors Buffalo Bill's Wild West Show. We base our program on the 1905 Paris Program.[19] As with that show, we depict the Drama of Civilization by offering a glimpse of pioneer life on the Western frontier. We tell the story of how the West was won by heroic cowboys who overcame the threats to civilization posed by outlaws and wild Indians (McNenly, 2012, pp. 144–145; also Moses, 1996; Warren, 2005, pp. 267–268).

Our Show has 12 performance scenes, as follows *(cowboy music plays)*:

1. Grand Entrance
2. Buffalo Bill
3. Annie Oakley
4. Mickey and Minnie (in disguise), Goofy, Chip 'n Dale
5. Sitting Bull
6. Buffalo Bill and Sitting Bull greet one another
7. Indians form drumming circle and dance
8. Cowboys herd cattle
9. Indians engage in buffalo hunt
10. Rodeo: Audience participation with cowboys and Indians
11. Attack on the Deadwood Stage by Indians and outlaws
12. Finale

ACT THREE, SCENE THREE
Indians Storm the Stage

Shouts from off-stage: NO NO NO NO THIS MUST STOP NOW—

A group of Crow and Sioux—the Imaginary Indians and the New Recruits—storm into the saloon and onto the stage. They jump over tables and bleachers.

Speaker One: **Imaginary Indians** and **New Recruits** as a Greek chorus—to Auguste Durand-Ruel

So, let's get this straight. We're supposed to be drumming, dancing, riding horses and attacking the white man's stage coach.

Speaker Two: **Imaginary Indians**

This may work for the New Recruits, but not us. They were hired to do these kinds of events. But there is no place for us in this story.

INDIANS IN COLOR

Speaker One: **New Recruits**

Let's be clear about this. We're not thrilled to just be Indians in some cowboy and Indian masquerade, either. But we need the money, and we're far from South Dakota

Speaker Two: **Secagawea**

People know us for the characters we've been playing—Tonto, Minnehaha, Pocahontas, Little Beaver, Hombre, Secagawea. But this is our worst nightmare, becoming the characters we are playing.

Speaker One: **Tonto**

Sacagawea is right. We are more than Indians playing cowboy and Indian games. We are thinking about calling ourselves the Seventh Generation Performers, or just The SGP's for short.

Speaker Two: **Imaginary Indians, aka the SGP**

We believe our performances should be judged by how they will benefit children seven generations from now. The seventh generation would not approve of this Disneyland Wild West Show.

With that both groups of Indians give three war whoops, jump off the stage, quietly step over bleachers and around tables and chairs, disappearing from sight.

ACT THREE, SCENE FOUR
Take Five, Let the Show Begin

Speaker One: **Auguste Durand-Ruel** (to Indians)

Quiet now. We have to let the show begin. Except for Sitting Bull, Colonel Cody did not advertise the names of Indian performers. His Indians were just Indians. Those are the kinds of Indians we have here today.[20]

** As Auguste is speaking, four cowboys charge into the arena waving flags representing the Gold Star Ranch in Texas, the Red River Ranch in

Chapter 2 ⚎ Disneyland Indians, Paris, circa 2014

Colorado, the Blue Moon Ranch in Wyoming, and the Green Mountain Ranch in Montana (McNenly, 2012, p.146).

**The new recruits arrive and race around the arena on their horses. Others form a circle and begin dancing to drumming music.

**Shouts and war whoops from off-stage are heard. The angry Seventh Generation Performers, in redface, have returned. They rush on stage and push the New Recruits, who are drumming offstage.

** Women and children scream and scramble for cover under the tables and bleachers.

Speaker Two: **Seventh Generation Performers, AKA Imaginary Indians**

This misuse of Native Americans must stop.

Speaker One: **Auguste Durand-Ruel**

If you don't stop, I'll call the police.

Speaker Two: **Seventh Generation Performers**

Hey, white man. This show MUST stop.

Speaker One: **Auguste Durand-Ruel** to audience

Dear audience. Forgive us. We are taking a brief intermission until we can get these unruly Indians off the stage. They call themselves the Seventh Generation Performers. I have no idea what they are talking about. Drinks are on the house!

Curtains come down; as the lights dim, armed policeman drag the kicking and screaming Seventh Generation Performers off stage.

Speaker Two: **Seventh Generation Performers** in unison

CUSTER DIED FOR YOUR SINS WHITEMAN (Deloria, 1969)

(Five minutes later the play starts back up.)

ACT THREE, SCENE FIVE
Take Five Again, or,
Let's Get This Show Back on the Road

The curtain comes up.

Speaker One: **Auguste Durand-Ruel** to audience

Dear friends. Our apologies. Come in, come in. The show is about to start back up. We are just about to start the section of our show where you as audience members get to participate. Just ignore the unruly Indians. I don't know why they complain. We pay them very well.

The following sequence appears on the giant drop down in the center of the arena. The scenes and narration run together at fast forward speed, as if in an old fashioned silent film, or a slick Powerpoint presentation. Descriptions of each scene appear in Times New Roman, 22 point font, at the bottom of the screen. Avatars (as alternate actor egos) perform on screen as stand-ins for real cowboys, Indians (new recruits and imaginary), audience members, Buffalo Bill, and Annie Oakley.

** The rodeo begins. Cowboys from the four ranches compete in a horse lassoing contest. Indians associated with each ranch cheer and race horses around the stage. In the medicine ball game audience members from each ranch cheer and pass a ball to one another, and then throw it into the arena where "the cowboys and Indians try to get their ranch's ball on top of a teepee" (McNenly, 2012, p. 148).

**Next is the attack on the Deadwood Stage. Four audience members are chosen to join Auguste Durand-Ruel to ride in the stage coach, which is carrying gold from the mines. Indians attack the stage and steal the horses. The passengers are blindfolded and tied up. The passengers struggle to get free. The James Gang drops into the arena on ropes and steals the gold on the stage. Buffalo Bill races to the rescue, chasing off the outlaws and the Indians and freeing the passengers (McNenly, 2012, p. 148).

** In the finale, Auguste Durand-Ruel and Buffalo Bill toast the show's success with champagne.

Curtains come down.

Lights dim.

** Back in real time, the country western band strikes up a new tune. The avatars step off screen and join the action on stage. The audience cheers and claps. Cowboy hats are thrown in the air. Couples in western dress dance to the music. Children chase one another around the arena. The children are joined by the two Disney star mice, as well as Goofy, Chip 'n Dale.

House lights dim. The curtain comes down. The band plays three western songs: "El Paso," "Home on the Range," and "Cherokee People."

ACT THREE, SCENE SIX
William and Alice Red Cloud

The curtain comes up. A spotlight sweeps the stage. Audience members take their places in the bleachers and at their tables in the saloon. Indian flute music plays softly. The spotlight stops center stage.

Speaker One: **Auguste Durand-Ruel**

Let's hear it for the Disney all-stars. It's all here for you, our fantastic audience. You just got to participate in a real Wild West show and experience the thrill of riding on the Deadwood Stage, playing the medicine ball game, being attacked by Indians and taken prisoner by outlaws, and being rescued by Buffalo Bill. This is a once in a lifetime experience.

The spotlight pauses, retraces itself, and stops on two riders on horseback. The horses and riders move slowly across the stage. The riders are William and Alice Red Cloud, aka Mickey and Minnie Mouse. William is dressed as Buffalo Bill and Alice is dressed as Annie Oakley. They are riding glorious palomino stallions. The audience cheers.

Speaker Two: **William and Alice Red Cloud** in unison

Hi, folks. We have to tell you something. We're going to step out of frame for a minute. We've got a little surprise for Auguste. We are not really Disney characters. We are brother and sister,

William and Alice Red Cloud. We like to dress up in western costumes. We are from Manchester, England; we are Sioux. Our parents performed in Buffalo Bill's 1887 Tour.[21] We've performed all over Europe in Wild West shows. Last year we found ourselves out of work, but read that Paris Disney was looking for actors to play Mickey and Minnie Mouse in their Wild West Show. Since we have been performing all our lives in these shows, or so it seems, we auditioned and got the job. We love it.

Speaker One: **SGP, aka Imaginary Indians and New Recruits**

This is getting too funny. Real Indians playing Disney mice.

Speaker Two: **Alice and William Red Cloud**

We needed work. The pay is pretty good.

Speaker One: **Imaginary Indians and New Recruits**

Are you Salford Sioux, or Disney mice?

Speaker Two: **Alice and William Red Cloud** in unison

Are you Buffalo Bill show Indians, or Lakota Sioux acting like Show Indians? Who is an Indian, and who is a mouse?

Speaker One: **Ms. Coyote**

Let's ask them.

Speaker Two: **SGP, aka Imaginary Indians**

Nothing new here. Disney has made a fortune using lovable talking birds, dogs, mice, bears, lions, cats, monkeys, raccoons, and rabbits. This often involved racial stereotyping, which has long been an issue—from *Song of the South* (1946) and the *Jungle Book* (1967), to *Pocahontas* (1995), *Mulan* (1998), or *Princess and the Frog* (2009) (see Giroux and Pollock, 2010).[22] They are just using us the way they have 'disneyfied' ethnic characters and people of color for almost a century.

Speaker One: **Imaginary Indians and New Recruits** in unison

We have to get out of these Disney stories.

The curtains come down.

Chapter 2 ⚏ Disneyland Indians, Paris, circa 2014

ACT FOUR, SCENE ONE
Is Disney Dead?

The curtain rises. House lights dim. The strains of Count Basie's band playing "April in Paris" can be heard over the sound system.

Speaker One:　**Norman K. Denzin** to audience

You want a new story? Unless you find a new place to start, unless Disney is dead and white writers stop writing Indian stories there are no new Indian stories. All we have are the same old stories about drunken bloodthirsty redskins, fat squaws, half-breeds, young bucks, and sexy Indian princesses, and maybe a senile chief or two. Just a bunch of stereotypes thrown together, over and over again. Sadly, you are out of luck if you are looking for white authors telling stories about a radically reinterpreted frontier or new Wild West. The stories are just not there; they can't be found anywhere. Left to Disney and Hollywood we only have the same old Wild West dime novels turned into Wild West shows with Indians on horseback attacking whites in re-enactments of the Battle of Little Big Horn, or kidnapping, murdering and raping white women (e.g., *The Missing*, 2003). Don't get me wrong. There are new stories, just not out of Hollywood.

Speaker Two:　**Ms. Coyote**

I agree this is pretty depressing, and it sure ignores a lot of new stuff. There are scores of fiction and non-fiction Native writers who are telling new stories, works that challenge official "narratives of Westernness, and Indianness. To name just a few—Alexie, Erdrich, Harjo, Howe, Silko, Vizenor, Welch (Trout, 1998; Warrior, 2005).

Speaker Two:　**Carter Yellowbird**[23]

When somebody asks me to throw on a headdress and dance around a fire, I tell them to go to hell. I tell them I'm not in the business of performing stereotypes. I'll go so far as to play my drums in a way that is not associated with warriors from

Hollywood westerns. Unfortunately, a lot of the current Wild West shows, like Disney Paris and Buffalo Bill Days, want us to perform in the old-fashioned ways. This is not the case for the shows organized by Native Spirit Production, Gordon Bronitsky and Associates, or Ho-Chunk Nation. Still, many Native Americans have to perform the stereotypes, whether they want to or not, because they are at the bottom of the Western capital economic pyramid.

Speaker One: **William and Alice Red Cloud** in unison to audience

We have to start over. For us this Disney Wild West stuff has to end (see Graves, 2014).[24] It is time to burn our Mickey and Minnie costumes.

ACT FOUR, SCENE TWO
Disney is Dead

Speaker One: **Alice and William Red Cloud** in unison to audience

If Disney is dead, what do we do with the Paris Wild West Show?

Speaker Two: **SGP** to audience

For the moment, we've decided to use the Paris Disneyland Wild West Show as an occasion to revisit the 19th-century tradition of Wild West shows (see Denzin, 2013). We have an idea for a play which would bring back to life famous literary and real 19th- and 20th-century Native American performers, from Sitting Bull to Charging Elk, from Winnetou[25] to Tonto and Little Beaver and Minnehaha, and Pocahantas.

Speaker One: **New Recruits** to audience

Shortly after we arrived we started working on the idea of bringing back the Ghost of Sitting Bull. We wanted to honor the great Chief. So in our play the Ghost of Sitting Bull has displaced Buffalo Bill as the leader of the Paris show. The Ghost has made friends with Mickey and Minnie Mouse, who we now know are Salford Sioux. Meanwhile, we are preparing notes on how to stage and perform traditional tribal dances for Parisian school children.

Speaker Two: **Seventh Generation Performers**

We want to get past the issues that have always been involved when Native Americans play Indian for white audiences. This Disney apparatus turns Indians into players in a minstrel play for white consumers. In bringing back Sitting Bull and 19th- and 20th-century Native performers, we want to show that, while a racist past is never dead, it could have been different. Sitting Bull and his ghost refused to give in to the Wild West story Buffalo Bill was selling to white audiences.

ACT FOUR, SCENE THREE
Back to the Beginning

Speaker One: **Seventh Generation Performers**

We can put the Disney part of the story on hold for now. Let's write new stories ourselves. We need no outside author to tell our story.

(Stage left, the Seventh Generation Performers remove their masks, name-tags, and costumes and place them on the prop table, and then step forward, in everyday causal street dress.)

Speaker Two: **Ms. Coyote**

We need to write stories and performances that take us back to our roots, stories that honor our children, our elders, and our tribal histories—stories that help us look seven generations down the road.

Speaker One: **Seventh Generation Performers**

We were trapped in stories defined by the fictional characters we were playing.

Speaker Two: **Mr. Coyote**

Fiction, reality, what's the difference? Ms. Coyote says it is real if I say it is real. This is the W. I. Thomas Theorem: "If people define situations as real, they are real in their consequences" (Thomas and Thomas, 1928, pp. 571–572). I can bend time, write from scenes of memory, rearrange and suppress the past, invent scenes, forgo claims to truth for deep meaning, fictional truths, a remaking of the past; testing the boundaries of creative nonfiction, I claim ownership of my past, changing it as I write (Denzin, 2013, p. 133).

Speaker One: **Seventh Generation Performers**

We need to write stories that show how our people are training to become new tribal leaders, including lawyers, professors, economists, teachers, environmentalists, artists, writers and scientists. We need stories about ordinary Indians—barbers, teachers, mechanics, carpenters, hairdressers (Howe, 2013a). We need stories about how we are forging intertribal alliances, and using internet-based technologies to create smart homes and schools and smart community centers in tribal communities. We need stories that address media stereotypes, intellectual property issues, and problems connected with the preservation of our cultural heritages.

Speaker Two: **Ms. Coyote**

We need stories that look at the dark side of Native life: alcoholism, drug abuse, family violence, spousal abuse, infant mortality, murder, divorce, poverty at Third World levels, high teen and adult suicide rates, 85 percent unemployment, school drop-out rates over 70 percent.

Speaker One: **Waylong Gary White Deer**

"In Indian Country we don't chase after stories or songs. They come around to where we are" (White Deer, 2013, p. 11, italics added).

Chapter 2 ⚙ Disneyland Indians, Paris, circa 2014

Speaker Two: **Seventh Generation Performers**

We called ourselves Six Indians in Search of an Identity. We said our writer had walked off the set. And we were looking for new story. In actuality we were carrying around a lot of baggage from the Pine Ridge Reservation and those Hollywood movies where we played pretend Indians.

We were carrying around the story we were looking for even before we walked on the set. The story is inside our skin, in our bones. We knew what had happened to us, but we did not have the words or the courage to tell the story. We had each experienced violence, betrayal, deception. We were trapped in lies and were looking for someone to write a new story. We had turned ourselves into actors playing pretend Indians for white audiences.

We were tangled up in the lives of the fake Indian characters we had been playing: Tonto, Hombre, Minnehaha, Pocahontas, Little Beaver, Sacagawea. We forgot that *we are* the story, and there are only two stories that matter, those we feel and those that we know.

We are tired of being characters in somebody else's story. These characters we have been playing have been part of an imaginary Wild West, an imaginary past that is no more.

Speaker One: **Waylong Gary White Deer**

Let the stories find you.

Speaker Two: **Sherman Alexie**

Be careful with your story. Don't get trapped into telling admiring stories about Indians. Try to avoid turning all Native Americans into superheroes, like "Hey, did you see what Tonto did to the Lone Ranger in that last episode?' (Hearne, 2012a, p. 265). We want stories of tricksters, postindian survivance, renunciations of white dominance, stories which have an active sense of presence over absence (Vizenor, 1999; 2008, p. 1).

ACT FOUR, SCENE FOUR
Where Next?

Speaker One: **Narrator**

Four reasons why we should stop staging Wild West shows:

1. They are racist, and they perpetuate stereotypes.

2. They make Indians historical re-enactors of a past that never was. Deloria calls this the dilemma of Indian modernity (2004, p. 67).

3. They foreclose any possibility that Indians as re-enactors will ever be able to occupy the same historical space as white audiences (Deloria, 2004, p, 67).

4. They foreclose any possibility that whites will ever stop appropriating Indian culture for white purposes.

Speaker Two: **Ms. Coyote**

We can add a fifth reason for terminating these shows. The contemporary Indian hobby movement draws its historical inspiration from the reenactments staged by Native American performers touring in Europe with Buffalo Bill's Wild West Show. Contemporary 'hobby Indians'[26] create and wear 'show Indian' costumes "so as to forge a link with this history" (Kalshoven, 2012, p. 191, paraphrase; see also Deloria, 1998, pp. 140–141).

Speaker One: **Gerald Vizenor** (1999, p. vii, cited in Strong, 2013, p. 4)

Never forget, the Indian is a simulation, a ruse of colonial domination. And there are many forms of simulation, including playing Indian in Wild West shows, being an Indian hobbyist, or painting red Indians on canvases that can be turned into commercials enticing tourists to buy tickets on the Atchison, Topeka, & Santa Fe Railroad. The postindian embraces survivance, resisting white domination.

Speaker Two: **Mr. Coyote**

So is this why white people still flock to these Wild West shows, Custer re-enactments, heritage events, Mountain Men

Chapter 2 ⁂ Disneyland Indians, Paris, circa 2014

Rendezvous and pow wows, and museum exhibits of paintings of Native Americans by white artists? Embracing the discourses of simulation, they live out a racist fantasy of colonial domination.

Speaker One: **Michelle H. Raheja**

Dear audience. Thank you for your patience. We wish you well. In closing, it would seem that the 'absolute fake' Indian will always be with us, at least this is the case for Disney, Buffalo Bill, and the Anglo painters who followed in Buffalo Bill's footsteps. (More on this in the next chapter.)

(Lights dim, the curtain comes down. Only the director and the narrator are left on stage. Slowly, from the right side of the curtain the Recruits and Second Generation Performers come back on stage. Their silhouettes are projected against a backdrop. The country-western band plays "Home on the Range." The director rushes from the stage. The stage is softly lit. From the right side of the curtain the Six Indians in Search of an Identity, aka SGP, come forward, stopping in the center of the stage, as if in a trance. The lift their arms and join hands, forming a circle, they slowly dance across the stage. The Six Native Americans turn, still holding hands, bow to the audience, leap off the sage, and disappear as the lights dim. The New Recruits follow the SGP. At the last possible moment they turn and take the steps leading off the stage. They run down the aisles between the rows of seats, laughing loudly as they leave the theatre [Pirandello, 1921/1998a, p. 74]. The director is left on stage, on the edge of darkness. The curtain comes down. The play is over. The audience looks perplexed, and then breaks out in cheers and clapping. The theatre goes dark.)

THE END

Chapter 3
Copper-colored Primitives

PROLOGUE

Speaker One: **Narrator** to audience

By way of introduction to this chapter, allow me to read the following statements:

We all drifted into Taos like skilled hands looking for a good steady job (Ernest Blumenschein, founding member of TSA, in Bickerstaff, 1955b, p. 25).

Actually, Ernest, for our travel brochures and calendars, we prefer a Indian subject with the Taos Pueblo in the background (William H. Simpson, Advertising Director for Atchison Topeka and Santa Fe Railway, quoted in Taggett and Schwarz, 1990, p. 137).

Indians in Color: Native Art, Identity, and Performance in the New West by Norman K. Denzin, 65–98. © 2015 Taylor & Francis. All rights reserved.

INDIANS IN COLOR

Walter, I can take a couple more of your paintings this year. They can both be 25 x 30 @$75 each or if you want I will take one 30 x 40 at $100 & let you use it for a while for exhibition purposes. But remember paint your Indians a little darker then you have been, copper-colored would be perfect (Carter Henry Harrison [1860–1953], five-term Chicago mayor (1897–1905, 1911–1915), art patron to TSA artists; letter to Walter Ufer, member of TSA, in Bickerstaff, 1955a, p. 142, paraphrase).

Speaker Two: **Norman K. Denzin**

From 1915 to 1927 the twelve artists who were founding members of the Taos Society of Artists produced a body of work (more than 400 paintings) that is popular and important to the present day (see Broder, 1980, pp. 312–321; Hassrick, 2008; 2009a, b; Lujan, 2003; Witt, 2003a, b). The TSA paintings of Taos Indians were presented to the public as accurate representations of an ancient, but dying culture.

In this chapter, a three-act play, Taos Pueblo Indians and native painters contest the way they and their culture were represented by the Taos Society of Artists. The play culminates in a play within a play, "A Protest on San Geronimo Feast Day," performed by the Seventh Generation Performers (SGP), Mr. Coyote, Ms. Coyote, the Forgotten Taos Painters, Carl Jung, and the San Geronimo Clowns. The performance takes place in the Taos Pueblo on San Geronimo Feast Day, September 30, 2015.

Stage Right: spotlights shine on this poster:

> **Regrettably our work helped turn the Taos Indian into a tourist attraction**
>
> (Walter Ufer, TSA artist)

Chapter 3 🎨 Copper-colored Primitives

ACT ONE, SCENE ONE
In Celebration of the Society of Taos Artists

The house lights go down. The curtains come up. The audience is seated in a large auditorium, facing a stage that looks like an artist's studio and an art gallery. The gallery is octagonal in design, with space to accommodate several large paintings. The program informs readers that the gallery is modeled after the Agnes Martin[1] Galley in the Harwood Museum. Stage right, a spotlight shines on The Taos Chamber Music quartet, which quietly plays a Schubert sonata.

The spotlight moves stage left to the center of the artist studio, which is filled with easels, stools, palettes, brushes, and a variety of props on tables and the floor, including Indian garments, headdresses, blankets, baskets, necklaces, and peasant sombreros. In the space designated as gallery, paintings and photos of artists are arranged in clusters on the white walls. Beautiful wood benches are located in front of select paintings. A young Taos woman enters from stage left, stops center stage, and strikes a pose for an imaginary painter. She is holding a ceramic bowl filled with ears of corn. A white scarf covers her hair. Her shoulders are draped with a flowing off-white shawl. She could have stepped off the canvas of Walter Ufer's painting, Indian Corn—Taos (1917) *(www.allposters.com/-sp/Indian-Corn-Taos-Posters_i7691675_.htm).*

The stage rotates clockwise. Activity moves from one site to another. The quartet keeps playing. The Indian model stands up and begins dancing with Walter Ufer,[2] who is painting her picture. The stage continues to rotate slowly. Pictures and photographs of Taos Indians, the Taos Pueblo, and persons identified as members of or friends of the Taos Society of Artists are projected on the giant drop down screen in the center of the gallery. Persons named in this montage include the 12 members of TSA, as well Fred Harvey, D. H. Lawrence and his wife Frieda, Georgia O'Keeffe, Martha Graham, John Collier, Elsie Clew Parsons, Alfred Stieglitz, Mary Austin, Mabel Dodge Luhan, Tony Lujan, Ansel Adams, Edward S. Curtis, and Thomas Moran.

The lights dim. The curtain comes down. The quartet continues to play softly. Georgia O'Keeffe, in a flowing dress, walks to center stage. The quartet stops playing. As Ms. O'Keeffe reads from the texts below a spotlight shines on Landscape with Indian Camp, *1920, by Ernest L. Blumenschein.*[3]

Speaker One: **Georgia O'Keeffe**

Dateline 15 July 1927. TAOS, New Mexico:
Let me take you to that historical moment when the Taos Society of Artists (TSA) was founded. The brilliant artists who formed TSA were all European trained and highly accomplished painters. They wanted to create a new vision of the American West and the American Indian. The purpose of the organization was primarily to stimulate general interest in art, to develop a high standard of quality among its members, and to promote the work of its members through traveling exhibitions. History will record the fact that these artists created a unique school of American Art. It was a national art that embodied a sense of the special relevance of the west and the vanishing Native American for American culture (see Bickerstaff, 1955a, p. 12, paraphrase). The founding artists were dear friends of mine: Bert Geer Phillips, Ernest L. Blumenschein, Joseph Henry Sharp, Oscar E. Berninghaus, E. Irving Couse, and W. Herbert Dunton (see Bickerstaff, 1955a). Later, the original six were joined by Walter Ufer, Victor Higgins, Jules Rolshoven, Catharine Critcher, Kenneth Adams, and E. Martin Hennings.[4] Tonight we honor their work by displaying their most famous paintings. Each artist is present and available to talk about his (or her) work.

ACT ONE, SCENE TWO
Taos—A Tourist's Genealogy[5]

Speaker One: **Narrator**

Let's pause for a moment. Consider the Tourist's Genealogy (also timeline) which is projected on the screen behind me.

Chapter 3 ⚜ Copper-colored Primitives

It gives more background to the history Georgia O'Keeffe is discussing.

1000–1450 AD	*Taos Pueblo is built.*
1540	*Pueblo is colonized by Spain.*
1847	*Taos Pueblo revolts against United States occupation of northern New Mexico.*
1872	*Atchison Topeka and Santa Fe Railroad (ATSF) completes line to Santa Fe.*
1876	*Fred Harvey forms alliance with ATSF to open trading posts, art galleries, tourist shops, and eating houses along the rail line.*
1879–1900	*U.S. Geological Survey creates Bureau of American Ethnology (BAE) headed by John Wesley Powell, who sends anthropologists and archaeologists into the field to study the Pueblos.*
1893	*Founding TSA member Joseph Henry Sharp visits Taos and produces* The Harvest Dance of the Pueblo Indians of New Mexico *for* Harper's Weekly.
1895	*Artists Ernest Blumenschein and Bert Phillips meet Sharp while studying in Paris.*
1898	*Blumenschein and Bert Phillips visit Taos. Their wagon breaks down twenty miles outside Taos. Phillips makes Taos his permanent home to begin the Taos art colony.*
1899	*Oscar Berninghaus sketches New Mexico landscape scenes for the Denver and Rio Grande Railroad, visits Taos and befriends Phillips.*
1900	*ATSF and Fred Harvey's Indian Detours aggressively promote the Pueblos as the "homes of the ancients." ATSF publishes a comprehensive guide to Indian tribes of the Southwest.*

1907	*School of America Research and the Museum of New Mexico is established in Santa Fe.*
1915	*July 1, 1915, Sharp, Blumenschein, Phillips, Berninghaus, Couse, and Dunton form the Taos Society of Artists (Broder, 1980, pp. 6, 9).[6]*
1915–1932	*Anthropologist Elsie Clews Parsons conducts her studies of the Taos Pueblo (Parsons, 1936, p. 5). She befriends TSA artists.*
1917	*The Atchison Topeka and Santa Fe Railroad purchases over 70 paintings by TSA artists, using them to illustrate brochures and calendars. The railroad provides free transportation to and from Taos for the artists, and arranges to bring tourists to their studios, as a way of promoting Southwestern travel (Bickerstaff, 1955a, p. 136).*
1915–1950	*Albert Looking Elk Martinez, Albert Lujan, and Juan Mirabal, self-taught Taos Pueblo painters, began exhibiting and selling their paintings to Taos tourists, but are shut out of Santa Fe markets.*
1927	*The TSA is dissolved.*
1962	*Lloyd Kiva New and Georg Boyce found the Institute of American Indian Arts (IAIA).*

ACT ONE, SCENE THREE
Taos—Another Opinion

Speaker One: **Seventh Generation Performers**

So these TSA guys all knew each other from their days in Paris. They had fat cat patronage. In truth, despite Georgia O'Keeffe's' noble-sounding statements, they were crassly commercial. TSA organized exhibitions where their work could also be sold to tourists riding on the Atchison Topeka & Santa Fe Railroad (see Taggett and Schwartz, 1990, p. 158; White, 1994, p. 67).

Chapter 3 ❖ Copper-colored Primitives

Speaker Two: **Peter Hassrick** (art historian)

You're wrong. It was not just a colony of painters out to make money, but an artist colony with literati, intellectuals and painters. They all contributed to a heightened intellectual environment that was challenging, creative, and rewarding, and that remains so to this day (Hassrick, 2009b, paraphrase).

Speaker One: **Harrison Eiteljorg**[7]

These wonderful paintings by the TSA are romantic representations of Indians and their culture ... and the other themes we associate with the Old West—landscapes, mountains, blue skies.

ACT ONE, SCENE FOUR
Taos—We Just Love Our Taos Indians

Speaker One: **Narrator**

We asked a number of prominent TSA painters to talk about what they like best about Taos, the Taos Indian, and what it means to be an artist in Taos.

Speaker Two: **Ernest L. Blumenschein**

As I write I see a primitive man, my first Taos Indian. He is a simple figure, picturesque, colorful, dressed in blankets artistically draped (paraphrase in Bickerstaf, 1983, p. 31).

Speaker One: **Bert Phillips**

Ah, the Taos Indian, simple yet so alien, yet they were the most perfect models I ever knew. They have a perfect kinship with wild animals (Phillips, paraphrase in Bickerstaff, 1955a, pp. 56–57).

Speaker Two: **Eanger Irving Couse**

I saw in Taos for the first time that copper colored Indian I had been looking for (in Bickerstaff, 1955a, p. 79).

INDIANS IN COLOR

Speaker One: **Oscar E. Berninghaus (Bernie)**

The Taos Indians are a splendid type: in fact the best I have ever seen, and if one wants to paint Mexican pictures, he can get a background near Taos just as picturesque as any spot in old Mexico (Berninghaus, paraphrase in Bickerstaff, 1955a, p. 94).

Speaker Two: **Walter Ufer**

I paint the Indian as he is. The Indian resents being regarded as a curiosity, as a dingleberry on a tree (Ufer, paraphrase in Bickerfstaff, 1955a, p. 129).

Speaker One: **W. Victor Higgins**

Here in Taos is the oldest of American civilizations. The manners and customs and architecture are the same today as they were before Christ was born. The Taos Indians are a people living in an absolutely natural state (Higgins, in Bickerstaff, 1955a, p. 180, paraphrase).

Speaker Two: **E. Martin Hennings**

I like it here in Taos. I love the adobe village with its Spanish people and of course the Taos Pueblo with its Indians with all the color and romance of their dress and history (Hennings, paraphrase in Bickerstaff, 1955a, p. 203).

Speaker One: **Kenneth Miller Adams**

Fellow artists, you must come to the land of enchantment and sunshine, picturesque subject matter, and inexpensive living. Be warned Taos has no paved streets and few houses have running water, but it is no primitive backwater, it is an outpost of civilization (Adams, in Bickerstaff, 1955a, p. 214, paraphrase).

Speaker Two: **Seventh Generation Performers**

There you have it. Primitives. A culture that has not changed since Christ was born. Simple copper colored Indians, endless sunshine, perfect models, splendid, colorful. And the artists were hired by patrons to paint a particular Indian, and they did what they were paid to do.

Chapter 3 Copper-colored Primitives

Speaker One: **Carter Harrison** (patron)

I told Walter to paint the Indians as they are today. Those were the paintings I wanted—Indians plowing with scrubby horses, Indians getting dirty digging in the field, Indians lying around the pueblo, and begging in the streets. This business of painting semi-naked Indians with bows and arrows and stalking game is a thing of the past (in Eldridge, Schimmel, and Truettner, 1986, pp. 83–84, paraphrase).

ACT ONE, SCENE FIVE
Taos Pueblo—We Don't Love These Painters

Speaker One: **Narrator**

We have now heard from the artists who used Taos models. A number of the prominent members of the Taos Pueblo modeled for TSA painters. We asked several of them to talk about being models and what being models for the Taos Society of Artists meant to them and the community.

Speaker Two: **Taos Models** in unison

We had had no experience as models. We did not know what was involved. They dressed us up in weird ways. Their stories misrepresented us. They used our pottery, blankets, and baskets as props for their paintings. They presented us as tourist attractions.

Then they did not want to pay us a fair wage. They were getting big money for their paintings from tourists in the Santa Fe galleries. We should have received at least half of what they were being paid (see Taggett and Schwartz, 1990, p. 170).

Speaker One: **Albert Lujan**

E. Irving Couse said I came to work drunk. That was a lie.

INDIANS IN COLOR

Speaker Two: **Albert Looking Elk Martinez**

> I started modeling for Mr. Couse, then I worked for Oscar Berninghaus, who gave me painting lessons. Before it was over I modeled for almost all of the original TSA painters. Being a model was hard work. The painters often insisted that I take almost all my clothes off and pose like I was an Indian brave from olden times. I am a modest man. I am easily embarrassed. I hated it when the young women of the Pueblo saw me with no shirt on. Whenever I could, I wore my own costumes and clothing.

Speaker One: **Juan Mirabal**

> It was comical and it was all make-believe. Mr. Sharp would have me wear the clothing of the Plains Indians and then ask me to wear the braids of the Taos Indians. Once he made White Wesel wear a Crow hat. Then he asked me to dress up like a Lakota Sioux because he had painted the Sioux. I said no (Taggett and Schwarz, 1990, p. 123).

Speaker Two: **Geronimo Gomez and Juan de Jesus** (models, and Taos carpenters)

> When Mr. Blumenschein had us pose for that painting he called "Star Road and White Sun," we did not know he was going to say that we were members of the peyote cult.[8] To outsiders this could convey the wrong impression. Peyote has special, sacred religious meaning for the Native American Church. It can effect cures. Peyote boys are always kind and clean (Parsons, 1936, p. 66; on the painting see Hassrick, 2008, p. 136).

Speaker One: **Taos Models** in unison

> The Taos Society painters wrote a joint letter to the publisher of the *Santa Fe N. Mexican* asking that he not print articles about them in which values and prices of their paintings were published. They were afraid we would see those prices and demand more money. It would jeopardize the whole Santa Fe-Taos Art movement. They would have to find models elsewhere (Taggett

Chapter 3 ▦ Copper-colored Primitives

and Schwartz, 1990, p. 170). Of course, that would be fine with us. We do not need them.

Speaker Two: **Narrator** sotto voice

We'll speak again with Albert Looking Elk Martinez, Albert Lujan, and Juan Mirable in Chapter Four. They became known as the Three (Forgotten) Taos Pueblo Painters and became quite famous in their own right.[9]

ACT ONE, SCENE SIX
A Second Opinion

Speaker One: **Mr. Coyote**

Truth be told, like all artists do, the TSA painters constructed their idealized version of Taos and the Taos Indian.[10] Here are two other versions of Taos.

Stage Right: Spotlight shines on photograph of Taos Pueblo, Frontpiece, and Plate 4 from Parsons (1936).

Stage Left: Spotlight shines on the text in a 1910 tourist brochure discussing the attractions in Taos (not to be read):

> Taos is a meeting ground for Indians of different Nations. It is a festival town, a marketplace where fairs are regularly held on the town Plaza, a place where Indians exhibit and sell colorful blankets with elaborate designs, beads, knifes, baskets. The Taos Valley is 7,000 feet above sea level. It is surrounded by the Sangre De Cristo Mountains. The valley is split by the waters of the Rio Grande River. It has a natural beauty defined by the lush land, the mountains, rivers, 'the lilac mist in the morning light shimmers above the sagebrush blue and bright gold of the upper mesas. And then you hear the laughter of living waters coming down from the mountain snows.' Welcome to heaven. (Laut, 1898, paraphrased in Taggett and Schwartz, 1990 p. 82).

INDIANS IN COLOR

Stage Right. Spotlight shines on this poster which replaces the previous photograph of Taos Pueblo:

Taos is no heaven for the Taos Indian
(Walter Ufer)

Speaker Two: **Mr. Coyote**

Taos is just a dusty old high mountain western town with high pretensions. It has Anglos, cowboys, tourists, artists, Taos Indians, Hispanic Americans, and the well-heeled women from the East Coast want to start a dance school. The *Taos Trading Post*, the one daily newspaper, advertises food for rich people—fresh fish, oysters, imported wines, liquors, and cheeses from San Francisco and New York. Kelly's Market sells San Francisco and New York newspapers (see E. Martin Hennings, "Taos Plaza, Winter," 1921. Oil, 34 x 40 inches. The Anschutz Collection, Denver, p. 81 in Broder, 1980).[11]

Speaker One: **Ms. Coyote**

Here is how the Taos Chamber of Commerce talks about today:

> Visit Taos—Soul of the Southwest! Take a moment to explore Taos and discover the beauty, the culture, the people that make Taos and Northern New Mexico the Land of Enchantment. Seated on the high-desert mesa at the foot of the Sangre de Cristo Mountains, Taos is rich with art and steeped in history. Home to Taos Pueblo, the Village of Taos Ski Valley and a colorful array of surrounding communities, Taos County has something for everyone. (www.taoschamber.com/Visitor-Info/Overview)

Chapter 3 Copper-colored Primitives

Speaker Two: **Mr. Coyote**

  In contrast, consider the following lines from the Taos Pueblo 'official website': "Taos is a sovereign nation within the United States; preserving our ancient traditions in the face of advancement of 'modernization' is our prime concern."[12]

Speaker One: **Ms. Coyote**

  Two versions of Taos—the Anglo, commercialized Taos versus Taos, the sovereign nation that resists commercialization and modernization.

Speaker Two: **Julie Schimmel** (art historian)

  The imaginary Taos Indians created by TSA appeared to integrate religious tradition, agricultural practice, and economic survival in a harmonious whole. In their paintings the artists often located the Taos Indian in an everyday setting which blended the architecture of the Pueblo with the surrounding Taos landscape. The paintings satisfied white consumers' fascination for images of noble Indians living in harmony with nature and community. The paintings fueled a hunger for the pristine, the alien, the sacred, and the pure. This was something that commercial America had lost. (Schimmel, 1994, p. xxiii, paraphrase)

Speaker Two: **Mr. Coyote**

  Just consider the titles of their paintings.

ACT ONE, SCENE SEVEN
A Genealogy of Titles

Stage Right: Spotlight shines on an incomplete list of painting titles by TSA painters (from Broder, 1980, pp. 312–321).

INDIANS IN COLOR

Other Medicine, Crow, War Bonnet Maker, Bear Goes to the Otter Ground (Sharp)	Water Carrier, The Rabbit Hunter (Phillips)	Prayer to the Spirit of the Buffalo (Sharp)
Apaches, Indian Girl with a Parrot and Hoop (Higgins)	Indian Dance, Feast Day (Blumenschein)	The Chief, Portrait of a Warrior (Dunton)
The Young Hunter, White Prince, Pawhyumma Umitilla Indian, Standing Indian with Child, Return of the War Party (Couse)	Taos Chief, Laguna Woman with Water Bottle (Ufer)	Indian Boy, Apache Camp at Boulder Lake, Indian Chief and Pony, Indian in White Robe (Berninghaus)
Mexican Child, Indian on Horse (Critcher)	Taos Indian (Hennings)	Taos Woman and Child (Adams)

Speaker One: **Mr. Coyote**

See what I mean. These titles are about Indians outside time and space—Mexican child, standing Indian, Indian boy, Indian girl—Indians as the object of the white painter's gaze.

Stage Left: Spotlight shines on select TSA paintings from the Smithsonian American Art Museum (americanart.si.edu/collections/search/artwork/?id=2247).

The Gift;[13] *Elk-Foot of the Taos Tribe;*[14] *Hand;*[15] *Making Sweet Grass Medicine, Blackfoot Ceremony;*[16] *Callers.*[17]

A stage hand enters stage right. She is pushing a media cart with a special edition Ziotek Media Carousel (ZT134150 134 1450). The Carousel is loaded with slides of the TSA paintings in the Smithsonian and the Eiteljorg Museum

Chapter 3   Copper-colored Primitives

of American Indians and Western Art in Indianapolis. Lights dim, a large screen drops down, the slide show begins. An off-screen announcer reads off the titles of the above paintings and artists names as they appear on screen.

Speaker Two: **Seventh Generation Performers**
How many times do we have to look at these paintings?!

ACT ONE, SCENE EIGHT
Who Is This Indian?

Speaker One: **Julie Schimmel**

The Taos Indian in these paintings exists in an imaginary unspoiled Western landscape. Dark-skinned female models in colorful dresses and white robes move through fields of corn. An Indian chief with hair in long braids stares at the viewer. He is frozen in time and place. The connection between the past, the present, and the future is fragile, and only somewhat make-believe (see Schimmel and White, 1994, p. 146).

Speaker Two: **Ms. Coyote**

Look carefully at these paintings. The painters are using native pottery and blankets as studio props. This allows them to introduce "bold design and color elements into their paintings" (Eldredge, Schimmel, and Truettner, 1986, p. 76).

Speaker One: **Mr. Coyote**

Pots, baskets, blankets, dances—you name it; these guys would use anything to represent Pueblo culture and to make their paintings look more authentic, including draping commercial English blankets over their models' shoulders. But, hey, this was also a way of creating a market for Indian crafts.

Speaker Two: **Taos Models** in unison

This was a rip-off! They turned us into fake, white Indians, and we stood for it!

INDIANS IN COLOR

Stage Right: Spotlight shines on a poster defining 'White Indian.'

White Indian: *The image of an American Indian painted by a white painter; a stereotypical 'Indian'—a noble savage, a fallen hero, an exotic Indian doing an exotic dance* (see Eldredge, Schimmel, and Truettner 1986, p. 33).

Speaker One: **Peter Hassrick**

You are all being too critical! These TSA paintings in the Smithsonian are outstanding works of art. *Still by the mid-1920s, American art critics were tiring of Indians in art* [italics added]. "The Indian, as a painter's subject, has gone a bit stale," wrote one observer in *Art News*. Blumenschein, and the other TSA artists, mindful of their need for national critical approbation, moved in a new direction. They did not abandon Indians, they simply made them a fundamental part of the larger scene, the New Mexico landscape. Thus, Blumenschein's (1920, 1929) *Landscape with Indian Camp*, with its exciting swirl of light and form, integrates the Indians into the pulse of nature, making them a crucial element in the otherwise abstract design. This solution would serve him and other TSA painters well in future years. (See Hassrick, 2008, p. 161; www.themagazineantiques.com/articles/ernest-blumenschein-and-the-indians/4/)[18]

Speaker Two: **New York Herald Art Critic** (November 12, 1921)

I'll answer you, Ms. and Mr. Coyote. We got tired of these paintings. For example, Mr. Blumenschein's *Superstition* (1921)[19] is a cheap and tawdry Indian picture. The Indians have suffered a good deal from the white man in times past, and it seems as though we were destined to hound them to the very end (quoted in Taggett and Schwartz, 1990, p. 225).

Speaker One: **Taos Models** in unison

They turned us into white Indians!

Chapter 3 ⊞ Copper-colored Primitives

ACT TWO, SCENE ONE
Rich Patrons and Their Imaginary Indians

Speaker One: **Ms. Coyote** (as cultural critic, in formal dress)

I'll chime in here. It is a mistake to lose your mind over these painters.

Speaker Two: **Gerald Vizenor** (Native American writer)

Couldn't agree more. With Indian art, for many white artists, rich patrons and reformers, Indian art is reverse imperialism at work. An old story. They attempt to honor Native culture, but encourage its marketing and consumption by white audiences, thinking that selling culture is the way to save it. There is also some selfishness at work. The Taos Indian was a marketable commodity. For many rich patrons and artists and writers the Taos Pueblo was also a source of their cultural renewal (Brooks, in Rudnick, 1984, p. 144).

Speaker One: **Mabel Dodge Luhan** (patron)

The true Pueblo Indian is gentle and stern, dignified, humorus, and at all times sincere and pure-hearted, a faithful friend. Indomitable, and unconquered, the Taos Indians are models for the spoiled and lost white man who has been buried under the accretions of objects that are destroying civilization (Luhan, 1947, pp. 12–15, paraphrase).

Speaker Two: **Mr. Coyote and Seventh Generation Performers** in unison

That pretty well sums it up. Once again white culture finds a way to exploit Indian culture for its own purposes!

Speaker One: **Henry McBride** (modernist art critic)

Mr. Coyote and SGP are correct in their critique. I'd even go a little farther. There is little recorded expression of deep feeling upon the part of the artist in these paintings (quoted in Hassrick, 2008, p. 140). Look at Ufer's *The Bakers*—there is no feeling here.

ACT TWO, SCENE TWO
Anthros and Artists

Speaker One: **Mr. Coyote**

The artists were following a stream of anthropologists, including Edgar L. Hewett, William Henry Holmes, Alice Fletcher, J. Walter Fewkes, Merton Miller, James Mooney, and Elsie Clews Parsons, who were there before or at about the same time as the painters. They were doing classical ethnographic research, taking pictures, making maps, recording Taos material culture, its kinship system, religious beliefs, ceremonies, rituals, and cosmology (see Eldridge, Schimmel, and Truettner, 1986, p. 70; Parsons, 1936, p. 121).[20]

Speaker Two: **Ms. Coyote**

In fact, some of the early anthropologists took the artists around and introduced them to village leaders and helped them find models and interpreters.

Speaker One: **Mr. Coyote**

So we had artists and anthropologists working together. Hewett felt it was the responsibility of the artists to recover and interpret the Pueblo arts, including the poetry, song, dance, music, masks, weaving, and embroidery, and to show the relationship between the arts and the sacred, religious-ritualistic aspects of Pueblo life. The anthropologists could help the artists better understand the complexities of Pueblo culture (Eldridge, Schimmel, and Teuettner, 1986, p. 70).

Speaker Two: **Ms. Coyote**

Ms. Parsons complained that nobody would talk to her. So how did she know what she was interpreting? Listen to what she says:

Speaker One: **Elsie Parsons**

I dedicate my book to my best friend in Taos, the most scrupulous Pueblo Indian of my acquaintance, who told me nothing

Chapter 3 ▦ Copper-colored Primitives

about the Pueblo and will never tell any white person, including me, anything his people would not have him tell (Parsons, 1936, p. 3, paraphrase).

Speaker One: **Vernon Lujan**

This is important, because those informants who did talk to her were ostracized for participating in her anthropological research. Some of the Taos natives were also stigmatized for modeling for the TSA painters (Lujan, 2003, p. 4).

Speaker Two: **Seventh Generation Performers**

This had consequences for the TSA painters. Even if they wanted to, they were not able to penetrate the inner side of the religious, cult, and clan systems in the Pueblo (Parsons, 1936, p. 36).

Speaker One: **C. C. Jung**

The Taos Pueblo Indians are unusually closed mouthed, and in matters of their religion absolutely inaccessible. They make it a policy to keep their religious practices a secret, and this secret is so strictly guarded that I abandoned as hopeless any attempt at direct questioning (1976, p. 40, paraphrase).

Speaker Two: **Taos Elder**

Our people have a detailed sacred oral history which is not divulged due to religious privacy.

Speaker One: **Ms. Coyote**

The TSA painters were reduced to producing colorful pictures of Taos Indians engaged in ritual performances, or crowd scenes outside the Catholic church.[21] They did not know what the scenes meant. These were the very paintings Harrison Eiteljorg bought and located in his museum.

INDIANS IN COLOR

ACT THREE, SCENE ONE
Another Announcement

Speaker One: **Georgia O'Keeffe**

> I have a major announcement. Mr. Coyote, will you please be quiet.
>
> I have some more text I need to read.

Dateline: 13 August 2013. *Denver, Colorado: Director of Denver Art Museum Announces Landmark Gift of Western Art:*

> *(ArtfixDaily.com) The Denver Art Museum (DAM) announced today that Denver collector Henry Roath has pledged to give the museum's Petrie Institute of Western American Art (PIWAA) his collection of approximately 50 artworks by masters of the American West, including Albert Bierstadt, Thomas Moran, Frederic Remington and Ernest L. Blumenschein. Considered one of the best private collections of western American art in the country, "Mr. Roath's generous gift establishes the museum's western American art collection as one of the best in the United States."*
>
> *PIWAA's mission is to recognize and promote the significance of the West and Western Art in the larger picture of American cultural development. Today DAM is home to one of the best collections in the country with specific strengths in early western American paintings, bronze sculpture, the Taos Society of Artists and early modernism in the American West.*
>
> *The Roath collection features paintings by three Taos Society of Artists; Landscape with Indian Camp, 1920, by Taos Society of Artists master Ernest L. Blumenschein; Black Bears, about 1933, by William Herbert Dunton; The Rendezvous, about 1930, by E. Martin Hennings.*
>
> *Mr. Roath stated, "I want the collection to be accessible to the public. I'm excited for visitors and the public to be able to experience the masters of the American West firsthand."*
> (www.artfixdaily.com/artwire/release/8480-denver-art-museum-announces-landmark-gift-of-western-american-art)[22]

Chapter 3 ⚞ Copper-colored Primitives

Speaker Two:　**Seventh Generation Performers**

WHAT?! This is it? This is your big announcement—the Blumenschein painting still has value and a prestigious museum like the Denver Art Museum wants to exhibit it with paintings by two other members of TSA?

Speaker One:　**Georgia O'Keeffe**

Don't be disrespectful. This is an important event!

Speaker Two:　**Mr. Coyote**

People are still paying good money to see these paintings!

Speaker One:　**Georgia O'Keeffe**

Of course, these are major artworks, and the Denver Art Museum is a major museum, one of the best in fact.

Speaker Two:　**Seventh Generation Performers**

Why all of this chest pounding over still one more museum buying Indian paintings by white artists?

Speaker One:　**Ms. Coyote**

I just do not get it. Joseph Sharp's *Squaw Winter* sold for $1,064,000, on July 24, 2004![23] (see taospainters.com/ TaosFoundersAuctionRecords.html)

Speaker Two:　**Georgia O'Keeffe**

My paintings sell at high prices, too. *Calla Lilies with Red Anemone* (oil on Masonite) sold for $6,166,000 on May 23, 2001. It would go for even more in 2015. (See www.georgiao-keeffepaintings.com/auction.html.)

Speaker One:　**Ms. Coyote**

But you don't paint Indians.

ACT THREE, SCENE TWO
A Little History

Speaker One:　**Norman K. Denzin**

I want to stop for a minute. Henry Roath's gift of the Blumenschein painting to the Denver Art Museum brings the story of the TAS artists and their paintings into the present. There is a smooth narrative at work here, one that brought art, capitalism, railroads and tourism together in the production of this artistic society (see also Denzin, 2008, pp. 115–117). Remember the timeline. With the completion of the transcontinental railroad in 1869, tourism emerged as a new form of cultural consumption. The soon-to-be-established national parks—Yellowstone, Yosemite, Grand Canyon—became points of destination for the European and American middle and upper classes. In order to entice people to travel to these sites, capitalists needed advertisements, photographs, paintings, and stories celebrating the beauty of the Southwest. Artists like Blumenschein, Phillips, Sharp, Couse, Dunton, Benninghaus, and Hennings supplied the necessary imagery for the establishment of Taos and Santa Fe as national tourist sites.

Speaker Two:　**Seventh Generation Performers**

And don't forget old Fred Harvey. The Fred Harvey Indian Department of Art was part of the Atchison, Topeka & Santa Fe Railroad, the rail line that funded the TSA artists. They wanted Indians painted in a certain way (Bryant, Jr., 1978; Taggett and Schwartz, 1990, p. 3).

Speaker One:　**Ms. Coyote**

Just like the Disney folks, they wanted their version of the Indian or no Indian at all. Listen to William H. Simpson, Advertising Director for ATSF:

Speaker Two:　**William H. Simpson** (to Ernest Blumenschein on June 8, 1911)

Chapter 3 ⏣ Copper-colored Primitives

We want Southwest pictures with Indians that have an advertising value apart from their art quality. Our goal is to enhance ATSF's image and promote tourism to the Southwest at the same time. We will buy these paintings from you, and this just helps avoid future conflicts over reproduction rights.

Speaker Two: **Stephen Fried**

Simpson started marketing the ATSF Calendar in 1907. They would buy as many as 50 TSA paintings a year for their calendars and magazine advertisements. Cynics said this is how the TSA painters supported themselves in their sweet little cowboy bohemia (Fried, 2010, p. 289, paraphrase).

ACT THREE, SCENE THREE
Painting Primitives

Speaker One: **Ernest Blumenschein**

Not so quick Stephen. We see ourselves as doing something more than railroad art. Those of us in TSA feel like we are following in the footprints of Gauguin and Van Gogh. We, too, have discovered the validity of the 'primitive' in our art. The Taos Indian is our primitive.

We are painting this Indian in the highlands of Taos, New Mexico. He or she is a simple figure, whether holding an Indian basket, riding a horse through the valley, harvesting corn, sitting on a bench, praying, dancing, building a fire, herding goats, or standing by a stream in autumn.

The art lies in the fact that the primitive has an unobtrusive place in an aesthetic space which we create. It is defined by color, spacing, pattern, composition, and decoration.

We are not just painting Indians. Indians are the raw material for a larger project, a truly higher national art (Blumenschein, in Bickerstaff, 1955b, p. 37, paraphrase; also Good, 1955, p.18).

INDIANS IN COLOR

Speaker Two: **Seventh Generation Performers**

This is all too familiar. In Paris Disneyland, Buffalo Bill's gang called us blood thirsty savages. That is not too far from being called primitive!

Speaker Two: **Walter Ufer**

I disagree with Ernest. We have to paint the Indian as he or she is today, trapped in an economic prison. But s/he is intelligent, s/he reads good magazines and the newspapers. S/he is a good at business. The Taos Indians have been turned into servants by whites, into waiters, maids, waitresses, auto mechanics, and ditch diggers. I don't want to paint noble savages sitting on pretty horses admiring lovely Western sunsets. (Ufer, paraphrased in Taggett and Schwartz, 1990, pp. 178, 180)[24]

Speaker One: **Seventh Generation Performers**

Hey, Walt, we could have used you and some of your paintings and arguments in Paris when we were tangled up with the Disney Wild West folks.

Speaker Two: **Carter Harrison**

Don't get too carried away with yourself, Walter. You never heard of Santa Clara, San Ildefonso, San Juan, or Taos until I made it possible for you to go there to paint. And when I asked you for a church painting, you gave me a desert landscape instead. That is not what I paid for! Remember, you begged me to buy your pictures (Harrison, quoted in Bickerstaff, 1955a, pp. 135, 146).

Speaker One: **Walter Ufer**

Begged. Indeed. I've been forced to paint for you at a price which barely gives me enough money to pay my expenses (Bickerstaff, 1955a, p. 147).

Speaker Two: **Carter Harrison**

Everybody has a price, Walter.

Chapter 3 ⊞ Copper-colored Primitives

Speaker One: **Walter Ufer**

I felt trapped in an unrevolved contradiction. I did not want to be part of an artistic project that exploited Indians. I wanted my art to show how Western capitalism was destroying Taos culture. That is why I painted Taos Indians as servants, as workers in low paying occupation, as menial laborers. I wanted to show the degradation. But I needed patrons to support my art, and they wanted only certain paintings. I was part of the exploitation that I opposed. I was exploited by the very capitalists that I loathed. I wanted to be a good guy, but I was a victim and kind of a bad guy at the same time!

Speaker One: **Joseph Henry Sharp**

Hold on, guys. It's not easy painting a Taos Indian. He gets drunk. He doesn't show up for work. He never holds a pose the way you want him to. Sometimes she goes on strike for more pay. She thinks she should get more than the established rate for models, which is 25 cents an hour, more than twice as much as an Indian can get for other work in Taos. I'm tempted to give the male models $10.00 and let them go off and drink themselves to death. (Sharp, paraphrased in Taggett and Schwartz, 1990, p. 119; see also Couse, in Taggett and Schwartz, 1990, p. 170)

Speaker Two: **Seventh Generation Performers**

Maybe they drink so they can deal with the pain of posing for your patronizing pictures.

Speaker Two: **Mr. Coyote and Seventh Generation Performers** in unison

This railroad calendar art stuff has to stop. It is demeaning to Taos Indians. Look at E. Irving Couse's *Wal-si-see (Good Medicine)*—This is a picture of an Indian in a loin cloth squatting in front of a fire. This was used in a 1914 ATSF calendar (www.qstation.org/Company_Calendars/1910s.html).

Old Ernest Blumenschein said that for more than 30 years Couse only painted Indians squatting (see Taggett and Schwartz, 1990, p. 229).

ACT THREE, SCENE FOUR
Disneyland West

Speaker One: **Mr. Coyote**

What's all the fuss about a bunch of white guys painting Indians. Nothing new here? You wrote about this in *Custer on Canvas* and *Indians on Display*.

Speaker Two: **Norman K. Denzin**

Those other books were about 19th-century painters creating their version of the Noble Savage. Their Indians had real names, and the painters located them within their respective tribal communities. The TSA are painting a nameless Indian with very little history or biography.

The Indian wars are over. The new Indian lives in poverty on reservations and in Pueblos. The TSA didn't paint that. Instead they painted an imaginary Indian in a Western landscape that was safe from the flood of tourists traveling west.

The tourists would travel to Arizona and New Mexico, visit the Grand Canyon, sign up for tours to Santa Fe and Taos, and stay in Fred Harvey Hotels, where they could buy the art work of the TSA painters and the craft work of Navaho, Zuni, Hopi, and Tano artists. In fact, as we noted in our time-line earlier, Fred Harvey operated a train-bus tour from Santa Fe to Taos—the Indian Detours—just so tourists could visit the TSA art colony and see the Taos Pueblos (see Fried, 2010, pp. 290–291).

Speaker One: **Seventh Generation Performers**

The Indian Detours to Taos were the closest thing America had to Disneyland in the 1920s (Fried, 2010, p. 291). Nothing like anything we ran into in Paris. Crowds flocked to Taos to see the Taos festivals and the rituals, to see the events during San Geronimo Feast Day, to watch the sacred clowns, to attend the Dance of the Sprouting Corn, to view the Hopi Snake Dance and buy pottery and paintings.

Chapter 3 — Copper-colored Primitives

Speaker Two: **D. H. Lawrence**

The Southwest in Taos is the great playground of the white American. The Indian, with his long hair, and his bits of pottery and blankets and clumsy home-made trinkets, is a wonderful live toy to play with. More fun than keeping rabbits, and just as harmless (Lawrence quoted in Fried, 2010, p. 289, paraphrase).

Speaker One: **Seventh Generation Performers**

Turn the tables, if we had won the Pueblo revolt, you'd be a sacrificial clown on San Geronimo Feast Day.

Speaker One: **Ms. Coyote**

RIGHT ON!

Speaker Two: **Mr. Coyote**

Now I get it! The painter's paintings are turned into ads for fat cat capitalist industrialists. Fat cats buy the original paintings and then donate them to museums for tax write-offs. Then the museums sing the praises of the painters and the capitalists. Nobody talks about the Indians in the paintings. Everybody assumes the painters had the right to paint the Indians the way they did, that they were doing the Indians a favor by using them as models and putting them in their paintings.

Speaker Two: **Gerald Vizenor**

Being Indian is just another way of saying the Indian is always the subject of colonial domination. The Indian is always the subject for one more painting by one more white man who sells his art and his Indian to the highest bidder.

Stage Right. Spotlights shine on these two posters:

> **The Taos Indian has been turned into a tourist attraction and we did it.**
>
> (Walter Ufer)

> They turned us into white Indians!
>
> (Taos Models as a chorus)

ACT THREE, SCENE FIVE
A Short Play—
"A Protest on San Geronimo Feast Day"

Speaker One: **Taos Models** in unison

It is time to stand up and say how we feel about being in those paintings.

Speaker Two: **Albert Looking Elk Martinez**

We were not paid fair wages. They made us look like pretend Wild West Indians, and that is not who we are. They never consulted us on how we wanted to be represented. It is an old story. They needed us, but we did not need them, except for the money they gave us. Poverty forced us to accept their terms.

Speaker One: **Albert Lujan**

They took advantage of us. On the one hand, our paintings helped attract tourists to Taos, and now we make money selling our paintings to white tourists! We get special exhibitions of our work. We have finally arrived.

Speaker Two: **Geronimo Gomez and Juan de Jesus** in unison

True, but don't forget Mr. Blumenschein made a lot of money from his paintings and never shared any of that money with us.

Speaker One: **Juan Mirabal**

Look carefully at the photographs of these painters. Their faces are cruel. Their lips are thin. Their noses are sharp, their faces furrowed. Their eyes have a staring expression. They always seem to be seeking something. I have to ask, what are they seeking? They always want something. They are restless, uneasy, unhappy. Some of them drink too much.

Chapter 3 ⚙ Copper-colored Primitives

Speaker Two: **Seventh Generation Performers**

It is a familiar story—the whites come to us for guidance, and then turn against us.

Speaker One: **Taos Models** in unison

We do not know what they want. We do not understand them.

Sometimes we think they are mad (Jung, 1976, p. 38).[25]

Speaker Two: **Seventh Generation Performers**

They do not know what they want!

Speaker One: **TSA Painters** in unison

You are being too hard on us. We are honest painters. We love Taos and its people. We are true artists. Critics said we did railroad art. Not true. We did the Taos Indians a big favor.

Speaker One: **San Geronimo Clowns** (with black and white body paint, wearing black and white costumes)

Maybe it is time for another Taos Revolt. The last real revolt was in 1847 when we fought against the United States occupation of the Pueblo.

The TSA painters are an extension of that occupation.

Speaker Two: **Seventh Generation Performers and Taos Models** as a chorus

We can stage a new revolt. We should sign a pledge. No more modeling for white painters. We should ask tourists to boycott their studios and not buy their paintings.

Speaker One: **Seventh Generation Performers**

Then their paintings will just hang there, outside history.

ACT THREE, SCENE SIX
Back to the Museum

Stage Right: The Taos Models, along with Mr. Coyote, the Seventh Generation Performers, and the San Geronimo Clowns, enter center stage. The sun is

setting. It is the second day of the 2015 San Geronimo Feast. The pole climbing competition has ended. Drummers are softly drumming. The Fancy Dancers are resting. The Feast Day director takes the microphone:

Speaker One: **Director**

Dear friends, we must come together as a community and honor the struggle that our artists are waging against how we have been represented by these powerful white artists.

Speaker Two: **Mr. Coyote**

You know we could ban the paintings from the Pueblo, and not permit them to be exhibited. But that is censorship, and it violates the principle of freedom of speech.

Speaker One: **Ms. Coyote**

Does freedom of speech give them the right to paint us any way they want? It is offensive and not good for our children, who wonder why they do not look like the Taos Indians in those TSA paintings.

Speaker Two: **Albert Lujan**

They did not help us when we wanted to be exhibited in the Santa Fe galleries and museums. They implied we were amateurs who did bad tourist art.

Speaker One: **Taos Models** as a chorus

We have a plan. We have our own museum here in the Pueblo. Harwood Museum has samples of the major paintings from each of the TSA artists. We could ask them to loan us one painting from each artist. We could mount our own exhibit. We would put their paintings in Plexiglass cases and line them in a long row in our main exhibit hall. On the opposite wall we would exhibit our own works.

Speaker Two: **Seventh Generation Performers**

We get it! You are putting them in your museum, even though they would not put you in their museum.

Chapter 3 Copper-colored Primitives

Speaker One: **Taos Models**

We are doing more than that. This exhibit will have a name: "Paintings from the Past." Before they enter the gallery, patrons are invited to listen to a pre-recorded interpretive lecture and watch a short film giving information about the odd, peculiar painting style of this group of early 20th-century American artists. Short biographies of each painter are given. At the end of the interpretive lecture and film, patrons will be guided through the exhibit by volunteers from the Taos Pueblo Culture Center. The volunteers will ask patrons to compare the TSA paintings to those done by the Native Taos artists. They will see two versions of the Taos Indian. First, they will see the imaginary TSA white Indian. Then they will see the humble ordinary Taos Indian, women in shawls, children playing in the plaza, men working in the fields.

Speaker Two: **Mr. Coyote**

We are still here. The TSA painters have died, only their paintings remain, and now we have them in our own museum, safe and sound. What they did in their heyday will not be repeated. But like William Faulkner (1950, p. 19) said, *"The past is never dead. It's not even past."*

We'll never be free of the representations of us in those paintings.

Speaker One: **Seventh Generation Performers**

These TSA artists were not activists. They claimed to be concerned about Taos and its culture, but they weren't. They argued that, like Gauguin, they were painting a vanishing primitive subject living in a natural state.

Speaker Two: **Ms. Coyote**

They were activist self-promoters, not activist artists using their art for social justice.

Speaker One: **Seventh Generation Performers**

Let's review the reasons why we should stop staging Wild West shows. Substitute white representations of Native Americans for Wild West shows, and these paintings, like the Wild West shows:

1. Perpetuate racial stereotypes.
2. Make Indians historical re-enactors of a past that never was.
3. Foreclose any possibility that Indians are able to occupy the same space and time as whites.
4. Foreclose any possibility that whites will ever stop appropriating Indian culture for white purposes.

Gerald Vizenor should have the last word.

Speaker Two: **Gerald Vizenor** (1999, p. vii, cited in Turner, 2013, p. 4, paraphrase)

Being Indian is just another way of saying the Indian is always the subject of colonial domination. The Indian is always the subject for one more painting by one more white man who is willing to sell his art and his Indian to the highest bidder.

ACT THREE, SCENE SEVEN
Setting Sun

Stage Right: The Taos Models, along with the San Geronimo Clowns, return to center stage. A red sun sets behind the mountain. The drummers are softly drumming. Fancy Dancers return to the stage and slowly dance. The San Geronimo Clowns begin another pole climbing contest. Stage lights dim. Dr. Jung walks on stage.

Speaker One: **C. C. Jung**

This is my fourth visit to the Pueblo. This morning I stood by the river and looked up at the mountains, which rise six

Chapter 3 ⚅ Copper-colored Primitives

thousand above this plateau. I was thinking, as I think the Taos Indian thinks, that this was the roof of world, and all life comes from the mountain, the water, the sun. If I set aside my European rationalism I can transport myself into this space. When I do that I know that the Taos Pueblo will continue to exist as long as her sacred mysteries and rituals are not desecrated by outsiders. (1976, pp. 40–43)

Speaker Two: **San Geronimo Clowns**

Right on, Dr. Jung, You got it right. This is our sacred home and we're not going any place.

Speaker One: **Taos Models**

As artists we were bound by an oath shared by all members of the Pueblo, to keep the sacred practices of the Pueblo secret. We would never paint in a way that would give whites access to this world.

Speaker Two: **San Geronimo Clowns** as chorus

Amen, and praise to St. Jerome, our patron saint.

Curtain.

House lights up.

San Geronimo Clowns enter stage left. They race across the stage, stop abruptly, turn, join hands, and bow to the audience. They then take the steps leading off the stage and run down the aisles between the rows of seats, laughing loudly as they leave the theater.

Applause.

The theatre goes dark.

THE END

CODA

I have troubled the concept of a unified Indian subject who patiently modeled for the TSA artists. In so doing I have challenged the fiction of the vanishing Taos Indian. (The only Indian in danger of vanishing was the fictional Indian painted by the TSA artists.) The Taos Indians resented being models, but doing so provided them with an income. Ironically, by watching the painters, they learned how to become painters themselves. As I show in the next chapter, when given the opportunity, they produced their own representations of the Pueblo. Their paintings were quite unlike those produced by the TSA artists, whose work was funded by wealthy patrons who directed their work and their subject matter.

Primarily illustrators, the European trained TSA artists painted Indians on demand—*copper brown not as dark skinned as the ordinary Red Man*—according to the wishes of their patrons. The artists were also dudes, dandies, and would-be cowboys. Their Wild West fantasies did not stop them from playing tennis and bridge and dressing formally for dinner by candlelight. They had servants, and often drank imported wines with their fancy meals (see Taggett and Schwartz, 1990, p. 3). Their paintings helped attract tourists to Taos and helped fund their upper-middle-class style of cultural consumption.

At a deeper level, this play, and the play within the play, has been about art, capitalism, museums, and tourism, and the destructive effects of these forces on our understandings of Native Americans today. Art is never innocent.

In the next chapter Albert Looking Elk Martinez, Albert Lujan, and Juan Mirable, the Three Forgotten Taos Pueblo Painters, tell their story (Lujan, 2003; Witt, 2003a, b).

Chapter 4
Taos Indians on Canvas

PROLOGUE

Speaker One: **Narrator**

> Since the publication of *Indian Painters and White Patrons* by Jerry Brody in1971, the large degree to which Anglo patrons shaped and eventually stultified Indian painting in the Southwest has generally been acknowledged. From Edgar Lee Hewett to Dorothy Dunn, Euro-American involvement in southwest Indian paintings has been ubiquitous. Native American painters whose work did not confirm to the accepted norms of the period were denied patronage by the major supporters of the movement and excluded from the history of Indian painting. (Watson, III, 1994, p. 62)

Indians in Color: Native Art, Identity, and Performance in the New West by Norman K. Denzin, 99–124. © 2015 Taylor & Francis. All rights reserved.

Speaker Two: **J. J. Brody** (art historian)

For Santa Fe trained Native artists, there was a basic philosophical problem that was never solved by the studio: not only how, but what does the Indian artist paint (Brody, 1971, p. 146)?[1]

Speaker One: **Ruth Phillips** (director of museum anthropology)

I have come to reject the scholarly apparatus that inscribes inauthenticity to commoditized Indigenous tourist art as a central problem in the way art history has addressed Native art (Phillips, 1998, p. x, paraphrase).

ACT ONE, SCENE ONE
Still Another Announcement

The lights briefly dim. The audience enters a darkened auditorium and sits quietly. The curtain rises. The Taos Pueblo drummers and three Native flute players enter stage left, take their places, and begin playing. The San Geronimo Clowns with black and white body paint, wearing black and white costumes, race across the stage. The stage makes a slow rotation, stopping in front of a set that looks like the entrance to a museum. Paintings hang on the wall. A large sign reads: Harwood Museum of Arts. *Georgia O'Keeffe steps forward. The music stops.*

Speaker One: **Georgia O'Keeffe**

Welcome to Taos and to the Harwood Museum of Arts. This is a historical moment. Tonight, by recognizing three important native Taos painters, we try to correct history.

Stage Right: Spotlight shines on a large poster announcing a new exhibit:

Dateline: January 24–April 20, 2014, Harwood Museum of Art of the University of New Mexico, Taos, New Mexico.

The Three Forgotten Taos Painters:
Albert Lujan, Albert Looking Elk Martinez and Juan Mirabal[3]

Chapter 4   Taos Indians on Canvas

Stage Left: Life-size photographs of the Three Forgotten Taos Painters (from Baca, 2003, p. 64) are projected.

Speaker One: **Georgia O'Keeffe** (cont'd) soto voice

Allow me to read the following text, which will introduce you to the three artists. Forty of their works will be on display for the next four months in the Harwood Museum:

> *The Three Forgotten Taos Painters were brilliant artists who celebrated Taos life while refusing to depict the sacred rituals and privileged themes of Taos culture (Baca, 2003, p. 66; Lujan, 2003, p. 4). Today, their paintings are regarded as "invaluable records of the pueblo and her people" (Baca, 2003, p. 68). In this respect they were not like the Taos Society of Artists, who focused on the sentimental themes of the vanishing and noble Indian, painting Taos natives as Plains warriors or Ancestral Pueblo sun worshippers (Baca, 2003, p. 65). Regrettably, the three forgotten painters were subjected to considerable criticism. And remember, they were models for the TSA painters before they became artists in their own right.*

Speaker Two: **Vernon G. Lujan**

The Taos Three provide an example of a Native artistic aesthetic. They painted the landscape, the buildings, and scenes from everyday village life in a naturalistic realistic style (Baca, 2003, p. 64).

Speaker One: **San Geronimo Clowns** as chorus

They were not like the European trained TSA painters who appropriated traditional Indian imagery for their own romantic representations of Pueblo life (Baca, 2003, p. 64).

Speaker Two: **Vernon G. Lujan**

As a historical reminder, the 1928 Miriam Report[4] recommended that the government encourage the development of

Native Indian art. The Santa Fe Indian School was selected to be the first training center for Indian Arts and Crafts.

Speaker One: **Elmo Baca**

True, but the Taos Three were not trained there. In fact their style of painting was discouraged by the Santa Fe School.

Stage Right: A spotlight moves back and forth across select paintings by the three artists (from Lujan, 2003, pp. 3–6; Witt, 2003b, pp. 7, 9 ,10, 11, 12, 13, 14, 15), and select TSA paintings where the Taos Three were used as models.

THE TAOS THREE:

Untitled painting of Taos Pueblo, *by Albert Lujan*[5]
Untitled oil, *by Albert Looking Elk*[6]
Xmas Eve, *by Juan Mirabel*[7]
Untitled, *by Juan Mirabel*[8]

TAOS SOCIETY OF ARTISTS (as models):[9]

A Son of the War Chief, *by Oscar Berninghaus*[10]
Elk-Foot, Taos Indian, *by E. Irving Couse*[11]
The Musicians, *by Henry Sharp,*[12] Collection Springville Museum of Art, Springville, Utah.

Speaker Two: **Albert Lujan, Albert Looking Elk Martinez, Juan Mirabal** in unison

It was not fun being models for the white painters. At times it was quite degrading. Irving Couse and Mr. Sharp had us take off our clothes and pose nearly naked, as if we were warriors from the olden days. Sometimes they had us dress up like we were Crow Indians or Lakota Sioux. It was not comical. It was

Chapter 4 — Taos Indians on Canvas

insulting. (see Schimmel and White, 1994, p. 147)

Speaker One: **Seventh Generation Performers**

These are the true Taos painters! They were too good to be models. It's about time they get some attention. For years we've only heard about those white TSA painters, or the Santa Fe trained Native painters. The Three Forgotten Taos Painters produced a substantial body of work.[13] Their work was not commissioned, endorsed, or supported by Santa Fe art patrons. (Hoxie, 2001, pp. 18–20; Schrader, 1983, p. 12)

Stage Right: Spot lights shines on this poster:

The Taos Indian is a simulation

(Gerald Vizenor)

ACT ONE, SCENE TWO
Albert Lujan

Speaker One: **Albert Lujan (1892–1948)**

I was a farmer before I became a full-time painter. Before I started painting I modeled for several of the TSA painters (Lujan, 2003, p. 4). I was well respected in the Pueblo. I was one of the five caretakers in the Taos Pueblo church. I was responsible for the overall maintenance and painting of the church interior. One day I tried painting a Pueblo landscape on a board. A tourist asked "if I sold my artwork." I said, "No I never had," but she persisted, and she bought my painting. Then she took me in to Taos and bought me some real oil paint and supplies. That is how I got started (Watson, 1994, p. 60). I was self-taught. My Tewa name, Xenalua, translated to 'Weasel Arrow' (Taylor, 2000, p. 59). I usually signed my paintings, Albert

INDIANS IN COLOR

Lujan Arrow, with a drawing of an arrow. When the tourists starting pouring into town and being general nuisances, I felt we should start charging admission. This way it was like the tourists were working for us, and not the other way around.

I started seeing myself as a particular kind of painter. I had modest goals, to paint the village as I saw it. None of the Taos or Santa Fe galleries would carry my work. I set up my easel[14] in the plaza and the tourists watched me paint. See my *Taos Pueblo*, oil on panel (Witt, 2003b, p. 13).

Stage Right: Spotlight shines on photograph of Albert sitting in front of his easel in the plaza, painting a scene from the Pueblo (from Taylor, 2000, p. 57).

Stage Left: Spotlight shines on an untitled painting by Albert Lujan —"Three Women Walking Toward Taos Pueblo." Done in muted colors, the painting depicts three woman walking past three trees and a horse on the way to the Pueblo, which is in the background.

Speaker One: **Albert Lujan** (cont'd)

I love this painting. I could have sold a 100 just like it. When I painted in the plaza I wore my hair in traditional braids and wore a white waistcoat atop my trousers. I painted the main pueblo houses, sometimes an isolated adobe residence framed by beehive ovens. I painted the mountains behind the Pueblo, and sometimes I painted human figures (Baca, 2003, p. 64). Later, I sold my paintings from my curio shop in front of my house, where I also sold pottery, and bows and arrows. I made money this way. I sold my paintings directly to tourists, with no middleman. Tourists from all over the United States and around the world bought my work. I was rather proud. Today, my paintings are in several museums: Millicent Rogers Museum, Taos Cowboy Hall of Fame, National Museum of the

Chapter 4 ⚞ Taos Indians on Canvas

American Indian, the Smithsonian, the Southwest Museum of the American Indian in Los Angeles. Not too bad, I'd say.

Stage Right: Albert turns right and steps back into his photograph. The lights shift to the next speaker.

Speaker Two: **Bradley F. Taylor**

Tony was a prolific artist. He was a highly successful salesman of authentic, contemporary art, and he sold it in his specialized niche—the white Taos tourist market. He had no middleman, no gallery that exhibited his work, no connection to the railroads. He made it all on his own (2000, p. 65).

ACT ONE, SCENE THREE
Albert Looking Elk Martinez

Speaker One: **Albert Looking Elk Martinez** (1888–1940)

I was modeling for TSA painters when I was twelve years old. I was the model for several of E. Irving Couse's paintings, including *Elk-Foot of the Taos Tribe, Klickitat Medicine Man, The Blanket Seller, The Pottery Decorator, Strange Gods, Indian Lessons, The Tom-Tom Lesson* (see Bickerstaff, 1983, following page 84). I was also the model for Oscar Berninghaus's *A Son of the War Chief* (Watson, 1994, p. 65). He mentored me. Perhaps because of his mentoring, I received early recognition as an artist in the *Taos Valley News*.

Speaker Two: **Art Critic**

Taos has a native artist ... Albert Martinez of the Pueblo... He has painted a number of pictures of merit, several of which he has been able to sell at a fair price (*Taos Valley News*, July 16, 1918; also Witt, 2003b, p. 11).

INDIANS IN COLOR

Speaker One: **Albert Looking Elk Martinez**

I had occasional showings (1923, 1930) at the Museum of Fine Arts in Santa Fe. I sometimes painted in the flat Santa Fe school style, and this offended some white collectors and curators. They said I had not been properly trained in that technique (Taylor, 2000, p. 59).

Stage Right: Spotlight shines on photograph of Albert Looking Elk Martinez sitting in front of his easel in his studio, painting a scene from the Pueblo (from Taylor, 2000, p. 64).

Stage Left: Spotlight shines on "Untitled oil" by Albert Looking Elk. Oil on Board. Courtesy National Museum of the American Indian (see Watson, III, 1994, p. 62). The "pueblo is steeped in shadows, set against the backdrop of the mountains" (Watson, III, 1994, p. 65). "The light suggests the time is early morning or late afternoon. The pueblo seems to be a desolate place, but there is a sense of calm in the emptiness. A women in a black shawl walks across the plaza. Her identity is unimportant, only her presence is noteworthy" (Watson, III, 1994, p. 65, paraphrase).

Speaker One: **Albert Looking Elk Martinez** (cont'd)

This is one of my favorite oils. I worked really hard to get the shadows and the light just right. I hope you like it. I got pretty good with my oils and my water colors, and I was getting exhibited in the big galleries in Santa Fe. Some people said I bridged the gap between the native painters in Santa Fe and Taos. I disagree. One Christmas, I think it was 1915, Oscar Berninghaus gave me a complete set of oil paints and brushes. That's really what got me started as a painter. Pretty soon I was selling paintings to the tourists in the Pueblo, for $5 or $10. Some of them were postcard size. In a few years I was winning prizes in the Santa Fe Fiesta.

Chapter 4 ⸬ Taos Indians on Canvas

Speaker Two: **Elmo Baca**

Albert Looking Elk, like Albert Lujan, lived a double or triple life. He appeared unnamed in Berninghaus's paintings as a Taos Indian. When he sold his paintings to tourists he was an artist and an entrepreneur. In the Taos community he was a leader and a maverick.

Speaker One: **Albert Looking Elk Martinez**

I was doing so well I stopped working as a model and just became a full-time painter.

Speaker Two: **Ms. Coyote**

Critics outside Taos said Looking Elk never developed the 'definable' Indian style preferred by the Santa Fe School. His oils were regarded as not "Indian enough." His water colors, including the fourteen paintings in his "Story of Indian Creation," were seen by wealthy patrons as ethnological artifacts, not art. One patron called him an informant, not an artist (Watson, III, 1994, p. 62).

Speaker One: **Mr. Coyote**

What is ethnography? What is art?

Speaker Two: **Mary Cabot Wheelwright**

I commissioned Looking Elk to create a series of paintings labeled "The Story of the Indian Creation." Looking Elk painted fourteen images. I purchased this series, not as an art patron, but as an ethnographic investigator. His paintings were the story of Indian creation. He was an ethnographer and a gifted talented artist, too. (Watson, 1994, pp. 67–68)

Speaker One: **Albert Looking Elk Martinez**

You could say I was selling my art and what my patron's regarded as ethnographic information. I believe a good artist has to be a careful observer, like an ethnographer.

107

Speaker Two: **Elsie Parsons**

All good ethnographers are artists and all good artists are ethnographers. I studied the art work of the Native Taos painters because they brought me close to the rhythms of daily live that I tended to overlook.

ACT ONE, SCENE FOUR
Ms. Parsons, the Painter and His Car

Speaker One: **Georgia O'Keeffe**

Albert Looking Elk Martinez was one of the first members of the Taos Pueblo to purchase an automobile—a Studebaker. He was criticized by Elsie Parsons, the anthropologist, who had been thwarted in her efforts to study sacred pueblo rituals.

Speaker Two: **Elsie Parsons**

During the recent sacred ceremonial period, Albert Looking Elk Martinez, chief of the Big-hail people and one of the Peyote boys, drove his own motor car to Albuquerque with a 'bunch of boys' to dance for the Mayor of New York, when his honor stopped off for an hour to be made a 'chieftain of the Thirty Tribes'. Of course there is a distinction between motoring and dancing outside the town and within the wall, but how long can the distinction be maintained (Parsons, 1936, p. 119)? These peyote boys were compromising their own cultural integrity when they drove to meet the mayor from New York in Albuquerque.

Speaker Two: **Ms. Coyote**

Take note, when Ms. Parsons criticizes Looking Elk for buying a car, she ignores his paintings.

Speaker One: **AlbertLujan**

Albert Looking Elk was not the only person from the Pueblo to buy a car. Lots of people from the Pueblo were buying cars.

Chapter 4 ⬚ Taos Indians on Canvas

Speaker One: **Albert Looking Elk Martinez**

Ms. Coyote, Albert, thank you for your support, but let me speak to the issues raised by Ms. Parsons. I bought my car with the money I made from the farmers' market and from selling my paintings to tourists. I am proud of this car. I worked hard to get that money. Many times I took trips to Santa Fe and Albuquerque with my friends in this car. We'd put the top down and just enjoy the rush of the wind on our faces. We'd look up at the blue sky, the white clouds, and the sacred mountains. We felt free. Did you think I was being too modern with my car, and did you think I should not be leaving the Pueblo?

Speaker Two: **Mr. Coyote**

Who is Ms. Parsons to talk about compromising cultural integrity? In her remarks she compromises her credentials as an anthropologist studying our culture. She is passing judgment on me and my friends from the Pueblo.

Speaker One: **Ms. Coyote**

Is Ms. Parsons saying it is OK for Albert to drive and dance in Taos, but not in Albuquerque? Some people say she is crying sour grapes, that she is still mad because of the tribal council's policy of forbidding recordings of any tribal ceremonies (Baca, 2003, p. 66).

Speaker Two: **Elsie Parsons**

You misunderstand me. I'm upset over what Albert represents. Albert and the Pueblo can't have it both ways. They can't live in the past and the present at the same time. You can't drive your motor car to Albuquerque and meet the Mayor of New York and still be a leader inside the walls of the Pueblo. When he does this Albert is telling the rebellious young people with their American boarding school education, their American shirts and trousers, and their non-Navaho-made jewelry that it is okay to abandon the sacred ways, buy American cars, paint and sell pictures to tourists and museums, and even open a curio shop. Where is ancient Taos in all of this?

Speaker One: **Albert Looking Elk Martinez**

Ancient Taos will always be here. We are going nowhere. We just need protection from outsiders like you.

Speaker Two: **Ms. Coyote**

Elsie, you should understand that Albert is a highly respected member of the Pueblo. You are treating him as if he is a rebellious teenager. What gives you the right, as an anthropologist, or as a non-Pueblo-member, to criticize the Taos Pueblo and leaders like Albert Looking Elk?

Speaker One: **Elsie Parsons**

I have every right. They are destroying something special. In ten years the use of the solar calendar will disappear. The American calendar will prevail. Whiskey will replace peyote. Their syncretic version of Catholicism will be diluted. Public ceremonies will break down. There will be more intermarriages, more Mexican half-breeds. The kiva groups will become clubs and look like vaudeville groups. Comanche and Apache dances will be danced on the Patron Saint's Day. In 50 years the sacred Pueblo customs may be remembered, but not practiced. In the end only a few old elders will be able to talk about them (Parsons, 1932, p. 120, paraphrase).

Speaker Two: **Albert Looking Elk Martinez**

The Pueblo has always adjusted and adapted to outside influences. When the Catholic priests came and built their churches, our ancestors listened and learned to blend our religion and rituals with those of the church. It's called synchronicity—the experience of two or more events as meaningfully related, where they are unlikely to be causally related (see Parsons,1936, pp. 72–73).[15]

Chapter 4 ❖ Taos Indians on Canvas

Speaker One: **Ms. Coyote**

Outsiders come in and introduce change and then blame the culture for changing. We are always changing.

Speaker Two: **Elsie Parsons**

I just say thank goodness the TSA painters have been able to record in their paintings this ancient culture and its people before it disappears. They could not have done it without the help of anthropologists like me and Edgar Hewett.

Speaker One: **Ms. Coyote**

We have always gotten along just fine without anthropologists telling us how to live our lives. Furthermore, we have our own artists; we don't need those TSA painters selling their images of us.

Speaker Two: **Vine Deloria, Jr.**

Ms. Coyote is correct. We have to fight back. For years I've criticized the anthropologists for their impersonal dissection of living Native American cultures.

ACT TWO, SCENE ONE
Juan Mirabal, Muralist

Speaker One: **Georgia O'Keeffe**

Ms. Coyote, are you quite done? We need to move on to Juan Mirabal.

Stage Right: As Georgia O'Keeffe speaks, the spotlight moves from her to the photograph of Juan Mirabal, who steps out of the photograph and joins her center stage.

INDIANS IN COLOR

Speaker Two: **Juan Mirabal** (1903–1970)
My history is a little different from the two Alberts, although I was also a model for TSA painters. I started my career as a model for Joseph Henry Sharp, and I was in a number of Sharpe's paintings.[16] I had formal training in the Taos Valley Art School, which was founded and directed by Luis Ribak.[17] I learned a lot from Luis, and I liked his radical politics. He taught me how to move from realism to the principles of abstract art. Luis was extending the work of the Cubist and expressionist painters. He was moving into non-objective abstractionism, into what some called 'lyrical abstract expressionism.' I learned how to use a bold, bright color palette. I learned how to suggest motion and movement with a few strokes. I learned how to use Indigenous symbols in my abstract representations of native dancers.[18] Luis was also a muralist. He worked with Diego Rivera. He taught me a great deal about mural painting.

Stage Left: Spotlight shines on three untitled paintings by Juan Mirabal— "Untitled," ca 1930, Oil on Panel, Harwood Museum Collection; "Untitled," Oil on Panel, private collection (p. 14 in Witt, 2003b); "Xmas Eve," ca 1932, courtesy of Charlotte Mittler, Photography, Santa Fe (in Witt, 2003b, p. 15). These are abstract and realistic representations of mountains, rolling mountain ranges, clouds, rivers, trees, the houses in the Taos Pueblo, Christmas dancers dancing in the square, barely visible humans walking across the plaza, trees, sacred dancers wearing masks dancing side by side in a closed space as little children and women with red and yellow shawls and white boots watch the dancers. The images are abstract, cubist, modernist, and realistic at the same time. The colors are bold, dramatic, and muted— tans, multiple shades of blue, green, orange, brown, beige, tan—complex design patterns are folded into other complex patterns; a white-faced dancer, an abstract figure, all angles and planes, holds two white feathers in each hand as he dances in place—movement, depth, shadows.

Chapter 4 ▦ Taos Indians on Canvas

Speaker Two: **Juan Mirabal** (cont'd)

In the 1930s I met and fell in love with Marjorie Eaton.[19] We lived together, but it was difficult. In those days white women and Indian men could not date or be intimate. Marjorie was a talented actress, a brilliant artist, a muralist trained by Diego Rivera. She taught me many of the techniques she had learned from Diego. I wanted to become a muralist and learn the true art of fresco painting (see Baca, 2003, p. 67; Witt, 2003b, p. 15).

Speaker One: **Marjorie Eaton**

I was absolutely infatuated with Juan. He was so handsome! We were so in love. We were both artists. We experimented with egg tempura, with fresco, with the new theories, like cubism. We did what we had to do to make ends meet. I got a job waiting tables at the Kit Carson Café. Juan got a commission to paint a large mural on the inside wall of the café. This was a little ironic, given what Kit Carson did to the Indians with the enforced long walk and his scorched earth policy.[20] While I waited tables, Juan painted his magnificent mural. It had mountains, dancers, churches, the river, the Pueblo, clouds, the blue sky. It was abstract and realistic and filled with bold colors (Baca, 2003, p. 67; Witt, 2003b, p. 15). I'd take a break and just watch Juan work. We'd have lunch together. That beautiful mural is still there. Later Juan painted a large mural on the veranda of the Adobe and Pines Bed and Breakfast. You can still see it. Pretty soon I started getting good acting parts in Hollywood and making a big salary.

Speaker Two: **Juan Mirabal**

We were a team, Marjorie and me. We got a lot of criticism for being a couple. Truth be told, she was the better artist, a much better muralist.

Speaker One: **Marjorie Eaton**

There are hypocrites in Taos, believe it or not. Some people were supposedly 'scandalized ' by our loving and mutually beneficial relationship, a relationship that lasted throughout our lives together, even after I got jobs in Hollywood acting in the movies and on TV (Baca, 2003, p. 67, paraphrase).

Speaker Two: **Juan Mirabal**

Marjorie gave me courage to experiment, to take what I had also learned from Luis and the two Alberts and try something new. I wanted to respect the culture of the Pueblo but find a style of painting that would let me paint the dances and the dancers in a new and bold way. I did this by engaging with the new philosophies, like cubism. Unlike the TSA painters, who did realist paintings of our dances, my pictures were abstract. My paintings were inspired by the Taos Pueblo culture, its drama, color, rituals, its beauty, and the beauty of the Pueblo structures. My paintings honor these features of our culture, our history, and this sacred landscape.

Speaker One: **Ms. Coyote**

Juan's experiments with contemporary art styles can be seen as a critique of Elsie Parsons and her fear that the Taos Pueblo was succumbing to the temptations of the modern, secular world. In fact Juan used secular art forms to celebrate the artistry of daily life in the Pueblo.

Speaker One: **Marjorie Eaton** (swooning)

Juan was a genius!

ACT TWO, SCENE TWO
Summing Up

Speaker One: **Ms. Coyote**

Summing it up, the three forgotten Taos artists were ignored by art historians and art critics until the 2003 major exhibit in the Harwood Museum in Taos. They exerted considerable influence over the next generation of Taos Pueblo painters (Lujan, 2003, p. 6; Witt 2003a, b; and below).[21]

Chapter 4 ⚏ Taos Indians on Canvas

Speaker Two: **Mr. Coyote**

Albert Lujan's *A Taos Pueblo Painting of a Group of Taos Indians at Taos Pueblo* just sold for $3,250, and his Taos Pueblo Village Scene sold for $7,500. [22]

Speaker One: **Ms. Coyote**

Hey, that is not a bundle of money, but it is money. It is time to celebrate! This exhibit is fantastic. We've waited a long time for this day to come, but never fear, the critics are out there.

Lights dim. Curtain comes down.

ACT THREE, SCENE ONE
Patrons and Museums

Lights come back up; curtain rises.

Speaker One: **Bradley F. Taylor**

I'm considered an expert on the three Taos Pueblo painters. I have collected their works and I have written articles about them (Taylor, 2000, p. 65). Ms. Coyote is right. The critics are out there.

Speaker Two: **Vernon G. Lujan**

From the very beginning critics jumped on this work. It was called bad tourist art.

Speaker One: **J. J. Brody**

The museum directors and the Santa Fe intellectuals said the only authentic Indian style could be traced to aboriginal roots seen in prehistoric murals and earlier Pueblo kiva paintings. The work of the Taos Three did not have these aboriginal roots.

Speaker Two: **Samuel W. Watson III**

Indeed, the forgotten Taos painters were denied patronage and excluded from the history of Southwest painting. Their work was defined as unschooled. Critics said the work was derivative of Pueblo kiva paintings and not pure Indian painting.

INDIANS IN COLOR

Speaker One: **J. J. Brody**

It's this whole notion that pervades the art history-museum business; namely, there is universal value and meaning to the objects we call art. That is sheer nonsense. The meaning of an artistic object is always socially constructed, and as Bourdieu and Darbel (1997) argue, art is just a class-based construct (Brody, in Garfield, 1995, p. 54). But this class-based notion shaped how the Santa Fe and Albuquerque museums treated the Native Taos painters.

Speaker Two: **Ms. Coyote**

The museums were especially disrespectful. Alexander Hogue, Director of the Museum of New Mexico in Santa Fe, said that painters like Albert Looking Elk and Albert Lujan would never get their works displayed in his museum.

Speaker One: **Alexander Hogue**

Occasionally, some Taos Indian painter comes to the museum hoping to exhibit his work done in oils after the white man's (TSA) manner. To us these are pitiful specimens. Our policy is clear. We refuse to show work like this. We send these painters away. Why, two of those tribesmen from Taos are turning out work that is atrocious. Those in power in Taos should stop this kind of drivel immediately (paraphrase quoted in Watson, 1994, p. 64).

Speaker Two: **Ms. Coyote**

Tribesmen, drivel, whiteman's manner. I am so insulted.
I do not know where to begin.

Speaker One: **Vernon G. Lujan**

I want to go back to J. J. Brody. He is right. With critics like Hogue, there were two or three issues involved. Because the work of the Taos painters was defined as bad tourist art, it was either discredited, mis-identified, or ignored by the best-known directories of Native American painters. The big shot art elite had the belief that there were only two types of authentic Indian

Chapter 4 🎋 Taos Indians on Canvas

painters. The first type were these with aboriginal roots; that is, the early Pueblo kiva painters. These painters had no formal training. They were just expressing skills they had inherited as aboriginals. The second type of authentic Native painter was formally trained in the style of the Santa Fe School. They were encouraged to paint native ceremonies and dances, or to follow the patterns found in ancient pottery designs (Baca, 2003, p. 64). The Taos painters did not fit into either of these 'authentic' Indian categories.

Speaker Two: **Alexander Hogue**

It was drivel for uninformed tourists.

Speaker One: **Ms. Coyote**

Hey, Mr. Museum Man, who were the big TAS painters painting for? I thought they were selling their paintings to rich tourists.

Speaker Two: **Mr. Coyote**

What is tourist art? Art sold to tourists.
What is Indigenous art? Obviously it is art produced by Indigenous artists. Any art that tourists buy is tourist art, so Indigenous art is tourist art.

ACT THREE, SCENE TWO
Being Patronized

Speaker One: **Mr. Coyote**

Critics said the Indians painted by the these three artists did not look like real Indians. They wanted romantic paintings of Noble savages, primitives doing ancient, sacred dances and painted in bold, vibrant colors (Baca, 2003, pp. 64–65).

Speaker One: **J. J. Brody**

In making these arguments, oddly, the intellectuals convinced themselves that they were not influencing the work of the true Indigenous artists. But this was an illusion. That is, if they were influencing Indigenous artists, then the art was no longer aboriginal and truly Indigenous.

Speaker Two: **Ms. Coyote**

It was an illusion and a lie to say there was no influence. There was irony at work. The Taos Indians caught on real quick. The museum directors may have told the Indians their paintings were worthless. And they may have denied ever telling an Indian how to paint, but the pictures were painted for Whites and the Indian painters knew what would sell. The museum directors may have said this art was unworthy of being collected, but the tourists bought it and collected it (Brody, 1971, pp. 115–116; Taylor, 2000, p. 56)!

Speaker One: **Mr. Coyote**

What is tourist art? Art sold to tourists. Art collected by museums.

ACT THREE, SCENE THREE
Natural Born Artist, but Not Really

Speaker One: **J. J. Brody**

We are back to the beginning, The self-taught Pueblo painters were allowed to be models for real TSA artists, but they could not be painters themselves.

Speaker Two: **Mr. Coyote**

Just listen to Edgar Hewett, the archaeologist and patron of Indian art. Today he sounds like a racist or a biological determinist. He is talking about Native artists trained in the Santa Fe school.

Speaker One: **Edgar Hewett**

The Indian painter is a born artist. No one knows how he came by his ability. The effect of instinct is obvious. He has talents that are inherent in the Mongoloid people. But his paintings

Chapter 4 ⚙ Taos Indians on Canvas

must be seen as the racial expression of a primitive (and inferior) people. Unfortunately, it is only slightly better than the so-called tourist art you might find in a curio shop on the reservation. (see Brody, 1971, pp. 90–91, paraphrased)

Speaker Two: **Ruth Phillips**

Tourist art! Nonsense! Critics like Hewett are using aesthetic concepts from the dominant culture. Calling something tourist art turns it into a souvenir, a curio, a trinket, a trivial inauthentic object produced for tourists. It says this is not 'real,' authentic, Indigenous Native art because it was produced for the tourist market (Phillips, 1998 p. xiii; also Graburn, 1976, p. 6; MacCannell, 1976; Pratt, 1992).[23]

Speaker One: **Mr. Coyote**

What is Indigenous art? Art produced by Indigenous artists. Is Indigenous art tourist art? Yes.

Speaker Two: **Ms. Coyote**

Let's turn this upside down. We should look at the paintings of the Taos Three as authentic Indigenous art, and as souvenir art at the same time. The paintings were consumed as souvenirs, as authentic representations of the Pueblo by a Taos painter. Because each artist represented himself uniquely through his own style, his paintings could be read as autoethnographic expressions of his relationship to Pueblo culture (Phillips, 1998, p. 17).

Speaker Two: **Mr. Coyote**

Let me elaborate. Their paintings were shaped by what they saw around them as members of the Pueblo. They reproduced the landscape of the Pueblo.

Speaker One: **Ms. Coyote**

These artists were also influenced by the practices of the Taos Society of Painters and the museum cultures of Santa Fe and Taos. But their art emerged out of interactions with tourists

INDIANS IN COLOR

in key 'contact zones' in Taos, especially the Pueblo Plaza (Phillips, 1998, p. 17; Pratt, 1992).

Speaker One: **Ms. Coyote** (cont'd)

All of these factors made their work 'visually' intelligible and desirable to the tourist consumer (Phillips, 1998, p. 20).

Speaker Two: **Nelson Graburn**

The forgotten Taos painters produced commercially fine art, not airport art, or ethno-kitsch, and they sold it to tourists—just as the TSA painters did. END OF STORY!

ACT THREE, SCENE FOUR
What Do You Call It?

Speaker One: **Edward Said**

Call it tourist art if you will, but the work of these Native Taos painters is important because of their expression of "native nationalism" (quoted in Taylor, 2000, p. 56). One way to interpret Native art in a colonial and postcolonial setting is to see it as an expression of local, Native values. The Taos Three gave us straightforward painterly expressions of the community, its architecture, buildings, homes, and citizens.

Speaker One: **Ruth B. Phillips**

Dr. Said is correct. Today the art work of painters like Lujan, Martinez, and Mirabal is recognized as an expression of the artist's efforts to blend native, local, and colonizing cultures. You can call it hybridity. Those who say it is inauthentic are dead wrong, and this remains a central problem in the way that art history and popular culture have addressed Native art (Phillips, 1998, p. x).

Stage Right: Spotlight shines on Bert Phillips, one of the original six TSA painters.

Chapter 4   Taos Indians on Canvas

Speaker Two: **Bert Phillips**

    These academics have it all wrong. They weren't there in the beginning, like I was. In the Taos Valley I saw my first dark-skinned Taos Indians, picturesque, colorful, dressed in blankets artistically draped. I came to understand that there are gifted artists among the aboriginal American Indians trained in Santa Fe. The effect of instinct is at once apparent. Their conceptions are as individual and full of racial character as those of the Japanese.

    I knew from the very beginning they would make great models, but I never thought they could be real artists (Phillips, in Scott, 1998, p. 3, paraphrase; also Phillips in Dunn, 1968, p. 225, paraphrase).

Speaker One: **Ms. Coyote**

    Really? Are you being just a little racist, Bert?

Speaker Two: **Samuel W. Watson III**

    Bert pretty well sums it up. Amazing! Models, but not artists.

Speaker One: **Bert Phillips**

    I stand my ground; good models, bad painters.

ACT FOUR, SCENE ONE
Another Setting Sun?

Stage Right: The Three Taos painters, along with the San Geronimo Clowns, enter stage right and walk to center stage. A scarlet red sun sets behind the mountain. Fancy Dancers enter stage left and slowly dance. The San Geronimo Clowns tumble across the stage. Stage lights dim. The dancing stops.

Speaker One: **The two Alberts and Juan Mirabal** in unison

We have already put the art work of the TSA painters in an exhibit which we called *Paintings from the Past*. Now we need to go one step further. The anthropologists, the Santa Fe Museum directors, the art historians, and the art critics need to go in this same exhibit. After all, they trivialized our art. They said we had no talent, or rather that any talent we had was inherited, was in our primitive genes.

We have all their names right here: Alexander Hogue, Edward Hewett, Elsie Parsons, Bert Phillips. Their names and pictures can go on the Hall of Fame wall in this new exhibit.

Stage Left: Spotlight shines on portraits of Hogue, Hewett, Parsons, and Phillips. As the off-stage announcer calls out their names, one by one each of the figures comes out of his portrait and carries it to the Hall of Fame.

Speaker Two: **San Geronimo Clowns**

Their criticisms reinforced the stereotypes created by the TSA painters. They said native artists like the two Alberts and Juan could model but not paint.

Speaker One: **Seventh Generation Performers**

This went along with the more general colonial critique of the museum directors, who called us tribesmen and said our paintings were atrocious.

Speaker Two: **Ms. Coyote**

Need I remind you what the critics said? The Indians painted by our artists did not look like real Indians, their art was no better than tourist trash.

Speaker Two: **Mr. Coyote**

We can't afford to wallow in these criticisms.

Chapter 4 ⌗ Taos Indians on Canvas

ACT FOUR, SCENE TWO
A New Chapter?

Speaker One: **Ms. Coyote**

We can't move on until we remember and honor the legendary Fritz Scholder[24] (Luiseno, 1937–2005; see Sims, 2008a and b), R. C. Gorman[25] (Navajo, 1931–2005; see Parks, 1983), as well as Woody Crumbo[26] (Citizen Potawatomi, 1912–1989), and non-Native artist Jim Wagner (1940–). They are called the Chapter Three painters, the third chapter after the Taos Founders (TSA, 1915–1927), and the Taos Moderns (1920–1960). www.harwoodmuseum.org/news/view/45[27]

Speaker Two: **Narrator**

A little history is in order. The so-called Third Chapter painters were agents of change in a larger social movement. During the 1960s, as J. J. Brody argues (1971, p. 204), things changed dramatically in the history of modern secular Indian painting. Several factors came together to produce radically different representations of Indians by Native American artists. These representations built on and repudiated prior traditions, from the 19th-century paintings of noble savages, by Catlin and others, to the romanticized Taos Indian painted by the TSA school, to the paintings of Indians by Indians taught in the Santa Fe School by Dorothy Dunn, to the landscape paintings of the Forgotten Taos Three.

The factors that produced these changes included: the emergence of angry young Indians as a result of the civil rights movements, the emergence of the Institute of American Indian Arts as a new institution designed to train and support a new generation of Indian artists, and a commitment to an aesthetic that said art could be both a tool of self-expression and an agent for social change. Together these factors set the conditions for the emergence of the so-called Third Chapter painters. They became agents of the very change their paintings embodied.

Speaker Two: Seventh Generation Performers

All right already. Enough of this fancy interpretive talk.

Before you extoll the Chapter Three painters, remember that in this play we are honoring three talented painters who were overlooked by the establishment. The Chapter Three painters stand on their shoulders, so to speak.

Speaker One   Ms. Coyote:

History, history, whose history?

Curtain.

Drumming music.

House lights up.

As in the last play, the San Geronimo Clowns enter stage left in front of the curtain, join hands, and bow to the audience. They turn and take the steps leading off the stage, laughing loudly as they leave the theater.

Applause.

The theatre goes dark.

THE END

CODA

Following the lead of Baca (2003), Watson (1994), Witt (2003a, b), and others, I have written the two Alberts and Juan into the history of art in Taos. At a fundamental level this play has been about honoring an art that preserves the ancient traditions that help define the sovereign nation of the Taos Pueblo. The next chapter turns to Fritz Scholder and a new generation of Native American painters, also called the Chapter Three artists.

Plates

Plate 1: Ernest L.
Blumenschein
Star Road and White Sun
1920
oil on canvas, 42 x 51 in.
Albuquerque Museum,
Museum purchase, 1985
General Obligation Bonds
Albuquerque High School
Collection, gift of the classes
of 1943, 1944, and 1945
1986.50.3

Plate 2: T. C. Cannon
Mama and Papa Have the Going Home Shiprock Blues
1976 (*circa*) Reproduced courtesy of the Estate of T. C. Cannon, Joyce Cannon Yi, Executor

Plate 3: T. C. Cannon
Collector #5
1975
Reproduced courtesy of the Estate of T. C. Cannon, Joyce Cannon Yi, Executor

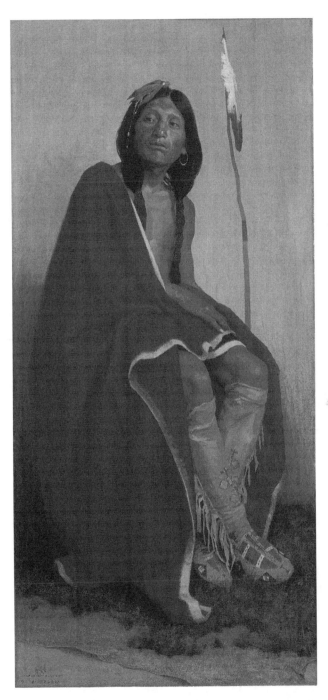

Plate 4:
Eanger Irving Couse
Elk-Foot of the Taos Tribe
1909
Smithsonian American Art Museum, Gift of William T. Evans
1910.9.5

Plate 5: Albert Lujan   untitled, *Taos Pueblo*   1940 (*circa*)

Plate 6: Kevin Red Star
Crow Indian Parade Rider
1982
oil on canvas
Buffalo Bill Center of the West, Cody, Wyoming, U.S.A.; Kevin Red Star, Crow Indian Parade Rider, 1982, Gift of Mr. and Mrs. W. D. Weiss, 7.94

Plate 7: Fritz Scholder
Indian with Tomahawk
1970
oil on canvas
Buffalo Bill Center of the West, Cody, Wyoming, U.S.A.; William E. Weiss Contemporary Art Fund Purchase, 15.77

Chapter 5
Postmodern Indians on Canvas

PROLOGUE

Speaker One: **Fritz Scholder**

You'll never get anywhere painting Indians. In fact, I'm never going to paint Indians again.[1]

Speaker Two: **Ms. Coyote**

For Native artists like Fritz Scholder and R. C. Gorman the artist's task is to paint him/herself into the sacred spaces of the culture and to honor those spaces and the persons who live there.

Speaker One: **Mr. Coyote**

For white artists like the Taos Moderns and earlier the Taos Society of Artists, the artist's task is different. They are following an aesthetic that is anchored in European notions of

---

Indians in Color: Native Art, Identity, and Performance in the New West by Norman K. Denzin, 125–150. © 2015 Taylor & Francis. All rights reserved.

beauty, artists, and art. The artist's commitment is to his/her art, not to his/her subject.

Speaker Two: **Ernest Blumenschien**

We, too, have discovered the validity of the 'primitive' in our art. The Taos Indian is our primitive, our subject. We are not just painting Indians. Indians are the raw material for a larger project, a truly original higher national art (Blumenschein, in Bickerstaff, 1955b, p. 37).

Speaker One: **Gerald Vizenor**

Postindian artists demand a place in national literature, history, and art (Vizenor, 2008, p. 17, paraphrase).

ACT ONE, SCENE ONE
Yet Another Announcement

The audience is seated in a large auditorium in the Harwood Museum. The house lights dim. The curtain rises. The Taos Pueblo drummers and Supaman[2] and three Native flute players enter stage left, take their places, and begin playing. The San Geronimo Clowns, wearing their usual black and white costumes, strut across the stage. The stage makes a slow rotation, stopping in front of a set that looks like the entrance to a museum. Photographs and paintings hang on the wall. A large sign reads:

Third Chapter of Taos Art Colony
celebrated by Harwood Museum of Arts

Jina Brenneman, curator of collections and exhibitions at the Harwood Museum, steps forward. The music stops.

Speaker One: **Jina Brenneman**

Tonight we honor the "Third Chapter of the Taos Art Colony." The play takes place in the town plaza on July 13, 2015, during the 29th Annual Taos Pueblo Powwow.

Chapter 5 ⚵ Postmodern Indians on Canvas

These artists turned the art world upside down. Indeed, because of them, regional Western art became global! The Taos art scene as we know it today did not exist at one time. The Taos Founders and the Taos Moderns tended to not sell their art in Taos. In the 1970s and 1980s Native American artists—Fritz Scholder, Woody Crumbo, R. C. Gorman (and Jim Wagner)[3]— opened Native-owned galleries in Taos and began showing and selling their own art. Art quickly became a major part of the town's economy (Pesquera, 2013). Soon, Hollywood celebrities trooped into town and started buying Native American artists' art (see www.harwoodmuseum.org/news/view/4).

Speaker Two: **Ms. Coyote**

Yeah, but what kind of art were they buying?

Speaker Two: **Narrator**

I keep thinking this Chapter Three notion is just a marketing category, a way for Steven Parks, a major gallery owner, to sell paintings.

Speaker One: **Mr. Coyote**

The art was the real thing. It was a wild, new art by very talented Native artists.

Lights dim, the San Geronimo Clowns enter stage left, pushing a speaker's lectern to the center of the stage. Lights come up.

ACT ONE, SCENE TWO
A Little History

Speaker One: **Steven Parks**

Actually, I coined the idea of 'Third Chapter.' It occurred to me that I had lived through an important period in art history, from the Taos Society of Artists, to the Taos Moderns, to the fantastic art of Scholder, Gorman, Red Star, and Crumbo. I called the latter the Third Chapter. In a sense their origins have to be traced back to the work of the Anglo artists who started coming to Taos in 1898. The foundational moment is given in this photograph.

Stage left spotlight shines on photograph, dated 1898, of Ernest Blumenschein next to a broken down wagon (from Coke 1963, p. 14). (See wikipedia.org/wiki/Bert_Geer_Phillips.) Off-stage music from the Native flute players can be heard as Parks continues to speak.

Speaker Two: **Steven Parks** (cont'd)

It is all here in this photo. The Anglo painter sits on the mountain side next to his broken down wagon. He looks dusty, dirty, and tired. He is in search of an Indian to paint, having been told about the colorful costumes and rituals of the Taos tribe (Coke, 1963, p. 14).[4]

Speaker One: **Ernest Blumenschein**

Making my way down the mountain on horseback, holding the broken wagon wheel in my arms, I was stunned by what I saw. No artist had ever painted what I was seeing—the Taos Indian and the incredibly beautiful landscape that surrounded him. It was all here, the brown-skinned Indian, the beautiful Sangre de Cristo mountain range, a clear blue sky, white clouds, the Taos valley green with trees, fields of alfalfa, and great lakes of sagebrush. I decided then and there that the Taos valley would be the end of our wagon trip. Here were the Indians and the landscapes that I had come to paint. These Indians were just like those Indians I saw in Buffalo Bill's Wild West Show in Madison Square Garden. (Blumenschein, in Bickerstaff, 1955b, p. 31, paraphrase)

The spotlight shines on Ms. Coyote.

Speaker Two: **Ms. Coyote**

So the origin story, what puts Taos on the map, is the story of a white painter and not the Taos Indians.

Chapter 5 ❖ Postmodern Indians on Canvas

Speaker One: **Steven Parks**
    Exactly.

Speaker Two: **Mr. Coyote**
    Got it. They painted a white person's Indian. Dark-skinned men, women and children in fields of corn, riding horses, hunting, dancing, and praying.

Speaker One: **Ms. Coyote**
    Got it!

Speaker Two: **Jina Brenneman**
    This is why the Third Chapter painters are so important. They helped create a new Indian, a new imaginary.

Speaker One: **Ms. Coyote**
    Don't forget Juan and the two Alberts. They painted an Indigenous Taos Indian. They had their own galleries and marketed their own art in their front yards and curio shops.

ACT ONE, SCENE THREE
An All-star Gallery

Stage Left: Native flute players softly play Hopi Rain Song #1. *The spotlight shines on a series of R. C. Gorman paintings, prints and lithograph (from Parks, 1983):* Navajo Woman *(1973),* Taos Man *(1977),* Pilar *(1980),* Anna *(1981),* Danya *(1980),* Miriam *(1981),* Kali *(1981),* Women from Ranchos *(1980),* Ruins *(1983).*[5]

Stage Right: Spotlight moves across a montage of Fritz Scholder's paintings, including: Monster Indian *(1968),* Indian with a Beer Can *(1969),* Custer and 20,000 Indians *(1969),* Screaming Indian Woman #2 *(1970),* Indian with Flag *(1970),* Indian with Tomahawk *(1970),* Dead Indians in a Wagon *(1970),* Massacre at Wounded Knee *(1970),* Super Indian #2 *(1971),* Portrait of a Massacred Indian *(1972),* Drunk Indian #2 *(1972),* Cowboy Indian *(1974),* Drunken Indian in Car *(1974),* Last Indian with

INDIANS IN COLOR

Flag *(1975)*, American Indian with Flag *(1979)*, White Indian *(1997)*, Self Portrait with Grey Cat *(2003)*, Heart Indian *(2004)*.[6]

Center Stage: Spotlight shines on a sequence of Kevin Red Star paintings: Rain the Face *(1980)*, Crow Indian Parade Rider *(1982)*, Family Shield *(1995)*, Crow Tipi *(2005)*, Three Absalooke Sisters *(2010)*, Black Eagle Northern Plains Warrior *(2013)* Shaman's Healing Helpers, Plains Indian Medicine Man *(2013)*, Evening Social Dance of the Crow Indians *(2013)*.[7]

Speaker One: **Ms. Coyote** (stepping forward)
These are our postindianist all-stars!

Stage Left: Spotlight shines on Red Star's Crow Indian Parade Rider *(1982) and Fritz Scholder's* Indian with a Tomahawk *(1970).*

Curtain lowers: Navajo flute music continues to play over the museum sound system.

ACT ONE, SCENE FOUR
Interpreting the New All-stars

Speaker One: **Christina C. Brindza**

In the summer of 2014 the just mentioned paintings by Kevin Red Star and Fritz Scholder were on display in the central gallery of the Whitney Gallery of Western Art. *Crow Indian Parade Rider* was displayed next to Scholder's *Indian with a Tomahawk*.[8]

We put these paintings side by side, placing mentor and student next to one another. The two paintings do not reproduce the Nobel Savage image of Native males. Each painting is a bold representation of a new Indian, even as it criticizes the classic Indian warrior pose.

130

Chapter 5 🎟 Postmodern Indians on Canvas

Painted in vivid pop art red, white, and blue colors, Fritz's *Indian with a Tomahawk* is a caricature, from his white and blue headdress that reaches to the ground, to his blue pointed shoes, his bright red pants, to his claw-like fist holding a long tomahawk that looks like a club. His face is painted white, his mouth a black gaping slit below an eye that seems barely open. His red shirt, dotted with white flecks, covers a slightly bulging stomach. This is a rundown Indian, stuck in time and place, barely holding on, his tomahawk his only link to a once proud past.

Kevin Red Star's *Crow Indian Parade Rider* is an exaggerated representation of a Crow Indian with a full white headdress sitting on a horse, holding a ceremonial staff that rests on the horse's shoulders and stretches nearly the width of the painting. A colorful red, grey and black thinly striped blanket falls on both sides of the horse's neck. The horse could be a wooden statue. The Indian parade rider appears weighted down underneath his huge headdress. He peers out of half-closed eyes over flared nostrils, and wide red lips. He wears a handsome breastplate. Seven white bone necklaces hang around his neck. His arms are enclosed in a deep blue fabric with reddish-orange flecks. It is as if he, like his horse, is a statue. Together, parade-rider and horse confront the viewer as if to say, take us as we are. We are proud to be who we are!

These two Indians are outside time and space. They have nowhere to go, except to mark a moment that should be honored and remembered. Scholder's Indian is the logical extension of Red Star's parade rider; indeed, at an earlier moment he was a parade rider, perhaps carrying a play tomahawk.

Stage Right: A spotlight shines on Supaman, who thanks Jina for letting him perform. Supaman also thanks Kevin Red Star for his art: "As a Crow Indian I found great courage from studying Mr. Red Star's paintings of Crow culture." Supamam then plays his award-winning "Prayer Loop Song," and the audience cheers.

Speaker Two: **Mr. Coyote**

This is art that comes from the heart. These are not Hollywood, Wild West Show Indians performing for whites. These are proud contemporary Indians inhabiting, performing, and critiquing a past that will never be again.

Speaker Two: **Ms. Coyote**

This is what the Third Generation painters do, unlike the Native and Anglo artists who came before them. Kevin Red Star uses the material artifacts of Crow culture for his art. R. C. Gorman did the same thing with Navajo culture, its women, their dress, and the mountains and mesas. Fritz took native culture to another place, showing how it had been distorted and commercialized in popular culture.

Speaker One: **Kevin Red Star**

I'm trying to capture an era. I listen to the stories about the days when the tribe followed the buffalo, stories of the family events that happened in this canyon or on that mountain. I always try to be respectful. Some things are private and should not be shared (Gibson and Leaken, 2014, p. 72).

Speaker Two: **Mr. Coyote**

In contrast, TSA painters celebrated the artist's ability to paint according to current conventions of Euro-American art. Indian models and the Taos landscape only provided the material for that project.

Speaker One: **Ms. Coyote**

Fritz Scholder, R. C. Gorman, and Kevin Red Star turn this approach upside down. Their Indian artist is called to paint the pain and the beauty in Native culture and to do so from personal experience. End of story.

Stage Left: Spotlight shines on the Taos Pueblo drummers who drum softly as the curtains come down.

Chapter 5 Postmodern Indians on Canvas

❖❖❖

ACT TWO, SCENE ONE
A New Generation, a New Art?

The lights dim. The curtain comes up. The drummers and flute players play softly. The Seventh Generation Performers walk to center stage.

Speaker One: **Seventh Generation Performers**

Where did this new art come from? Because the Seventh Generation looks seven generations into the future, we must look to the past, to guide us to this new place.

Speaker Two: **J. J. Brody**

Of the several factors that came together to produce this new Indian art, perhaps the Institute of American Indian Arts (IAIA) was the most important. The result of the training at the IAIA was the emergence of a radical art that is vital and expressive, though sometimes not pretty, even un-Indian, polemical, but always stylistically varied (Brody, 1971, pp. 204, 206).

Inspired by their work at the IAIA, this new generation of artists became the agents of the very change their paintings represented. As a result, a new Indian unlike any Indian before emerged on canvas. This Indian—wild, reverential, somber, joyous, beautiful, bold, drunk, dying, brave—became an inspiration for others.

Speaker One: **Fritz Scholder, Woody Crumbo, R. C. Gorman, Earl Biss, Kevin Red Star, T. C. Cannon, Charlene Teeters**, aka Alumni of IAIA (in unison)

Some say it all started with Lloyd. Lloyd Kiva New recruited some of us as teachers and some of us as students. Like W. E. B. Du Bois (1926) who wanted black art about blacks written and performed by blacks for black people, Lloyd wanted Indian art for Indians, art painted by Indians who were trained by real Indians. He wanted a new generation of

INDIANS IN COLOR

teachers, and a new generation of students. He wanted representations of real Indians painted by real Indians.

Speaker Two: **Lloyd Kiva New**

I believe that each generation of Indian painters must evolve its own art form to reflect its own times and conditions, rather than turn to the hopeless prospect of mere re-manipulation of the past. This will allow them to avoid the stultifying clichés endorsed by purists who resent and resist any evolution of forms and techniques applied to new Indian art. The Indian artists who draw on tradition learn to stand on their own feet (New, quoted in Hill, 2008, p. 131, paraphrase).

Speaker One: **Ms. Coyote**

Lloyd argued that because of forced relocation, urbanization, and assimilation, generations of Indians believed that to be an Indian was a disgrace. This led to shame and self-destructive behavior. Lloyd felt that the future of American Indians was at risk. He wanted to help create a new Indian. He wanted to see Indians succeed as Indians, with pride and dignity. A new art was a path to this end. His experiment at the IAIA was an attempt to break this self-imposed stereotype of Indians as second-class citizens, broken-down wards of the federal government. Artists like Scholder, T. C. Canon, Kevin Red Star, R. C. Gorman, and others charted a positive path forward from their training at the IAIA (Hill, 2008, pp. 131–132, paraphrase).

Speaker Two: **Kevin Red Star**

The Institute brought people from all the different tribes together. They took us to the surrounding pueblos for seasonal celebrations and feast dances—Santa Clara, Zunu, San Ildefonso, Taos, Chaco Canyon. They wanted us to experience the great mesas and landscapes. They took us to Navajo trading posts. They wanted us to experience different kinds of Native arts. We were a community. We ate together, worked

Chapter 5 🎴 Postmodern Indians on Canvas

together, hung out together, shared colors, ideas, stories. We were painters, sculptors, dancers, jewelers, dancers, musicians, composers. We were Native American artists and proud of it! (Red Star, in Gibson and Leaken, 2014, pp. 41, 43, paraphrase)

Speaker One: **Fritz Scholder**

We all agreed with Lloyd, and we learned from each other and from our students. Too many earlier Indian artists were pressured to assimilate to American culture and to create an entirely artificial art. I was opposed to this. This kind of tourist art was simply no more than decoration for white living rooms (Scholder, in Cowen, 1981, paraphrase).

Speaker Two: **J. J. Brody**

Don't be so critical. No matter what style, subject matter, or form, no matter whether it fulfilled a commission or was a speculative venture, the usual assumption was that this art would be purchased by a white patron for use as a decorative object. This was the case no matter whether it was called tourist art or art made by a serious artist, like yourself or by Gorman or Cannon. Nothing new here. This is always the way Anglo artists, Native artists, and craft persons have to make money to remain artists, and wealthy patrons are the key audience to sustain them (Brody, 1971, pp. 189–190, paraphrase).

Speaker One: **Fritz Scholder**

I agree, J. J. I want to make money, but still too many Indian artists have been integrated too deeply into Anglo life. As artists (and Indians) they confront a major problem—namely, rediscovering those identities and traditions that have been lost in the integration process. Lloyd and the IAIA helped many of us find a path to this hidden or repressed identity (Scholder, in Cowen, 1981).

Speaker Two: **Eva Mirabal** (Eah-Ha-Wa)

I'm one of those Indian artists you are talking about. I don't think I sold out. I was a WAC during WWII. My G. I. Gertie posters were used to sell war bonds.[9] So what does it mean to assimilate? I was the first female Native American cartoonist, and one of the first female creators to have her own strip. But I found an artistic identity in my cartoons that worked for me. I was setting a path for a new generation of female Native American cartoonists.

Speaker One: **Fritz Scholder**

I'm going to shut up.

Stage Left: Spotlight circles the stage, moving back and forth across the political cartoons and G. I. Gertie posters of Eva Mirabal. The spotlight moves from poster to poster. Coyote steps forward.

ACT TWO, SCENE TWO
Drunk Indians, Half-Breeds, and Prairie Niggers[10]

Speaker One: **Mr. Coyote**

Who and what does an Indian painter paint? J. J. Brody asked this question many times.

Speaker Two: **Ms. Coyote**

Fritz, somewhere you said the Indian has no homeland, the Indian lives in a homeland that is possessed by the dominant culture (Scholder, quoted in Smith, 2008, p. 39).

Speaker One: **Fritz Scholder**

I paint vampires, and grotesquely distorted Indians holding beer cans, Indians sleeping in old cars in dirty junk-yards. We have been devoured by vampires sent by white culture. We are tarnished angels. We have become homeless alcoholics, derelicts lost in a cultural wasteland. We have become monsters to ourselves and non-persons to society at large.

This is what Lloyd was talking about. I guess you can say my paintings of drunken Indians in bars represent a response to Lloyd's challenge. This is the image of the American Indian

Chapter 5 ⁜ Postmodern Indians on Canvas

> Lloyd feels we must get past. I feel we have to look this Indian in the face (Scholder, in Smith, 2008, p. 33, paraphrase).

Speaker Two: **Kevin Red Star**

> Fritz was way ahead of many of us when we got to Santa Fe and the IAIA. We were just fresh from the rez. I was happy to be somewhere else other than on the reservation.

Speaker One: **Fritz Scholder**

> I was not raised on areservation. Being only one-quarter Luisano, I would be called mixed-race today. In 1974 I did a painting, a portrait I called *Half-Breed*.[11]

Stage Left: Spotlight on photo of Half-Breed *(1974) by Fritz Scholder (see centerofthewest.org/explore/western-art/research/fritz-scholder/).*

Speaker One: **Fritz Scholder** (cont'd)

> Maybe it was me. Later in my life I would do other self-portraits. My 1974 half-breed is a red-skinned male with long braids in western dress with a yellow scarf around his neck. I did not have to live through being an Indian student in a government boarding school where teachers told students they were never going to amount to anything. I did not have to go through what Kevin, T. C. and other reservation Indians had to go through.

Speaker Two: **Kevin Red Star**

> We felt we were at the center of a new movement. Back in Montana we were dealing with racism while competing with the legacies of white artists like Charlie Russell and Russell Chatham. At the IAIA I was encouraged to turn to Crow culture for my inspiration, and I did. In my paintings I incorporated beads, leather, feathers, tipi liners, porcupine quill bags, headdresses, and the colors of Crow ritual found in dance, song, and legend. I learned to be proud of the fact that I am an American Indian, a proud member of the Crow Nation.

137

I'll never forget the fact that when my teenage daughters came to live with me near Crow Reservation in the mid-1990s they were called 'prairie niggers' in the local Roberts school. I had a studio in that time in that town, and I did business with local townspeople. Prairie Niggers!!!!

ACT TWO, SCENE THREE
Custer, Vietnam, and Alcatraz

Stage Right: Spotlight shines on Supaman, who steps forward and softly plays selections from his new CD.

Stage Left: Spotlight shines on Kevin Red Star's Rain in the Face *(1980) and Fritz Scholder's* Custer and 20,000 Indians *(1969) and* American Landscape *(1976).*

Speaker One: **Mr. Coyote** (to Kevin Red Star)

You were at the IAIA about the time of Vietnam. The anti-war movement was in full force. The American Indian Movement (AIM) and the Red Power movements were mobilizing. Indians occupied Alcatraz Island. They took over the Bureau of Indian Affairs offices in Washington, D. C., and initiated a 71-day siege of Wounded Knee in 1973 (Smith, 2008, p. 28). Where were you in all of this?

Speaker Two: **Kevin Red Star**

I went for a visit at Alcatraz when it was occupied. A number of us at the San Francisco Art Institute were invited over. I found it very depressing. Many Indians had been in prison on Alcatraz. Many had died there. It reminded me of a reservation. When I left, I felt committed more than ever to my art and my artistic career. I felt my calling was to celebrate Crow culture in my art. I was not a political radical or a leader, in that sense (Red Star, paraphrase in Gibson and Leaken, 2014, pp. 51–52).

Chapter 5 ⚙ Postmodern Indians on Canvas

Speaker One: **Fritz Scholder**

My entire project has been devoted to rejecting the image of the Noble Savage, demolishing the myths surrounding Custer and his Last Stand, and doing a form of political art that empowers. When I paint Indians wrapped in the American flag, I'm making a strong political statement. That flag and all it stands for helped kill Indians (Gover, 2008, pp. 9–10, paraphrase).

My early work (1967–1972) is situated alongside the political activities Coyote has just listed—Vietnam, Wounded Knee, Alcatraz. I got very political. I did several paintings about Wounded Knee, including the *Massacre at Wounded Knee, No. 1* (1970).

I did two anti-Custer paintings: *Custer and 20,000 Indians* (1969) and *American Landscape* (1976). Both paintings mock the myth of Custer, turning the Battle of Little Bighorn into a nightmare and Custer into a comic figure (see collections.centerofthewest.org/treasures/view/custer_20000_indians; collections.centerofthewest.org/treasures/view/american_landscape; Denzin 2011, pp. 106–107).

Speaker Two: **Kevin Red Star**

I did *Rain in the Face* (1980), my anti-Custer painting, over a decade after Frtiz's *Custer and 20,000 Indians*. My painting honors the Lakota leader who killed Custer. When TSA painters took up the topic of the Battle of Little Bighorn, they frequently celebrated Custer and his soldiers.[12]

Stage Right: The spotlight shines on Fritz Scholder's Massacre at Wounded Knee, No 1 *(1969) (see also Sims, 2008b, p. 91).*

Speaker One: **Christine C. Brindza**

Massacre at Wounded Knee is a painful painting. It is hard to look at. An apparently dead Indian lies prone, his face a grotesque skeleton, one hand in the shape of a gun is pointed at his head. Clearly, the anti-Custer paintings of Kevin Red Star and Fritz Scholder disrupt the smooth narrative that honors Custer by bringing a Native interpretation to this historical event.

Speaker One: **Ms. Coyote**

There are at least two sides to the art of Kevin Red Star and Fritz Scholder: the political and the artful—art as resistance, art as critique, art as celebration of a paradise lost and sometimes found.

Curtain lowers.

ACT TWO, SCENE THREE
Fritz Scholder

Speaker One: **Fritz Scholder**

I did not want to get trapped in the 'Disney' or 'Bambi' style of the older Santa Fe Indian School. At the new Institute of American Indian Art we were asking hard questions:

** 'What is Indian Art?'

** 'Who is an Indian artist?' 'Is it an Indian who is an artist?'

** 'Must you have lived an unassimilated Indian life to be an Indian artist?'

** 'What about a non-Indian who employs traditional Indian styles or takes up Indian subjects?'

** 'Are these just different forms of Indian art?'

(Gover, 2008, p. 10)

Speaker Two: **Kevin Gover**

Norman raised these questions in Chapter One. Fritz's work raised all of these questions. He was outraged over the history of

Chapter 5 ▦ Postmodern Indians on Canvas

the ill-treatment of Indians by the U. S. government and the devastation caused by the California gold rush to Native Americans and their homelands in California. He was depressed and excited about the American Indian Movement and mourned the deaths of Native American warriors who fought for America in every 20th-century war (Gover, 2008, pp. 9–10).

Speaker One: **Fritz Scholder**

I tried to create a style that commented on the historical 'Indian' painted by 19th-century artists like King and Catlin and the Taos Indian painted by Sharp, Blumenschen, Couse, and the other TSA painters. I wanted to go beyond the photographic images created by white photographers like Edward Curtis and Mathew Brady—the noble savage, the high plains warrior, the solitary hunter. Initially I worked from old Curtis and Brady photographs of Indians supplied by the Smithsonian. I wanted to turn those images on their heads (see Sims, 2008b, p. 95; Wasserberger, 2008, p. 42). These photographs were historical documents showing how whites wanted Indians to be represented to white culture. It was important to critique those images, especially so for a younger generation whose link to their past had been compromised during the period of forced assimilation. This generation had to ask if any Indians they knew actually looked like the Indians in a Curtis or Brady photograph (Sims, 2008b, p. 97).[13] The TSA group was especially problematic.

At the same time I did not want to confine my work to Indian dancers, or reproductions of the Taos and Santa Fe landscape. My Indians are outside time and place. They are from another planet: derelicts, loafers, drunks, ghosts, fallen angels, and female avatars. Frequently, they are negative stereotypes.

I'm after a political art, an art that goes beyond noble savages and tourist pleasing clichés; I wanted to depict Indians as 'real' rather than 'red' (Sims, 2008a, pp. 19–20; Wasserberger, 2008, p. 46).

141

INDIANS IN COLOR

Speaker Two: **Ms. Coyote**[14]

Fritz's paintings make caricatures of the representations of Indians painted by the TSA artists and the Indians painted by Indians trained in the Santa Fe School. Fritz's Indians are not stoic. They are not posed in front of outdoor landscapes. Fritz's Indians hang out in bars. They pose in front of rhinoceros and hold huge tomahawks decorated with little valentine hearts. They sit slouched on wood stumps, holding melting ice cream cones.

Speaker One: **Mr. Coyote**

Fritz's Indians have sunken cheeks, huge hands and feet that look like animal paws. Some have been massacred, others are dying, others are wounded, bleeding, crying, pleading for help. Some are pensive, others are colorful, hopeful, proud, passionate, full of energy—wild lovers filled with desire.

Speaker Two: **Fritz Scholder**

When I was invited to participate in the Rockefeller Indian Art Project at the University of Arizona in 1961, I said, 'I don't paint Indians,' but I revised that. I needed to learn how to paint Indians differently. I accepted the position of instructor in Advanced Painting and Contemporary Art History at the Institute of American Indian Arts in Santa Fe in 1964. Everybody was doing Indians, but not the way I wanted. That is when I started my Indian series, depicting the 'real,' not the 'red,' Indian. I wrapped Indians in the American flag, and people thought I was making a political statement. People forget that in the old days surplus flags were sent from Washington to the reservations and the old chiefs made them part of their wardrobes like blankets (Scholder, in Sherman, 1981). I gave my first Indian green hair. I stenciled the word Indian at the top of the painting, so people would know that this was a painting of an Indian.

Chapter 5 ⬛ Postmodern Indians on Canvas

Speaker Two: **Ms. Coyote**

The art critic Paul Chaat Smith is quoted as saying your *Indian with Beer Can* (1989) is the most influential painting in the history of Indian Art (Smith, 2008, p. 30).

Speaker One: **Fritz Scholder**

I don't know how important the painting is, but it freed me to become a painter who painted what had happened to Indians in American society.

The TSA painters made good money painting Indians for white people. So did I. But the TSA painters were hip-deep in the project that led to the demise of the Native American in America.

ACT TWO, SCENE FOUR
R. C.'s Solitude

Speaker One: **R. C. Gorman**

I don't have Fritz's fever. I want to paint a home place that is already here, but maybe disappearing. There is a magic in Taos, a spiritual power, a unity, from the Pueblo, to the Ranchos Church, to the Sangre de Cristo (blood of Christ) Mountains, the mesas, the Taos people themselves. Taos is a home for Indians from many different tribes and pueblos— Apache Navajo, Potawatomi, Luiseno, Ute, Zuni, Crow, Santa Domingo Pueblo. Like all Navajos, I have a great reverence and respect for the people of Taos Pueblo. They love color and ceremony. They are very religious. They include religion in everything they do (Gorman, in Parks, 1983, pp. 75–77, 195, paraphrase).

Speaker Two: **R. C. Gorman** (cont'd)

To outsiders we may all look alike, just Indians in Taos. But we are from different tribes with different cultures.

143

INDIANS IN COLOR

Speaker One: **Margaret Kovach**

Every tribal culture is unique, tied to a specific sense of place, *Wisdom Sits in Places*, as Keith Basso (1996) argues, and place is sacred. Indigenous painters bring this sense of place to their work.

Speaker Two: **R. C. Gorman**

Back home at Chinle, Canyon de Chelly, and Black Mountain I am Navajo, and I do as Navajos do. I am at home in the dessert, the hills, in Canyon de Chelly. And there, as a Navajo, I paint Navajos, primarily women. Maybe this is why they call me the Picasso of American Indian art. Picasso painted women in sacred spaces, too.

Speaker One: **Eva Mirabal** (Eah-Ha-Wa)

The Taos people believe in being in harmony with the world, not separating themselves from other people or nature. There is a life spirit in everything—rocks, trees, animals, rivers, and mountains (see Parks, 1983, p. 110, paraphrase).

Speaker Two: **R. C. Gorman**

This sacred sense of place is what I try to capture in my art. I want to paint something that may well be destroyed, lost— a special beauty that embodies a harmony with the world. (Gorman, in Parks, 1983, p. 65, paraphrase).

Speaker One: **Fritz Scholder**

R. C. was called to a space I could not see. At first I did not want to paint Indians or landscapes. I felt I had to negate those topics because they had become such visual clichés (Hill, Sr., 2008, p. 130).

Speaker Two: **Margaret Kovach**

What has happened to all the sacred places? How can they be painted, preserved, honored?

Chapter 5 ⌘ Postmodern Indians on Canvas

Speaker One: **Ms. Coyote**
> Good point, Maggie. It's pretty clear that Fritz's Indians have no sacred homeland to return to. His fallen angels are outside time and space.

ACT THREE, SCENE ONE
A One-Act Play:
Native Artists Attempt to Take Back the Day

Lights dim. A spotlight shines on a stage set constructed as the Taos Town Plaza. A banner hangs across the stage, announcing the date and the event:

July 13, 2015
29th Annual Taos Pueblo Powwow

The San Geronimo Clowns enter stage left and dance slowly in a circle around the plaza.

The Seventh Generation Performers (SGP) enter stage right, and push a speaker's lectern to the center of the stage.

Off-stage the Taos Pueblo drummers softly play, accompanying the three Navajo flute players.

Lights come up.

Speaker One: **Seventh Generation Performers** (approaching the podium)
> We hold that tribal actions should be judged by how they will benefit children seven generations from now. This applies to our artists as well. We must ask how an artist's work will impact our children in the near and distant future. We know that the paintings of Indians by the 19th- and early 20th-century Anglo artists created an imaginary white man's Indian. This does not have a positive impact on our children. They have problems recognizing themselves in those paintings.

Accordingly, we are here today to praise the work of the Chapter Three painters. This body of work is bold, radical, and thoughtful. It honors Native culture, but it is not afraid to criticize the effects of the dominant culture on Native life.

Stage left: The San Geronimo Clowns summersault across the stage. Supaman fancy dances in front of the podium.

Speaker Two: **Ms. Coyote** (from the podium)[15]

Let's hear it for Supaman, Fritz, R. C., and Kevin!!!!

Speaker One: **Fritz Scholder**

The past is past. We must think ahead, into the future. What does our art mean for future generations of our children? How will our children benefit from what we do? This is an enormous responsibility. (Benally, 2013, p. 1)

Speaker Two: **R. C. Gorman**

It is huge! As Native artists, we must assert our rights to make art that makes a difference. Our art can help give a voice to our youth. Many of them are seeking new art forms that will help them better express their Indigenous identities. We must be strong role models. We can show our youth how to take back the day, how to take credit for what they are accomplishing in these difficult times. (Benally, 2013, p. 1)

Speaker One: **Kevin Red Star**

What will they be able to learn from our art?

Will they be proud to claim it as part of their heritage?

Where will our art take them?

Speaker One: **Fritz Scholder**

Taking credit also means getting credit for what we and they have done.

Chapter 5 ▦ Postmodern Indians on Canvas

ACT THREE, SCENE TWO
The Eiteljorg Museum and Little Progress

Speaker Two: **R. C. Gorman**

We have demolished the traditional style of Indian art promoted by Dorothy Dunn's Studio at the Santa Fe School (Scholder, in Smith, 2008). We mocked the Indians painted by the TSA.

Speaker One: **Fritz Scholder**

We need to protest when a major art museum like the Eiteljorg Museum of American Indians and Western Art in Indianapolis, Indiana, devotes several rooms to the art of the Taos Society of Artists but has no space for artists trained at the IAIA. It is as if we never existed. Yet Native art and Native history are there in other ways. [16]

There are at least two versions of art in the museum. Native art and non-Native art. Non-Native art is 'real' art. It is in the Art of the American West gallery on the first floor. Native art is on the second floor (The People's Place) and is devoted not to Native art forms per se, but to Native material culture, to the history of Native people who originally lived in Indiana. There are exhibitions and dioramas devoted to different tribes, Native artifacts, pottery, hides, blankets, tipis, and samples of treaties that were signed and broken.

Here is the dilemma: when it comes to traditional museums, we still find ourselves outside looking in. We thought we had made progress (see Strong, 2013, p. 178).

Speaker Two: **Kevin Red Star**

I agree, Fritz, with Scholder—two steps forward, three steps back. We left the older Santa Fe style behind. No more stick figure dancers painted in a flat two-dimensional style. No more imitations of pre-historical pottery designs. We challenged the TSA painters with their romantic, sentimental themes

147

INDIANS IN COLOR

involving noble Plains warriors, lovely Indian maidens, and Anasazi sun worshipers (Baca, 2003, p. 65). And yet, here on the Eiteljorg in a room filled with TSA paintings there is not one mention of our work and what we have accomplished.

Speaker One: **R. C. Gorman**

We challenged the so-called moderns, the Cubists and expressionists who looked to Europe and elsewhere for a new art. At the same time, we borrowed from everywhere. Fritz, for example, was influenced by the famous British painter, Francis Bacon.[17]

Speaker Two: **Fritz Scholder**

We stole from everything in the 1950s and 1960s art world: pop art, Andy Warhol, Jaspar Johns, O'Keeffe, Pollock, Robert Rauschenberg, Francis Bacon, West and East Coast expressionism, European modernism. We borrowed from the past: Mathew Brady and Edward S. Curtis photographs, Homer Winslow, Monet, Van Gogh, Egyptian images, you name it—I mean everything. Maybe we were overlooked or neglected by some of the museums, but we had a message, a new way of doing Indian art. We inspired a generation of Native artists and we made good money. So who can complain?

Speaker One: **Ms. Coyote**

Don't forget the Forgotten Three Taos Painters. They created the space for you guys, a new generation of Native painters who would paint real Indians.

Speaker Two: **Seventh Generation Performers** (approaching the podium)

This is how you think your way into the future. You use the very best from the past to create a new art that has yet to be imagined.

Chapter 5 ▦ Postmodern Indians on Canvas

ACT THREE, SCENE THREE
Taos is Still a Disneyland

Speaker One: **Mr. Coyote**

> The Third Chapter painters made a living in Taos (and Santa Fe) as artists. They brought new energy to the town. Their paintings were displayed and sold in prestigious galleries.[18]

Chapter Two: **Ms. Coyote**

> You said in Chapter Three that the Indian Detours from Santa Fe to Taos was the closest thing America had to Disneyland in the 1920s. Taos is still a Disneyland, a little more dirty and dusty, but just as touristy. But, oh, the views, those mountains! And Blue Lake! (see Wasserberger, 2008, p. 50)

Speaker Two: **Mr. Coyote**

> Does anybody see a contradiction here? Taos, a sacred site, is turned into commercialized space for celebrity tourists who buy art that criticizes the very act of consumption.

Speaker One: **Ms. Coyote**

> At one level Kevin, R. C., and Fritz are laughing all the way to the bank.

Speaker Two: **Mr. Coyote**

> Who wouldn't want a Gorman and/or a Scholder or a Red Star in their house?! I mean, really!

House lights dim. The stage is bare, no scenery, no props, just a folding table, an artist's easel and palette and one chair.

Stage Right: The San Geronimo Clowns return to center stage. The Taos Pueblo drummers and Supaman and three Native flute players enter stage left taking their places and begin playing and dancing. Fancy Dancers walk on stage and join hands with the San Geronimo Clowns. Stage lights dim. Outside the theatre a scarlet-red sun sets behind the Sangre de Cristo Mountains.

The curtains come down.

THE END

Chapter 6
Indian Painters, Patrons[1] and Wild West Shows
A New Imaginary[2]

PROLOGUE

Speaker One: **Anonymous**
Has Indian art at last arrived?

Speaker Two: **Bert Phillips**
There are many gifted Indian artists (Bert Phillips, TSA painter, quoted in Dunn, 1968, p. 253).

Speaker One: **Annette Fassnacht**
Art is a serious business for the Indian (Fassnacht, 1936).

Speaker Two: **Edgar L. Hewett**
Indian painting is heading in the right direction. It is new, but it is Indian (Edgar L. Hewett, quoted in Dunn, 1968 p. 290).

Indians in Color: Native Art, Identity, and Performance in the New West by Norman K. Denzin, 151–179. © 2015 Taylor & Francis. All rights reserved.

Speaker One: **Paul Chaat Smith**

What of the larger dream of a new Indian art that would take the world by storm (Chaat Smith, 2008, p. 34)?

ACT ONE, SCENE ONE
Just Getting Started

The audience is seated in a large auditorium in the Harwood Museum. The lights dim. The curtain rises. The Taos Pueblo drummers and three Native flute players enter stage left, take their places, and begin playing. The San Geronimo Clowns, wearing their usual black and white costumes, mingle with the audience, giving autographs and posing for selfies. The stage makes a slow rotation, stopping in front of a set that looks like the entrance to a museum. Photographs and paintings hang on the wall. A large banner reads: Indian Art: Past, Present, Future. *The spotlight turns to center stage, focusing on a long table where several distinguished looking speakers are seated. The San Geronimo Clowns enter stage left, pushing a speaker's lectern to the center of the stage. Lights come up. Ms. Coyote steps forward.*

Speaker One: **Ms. Coyote**

Tonight's short three-act play, "Indian Painters and White Patrons," was performed in the historic Santa Fe town plaza on August 25, 2015, during the 93rd annual Santa Fe Indian Market.[3]

Speaker Two: **Mr. Coyote** (stepping forward, to Norman)

In Chapter One you discussed three artistic discourses: premodern, modern, and postmodern. Then you asked:

** Whose racialized Indian is being painted in each of these discourses?

** Can white artists any longer claim the uncontested right to paint Native Americans?

** Can the legacies of postmodern Indian art serve to advance an agenda of empowerment, can it function as a pedagogy of liberation (Friere, 1992)?

Chapter 6 ⚏ Indian Painters, Patrons, and Wild West Shows

Speaker One: **Norman K. Denzin**

Clearly we can use these questions to guide the conversations tonight.

Speaker Two: **Tonto**

It is all about ending the practice of redfacing. It is about a call for a new politics of representation. It is about ending the practices of creating images of a vanishing, imaginary, dark-skinned noble savage (Raheja, 2010, p. xiii).

Speaker One: **Ms. Coyote**

We are pretty clear on redfacing. Only Indians should paint Indians.

Speaker Two: **Mr. Coyote**

Are you saying Indians should never paint whites?

Speaker One: **Ms. Coyote**

I'm saying while race is socially constructed, whites have a normative privilege, whether they claim it or not (see Madison, 2012, p. 88). Whites can impose the privileges of whiteness on others—white painters painting Native Americans. The reverse case is contested. Non-whiteness affords few privileges. Native Americans were taught to only paint Native Americans. I contest this injunction. We need a moratorium. Only Indians should paint Indians. But Indians also have the right to paint whites. This is an extension of what some call strategic essentialism, deploying difference for political purposes (Madison, 2012, p. 85).

Speaker Two: **Mr. Coyote**

So Indians should paint whites.

Speaker One: **Ms. Coyote**

Of course. Art is always political, even when it claims to be just art. If you have any doubts, just look at the red Indians painted by the TSA artists. Or look at the how Disney Paris

153

presented Indians in 19th-century garb. And never forget what Hollywood and the movies can do to an Indian. Consider what happened to Tonto in all those Lone Ranger shows, including the latest Disney *Lone Ranger*. Why did he have to be a white man's sidekick who spoke pidgin English and walked around with a stuffed dead black crow on his head? (see Disney.com/The LoneRanger)

Speaker Two: **Johnny Depp**

Ms. Coyote, Tonto. I did the best I could with what they gave me. You know I am an honorary member of the Comanche nation.

Speaker One: **Tonto**

At least Jay Silverheels was a real Indian (Mohawk). Only a Hollywood movie producer would give you the right to play a Native American.

Speaker Two: **Ms. Coyote**

Calm down, Tonto. We all agree with you. It's always the same story, what Gerald Vizenor calls 'survivance,' overcoming colonial images of playing Indian, rejecting simulations of redness that turn us into victims and toys for the white imagination (Vizenor, 1999). We must always ask, "Whose Indian, whose memory, whose history?"

ACT ONE, SCENE TWO
Georgia O'Keeffe Moderates

Georgia O'Keeffe steps forward to the lectern.

Speaker One: **Georgia O'Keeffe**

Ms. Coyote has asked me to moderate our discussion tonight about Indian art with representatives from our three Taos artistic movements.

Chapter 6 ▦ Indian Painters, Patrons, and Wild West Shows

Speaker Two: **Fritz Scholder**

Can we go back to the questions I raised earlier, namely "What is Indian Art?" and "Should only Indians paint Indians?" (Gover 2008, p. 10).

Speaker One: **Lloyd Kiva New**

Anybody can paint anything. Of course this is what white artists have always believed. This is not what we teach. Indian art is art produced by an Indian artist. Period. Good Indian artists must draw on their tribal cultures and lived experiences. They must avoid clichés and stereotypes. Their art should empower and stir the critical imagination. It must speak to men, women, and children and help them resist structures of domination while encouraging them to imagine utopian spaces where Native life is celebrated and honored. This is art that is wild and unruly, beautiful and political.

Speaker One: **Fritz Scholder**

When I first started painting, I said, "I'm never going to paint a white man's red Indian. I only paint real Indians, and they are not RED." Sometimes I call my Indian monster Indian.

Speaker Two: **Kevin Red Star**

My *Crow Indian Parade Rider* is on one side of a coin. Fritz's *Indian With a Tomahawk* is on the other side. Our two Indians honor Crow/Native culture. Both Indians stand outside history. Both Indians mark the disappearance of an Indian who may never be again. Fritz's grotesque Indians may always be with us.

Speaker One: **R. C. Gorman**

Extending Lloyd and Fritz and Kevin, my version of Indian art honors the landscapes and sacred spaces of Indian life. I want my paintings to inspire the imagination. I want my art to honor the beauty, shapes and colors that define our beautiful land, the sky, dessert, canyons, rivers, hills, rocks, boulders, clouds. I want my art to honor our tribal rituals, ceremonies, religions, and the pueblos themselves.

INDIANS IN COLOR

Speaker Two: **Georgia O'Keeffe**

I love the Taos landscape. That is basically all that I paint. Oh, I paint flowers, too. How is our art different? I have also painted pueblo landscapes. One example of many: eyelevel. si.edu/2008/12/it-takes-a-pueblo-georgia-okeeffe-and-ansel-adams.html

Speaker One: **R. C. Gorman**

Maybe we both focus on shape and color, but I'm painting the Navajo landscape through the eyes of a Navajo. Naturally, you see this landscape through gendered white eyes. We do not see the same landscape.

Speaker Two: **Georgia O'Keeffe**

I can't agree, R. C. You have no ownership over this landscape.

Speaker One: **R. C. Gorman**

It's not about ownership, Georgia. We do not own the land; we live on the land and cherish it. For us the land is sacred. I feel that this is not the case for you.

Speaker Two: **Ms. Coyote**

R. C., you see sacred spaces of great beauty. That is what you paint. I feel like Georgia brings her sense of beauty to the landscape. Some feminists celebrated Georgia as the originator of a 'female iconography.'

Speaker Two: **Georgia O'Keeffe**

I love this land.

Speaker One: **Fritz Scholder**

My monster Indian has no sacred landscape to return to.

Speaker Two: **Mr. Coyote:**

There is much to explore here. Who owns the landscape? White lenses on landscape are different from Indian lenses, and this is not just a matter of differences between artists. The whites stole

Chapter 6 — Indian Painters, Patrons, and Wild West Shows

much of this land from our people. Should it be painted differently because it was stolen? Does this make it any less sacred?

Speaker One: **Ms. Coyote**

Let's go back to Lloyd Kiva New. He said our art should empower. He said we should use the beauty of our natural landscapes to inspire the beauty that is in each of us. Georgia O'Keeffe finds a beauty that inspires her. R. C. Gorman finds a different beauty. Fritz Scholder forsakes the beauty of landscapes that have been stolen by whites.

ACT ONE, SCENE FOUR
Authentic Art?

Speaker One: **Fritz Scholder**

You have to have lived as an Indian in order to be an Indian artist. But then I am only one-quarter Indian! What do I know?

Speaker Two: **Lloyd Kiva New**

In Chapter Four we talked about several kinds of art: authentic, inauthentic, Indigenous, non-tourist Indigenous, non-Indigenous art. We even borrowed from an art historian and used the categories of ethnic art, tourist art, commercial fine art, assimilated fine art (Graburn, 1976, pp. 5–7).

Speaker One: **J. J. Brody**

You can have as many categories as you want. There has always been a basic philosophical problem that has never been solved with satisfaction: not only *how*, but *what*, does the Indian artist paint (Brody, 1971, p. 146)? Anglo patrons ruined Native art by insisting that Indians paint in only one way. Work that did not confirm to the patron norms was denied financial support.

Speaker Two: **R. C. Gorman**

So these categories Lloyd lays out are useless. Just a lot of mumbo jumbo.

INDIANS IN COLOR

Speaker One: **Lloyd Kiva New**

They aren't mumbo jumbo. But J. J. Brody's questions may take us in the wrong direction. Step outside the box for a moment. We are talking about Native American art that honors native culture. Ignore what the art critics say about authentic or inauthentic.

Speaker Two: **Walter Benjamin**

Historically, 'authentic' has been a term that is reserved for an original work of art, not a mechanical reproduction, like a print or lithograph. An original has an aura that is absent in a reproduction. Still, the reproduction inherits an aura invoked by the original; for example, a print of a famous Georgia O'Keeffe painting.

Speaker One: **Tonto**

This gets real complicated with Native art, where every original is, at one level, also a copy and also authentic.

Speaker Two: **J. J. Brody**

I agree with Lloyd and Tonto. But let's cut to the bottom line. ALL ART, Native, non-Native, no matter what time period, is shaped by European colonialism and economic market conditions. Somebody is always paying somebody for a painting or some work of art, and nothing is ever pure.

Speaker One: **Georgia O'Keeffe**

J. J., I'm not going to go there. The work of a true artist is always authentic.

Speaker Two: **J. J. Brody**

You have not been listening to our conversation. 'Authentic' is an invented category, a marketing device.

Speaker One: **Mr. Coyote**

In my book Georgia is an original and a true, authentic artist.

Chapter 6 🟦 Indian Painters, Patrons, and Wild West Shows

Speaker Two: **Ms. Coyote**

OK. OK. But don't forget there are authentic replicas, forgeries, copies, and inauthentic replicas. So there you have it! (See Kalshoven, 2012, pp. 204–205.)

ACT TWO, SCENE ONE
Let's Hear It for TSA

Speaker One: **Georgia O'Keeffe**

Blumie, how did the TSA artists see these questions?

Speaker Two: **Ernest Blumenschein**

For us art answers to a true aesthetic of beauty. We knew we were making real art. Remember, we were European trained. We felt like we were following in the footprints of Gauguin and Van Gogh. The art we created was not about the primitive, per se. The primitive, this simple dark-skinned figure riding a horse through the valley, had an unobtrusive place in the artistic space we created. That space was not defined by the content of the painting—that is, by the Indian. The Indian was raw material for a larger project. We were creating a truly American national art. (Blumenschein in Bickerstaff, 1955b, p. 37, paraphrase; also Good, 1955, p.18)

Speaker One: **Tonto**

Hey, Blumie, whose nation, whose art? Surely not our nation, and not art for us.

Speaker Two: **Ms. Coyote**

Right on, Tonto! Critics called it railroad art for rich tourists.

Speaker One: **Ernest Blumenschein**

It was not railroad art. It was true art.

Speaker Two: **Tonto**

Hey, you sold it to the railroads and they turned it into advertisements.

Speaker One: **Ms. Coyote**

Painters like Juan, and the two Alberts, Fritz, Kevin, and R. C. had no rich patrons telling them what or how to paint.

ACT TWO, SCENE TWO
Not a National Art

Speaker One: **Georgia O'Keeffe**

Blumie, what do you mean by a national art?

Speaker Two: **Ernest Blumenschein**

It is art that is recognized by the national museums, the National Arts Club, the National Academy of Design, the Chicago Art Institute. Only formally trained artists can produce a truly national art.

Speaker One: **Georgia O'Keeffe**

What about Native artists?

Speaker Two: **Ernest Blumenschein**

Those Taos Indians who modeled for us could never do this. They were models, not artists. They had no artistic training,

Speaker One: **Georgia O'Keeffe**

Wow! Really?! There is a new generation of Native painters out there, Blumie, and they are getting a lot of attention—Fritz Scholder, R. C. Gorman, Kevin Red Star.

Speaker Two: **Ernest Blumenschein**

I know their work. They were not formally trained, either. Their techniques are questionable, especially their use of form, color, space, movement, balance, rhythm, symbolism. Their

Chapter 6 ⚏ Indian Painters, Patrons, and Wild West Shows

art is not controlled. It violates too many rules of composition (see Taggett and Schwartz, 1990, pp. 206–207).

Speaker One: **Georgia O'Keeffe**

People love Fritz's wild, bold Indians, his Pop Art images, his dead Indians that appear to fall off the canvas. They love R. C.'s canyons and Kevin's horses and Indian parade riders.

Speaker Two: **Ernest Blumenschein**

Georgia, people may love this work, but people are not trained art critics. They do not know what good art is. They do not understand the difference between aesthetic and illustrative reality, the difference between a thing as a recognizable object and the emotional idea of the thing. With aesthetic reality there is no representation of the thing as a recognizable object (see Taggett and Schwartz, 1990, p. 207).

Speaker One: **Georgia O'Keeffe**

Maybe they are following a different set of rules. Fritz's drunk Indians are caricatured Indians, and Kevin's Crow parade rider is an idealized warrior. But people relate to the power of these representations.

Speaker Two: **Ernest Blumenschein**

They don't even know what the rules are. These Indian activist artists will never find a home for their work in the great museums.

Speaker One: **Georgia O'Keeffe**

Lloyd, can you step in here?

Speaker Two: **Lloyd Kiva New**

At IAIA we told the students we wanted an art that made a difference for Native Americans. We want this art to come out of Native culture, out of the artist's life. You can call this activist art if you want to. Activist art can be great art, because great art moves people to thoughtful reflective action.

INDIANS IN COLOR

Speaker One: **Ernest Blumenschein**

Lloyd, I don't want to be disrespectful, but this art will never get off first base with the big museums.

Speaker Two: **Seventh Generation Performers**

Blumie is only partially correct. Some of the major museums have bought and are exhibiting works by Native artists, including the Heard Museum of Native Cultures and Art in Phoenix, the Eiteljorg in Indianapolis, and the National Museum of American Indian Art. Of course, we have always been marginalized, ignored, and told that our art was only good enough for train stations, airports, tourist shops, and ethnographic exhibits. But times are changing.

Speaker One: **Fritz Scholder, R. C. Gorman, and Kevin Red Star** in unison

Lloyd told us to paint from the heart. You cannot say that about the art of the TSA. We learned from the two Alberts and Juan to paint in a way that spoke directly to our communities. We were never painting for a national audience.

ACT TWO, SCENE THREE
The Forgotten Taos Three's View

Speaker One: **Juan Mirabal**

We were Native artists who loved the Taos Pueblo and painted scenes from the village. We experimented with various approaches and styles, from realism, to cubism, to lyrical abstract expressionism.

Speaker Two: **Georgia O'Keeffe**

Your experiments were amazing, but until the 2003 exhibit in the Harwood you never got proper credit for what you were doing.

Chapter 6 ⧉ Indian Painters, Patrons, and Wild West Shows

Speaker One: Albert Looking Elk Martinez

Georgia is being very nice, and we appreciated all the attention we got in 2003. But for the record, I think I need to mention the stories about how we were treated as models by the TSA painters. They had us take off our clothes and pose almost naked, as if we were warriors from ancient times. They had us dress up like Lakota Sioux or Apaches, or Crow Indians. They knew very little about Native culture and our many different tribes.

Speaker Two: Mr. Coyote

Today this all seems funny, but it was not funny. It revealed a fundamental disrespect for Taos and the native Taos Indian culture.

Speaker Two: Elsie Parsons

Allow me to come forward. It was disrespectful. I took some of those artists around and made introductions for them. If they had at least read my book, they would have learned about Taos culture and its customs.

Speaker One: Seventh Generation Performers

Remember, by their own admission they were not painting Indians.

Speaker Two: Mr. Coyote

They were not interested in painting Taos as it was. They had a pre-conception of an Indian based on the paintings of George Catlin, Charles Bird King, Karl Bodmer, and that was the Indian they set out to paint.

Speaker One: Albert Lujan

I was the "Grandma Moses" of the Taos Pueblo. My paintings were miniature, postcard size scenes from the village. I painted scenes from the village as I saw it. I painted for the white tourist market. No gallery would show my works. The Santa Fe and Taos art dealers called me an amateur easel painter, so I set up a gallery and sold my paintings there in my house.

163

Speaker Two: **Albert Looking Elk Martinez**

    I got criticized from all sides. Elsie Parsons criticized me for using money I made from my art to buy an automobile and taking trips to Albuquerque with my friends. Gallery owners in Santa Fe said my Indians were not Indian enough.

Speaker One: **J. J. Brody**

    The art critics also rejected the work of these Taos painters because it did not have proper aboriginal origins, it did not conform to aboriginal patterns in either form or function. They called them primitive tribesmen. The Santa Fe museum directors said their work was drivel that would only sell to uninformed tourists (1971 pp. 82, 90–91).

Speaker Two: **David Witt**

    This judgment was a mistake; Albert Lujan, Albert Looking Elk Martinez, and Juan Mirabal were among the most important painters to emerge in the Taos Pueblo from the early to mid twentieth century. Theirs was a representational art that departed from the traditional buffalo hide, teepee, and kiva paintings and ledger art of Indian artists trained at the Santa Fe Indian School (Witt, 2003b, p. 8). The art of the Taos Three is an integral part of the art history of Taos. They forged a path for a new generation of Taos Pueblo painters.

Lights dim, curtain comes down.

ACT THREE, SCENE ONE
Where Are We Today?

Lights come up, curtain rises.
San Geronimo Clowns tumble across the stage.
Georgia steps up to the speaker's lectern.

Speaker One: **Georgia O'Keeffe** (to audience and the speakers)

    We started by asking: Whose racialized Indian is being painted

Chapter 6 ◫ Indian Painters, Patrons, and Wild West Shows

by these three groups of artists? We've seen that there are three kinds of Indians: the TSA noble savage; the everyday, ordinary Taos citizen painted by the Forgotten Three; and the wild, radical postmodern Indian of Scholder and Red Star.

Speaker Two: **Mr. Coyote**

Georgia, we have more than three different types of Indians going on here. We have to ask who has the right to paint a Native American, and for what purposes. The TSA painters practiced a form of redfacing. We challenged this practice from the beginning. Our project is all about painting a new postindian, while honoring the work of Indigenous artists like the Forgotten Three Taos Painters.

Speaker One: **Ms. Coyote**

To repeat, only Indians should paint Indians. Postmodern, postindian art is activist art. It is intended to advance an agenda of empowerment.

Speaker Two: **Mr. Coyote**

We are calling for a moratorium. We need an extended time-out period from white artists painting Native Americans.

Speaker Two: **Tonto**

But of course they continue to claim this right. White artists who paint Native Americans still make a good living, just like the TSA old boys did in the 1920s.

Speaker Two: **Ernest Blumenschein**

You are correct. We have the right to paint anybody and anything. That is the TSA position. Always has been, always will be. Nothing has changed.

Speaker One: **Seventh Generation Performers**

Blumie is right. Nothing has changed! For example the website for the Autry National Center of the American West 2015 Masters of the American West Fine Art Exhibition and Sale

INDIANS IN COLOR

(January 31–March 8, 2015) reproduces a copy of Howard Terpning's painting, *The Patrol* (oil, 50 x 52). This is a post-Civil War painting. In the center three union military officers and a Native American look down at a fallen military officer on the prairie grass. Two Native Americans on horseback look on, as do four other union military officers, three on horseback. Terpning (1927–present) is a leading contemporary white Western artist who specializes in painting Native Americans. His painting, Major North and the Pawnee Battalion, recently sold for $1,496,000 at the 2014 Jackson Hole Art Auction (see jacksonholeartauction.com/news/untitled8.html; theautry.org/masters-of-the-american-west/masters-of-the-american-west).

Speaker Two: **Jen Graves**

This is contemporary Western art in the service of Western myth. The presence of the warriors lends a sense of Indian-ness to the scene, suggesting that they are allies of the military.

Speaker One: **Philip Deloria**

This is an assimilation narrative. Time stands still, and once again the pacified Native American is locked out of contemporary history. Contemporary audiences only know him thorough his presence in these staged scenes of violence. His fate is to be painted over and over again into war scenes by white artists who keep telling the same story (Deloria, 2004, pp. 65–67).

Speaker Two: **Seventh Generation Performers**

The master economic narrative that rules the North American Indian art world is the same today as it was 30 years ago when Jamake Highwater observed (Highwater, 1986, quoted in Chaat Smith, 2008, pp. 34–35):

Speaker One: **Jamake Highwater**[4]

Most of the Indian artists now are trying like Fritz Scholder himself, to get out of the field as quickly as possible. In 1985

Chapter 6 ⁂ Indian Painters, Patrons, and Wild West Shows

it is apparent to anyone who works as an art critic in New York City that Indian art has almost no chance of making an impact on the booming cosmopolitan art market; that it is very unlikely that anything called 'Indian art' will soon be exhibited by the reigning international entrepreneurs of contemporary art; or that at this moment in time the Indian artist has any hope of altering the emphatic indifference of the powerful East Coast clique of contemporary art promoters, critics and exhibitors. There is not a single fine arts museum of significance in Boston, Los Angeles, San Francisco or Washington, D. C. that currently has a single painting or sculpture by an American Indian on permanent exhibition. In talking to critics there is real doubt that any Indian has produced art of the first rank.

Speaker Two: **Paul Chaat Smith**

It is twenty years later. These problems still remain (Smith, 2008, p. 35).

Speaker One: **Tonto**

Paul published those lines in 2008. It's 2015. Time stands still. With few exceptions, Native art is primarily exhibited in regional museums[5] and select galleries in the Southwest: Santa Fe, Albuquerque, Phoenix, Tucson, Jackson Hole.

Speaker Two: **Ms. Coyote**

What does this mean for Lloyd's dream of a postmodern Indian art that makes a difference. Is that dream dead? Can this art function as a pedagogy of liberation?

Speaker One: **Mr. Coyote**

Liberation? Of course. A new generation of Native painters can study Scholder, Gorman, Red Star and create a new art that speaks from the heart and the soul of Native culture. This is how a pedagogy of liberation works.

Lights dim, curtain comes down.

INDIANS IN COLOR

ACT THREE, SCENE TWO
How Wild West Shows (and the Taos Society of Artists) Sold Out the West[6]

Lights come up. The curtain rises.

Soft Navajo flute music plays over the sound system. Supaman and the San Geronimo Clowns line-dance across the stage. The sun is setting in the West, casting shadows across the Santa Fe town plaza. Jen Graves steps forward:

Speaker One: **Jen Graves**

   I'm here to pick up on Lloyd's dream by introducing you to a new Crow artist named Wendy Red Star. She has her own Wild West show.

Speaker Two: **Wendy Red Star**

   Welcome to my show. Like Buffalo Bill, we are combining genres—buffalos, cowboys, Indians, attacks on white settler cabins, cowboy music, and lady sharp shooters. But unlike Buffalo Bill, we have art exhibits and installations, performance artists, Indian music and fancy dancers. However, with the title of my show I'm following Buffalo Bill's lead. He called his show "Buffalo Bill's West Show & Congress of Rough Riders of the World."

Stage right: Spotlight shines on the following poster.

Wendy Red Star's Wild West & Congress of Rough Riders of the World
Bumbershoot 2014—Fisher Pavilion
August 30–September 1, 2014

168

Chapter 6 ⚏ Indian Painters, Patrons, and Wild West Shows

Speaker Two: **Wendy Red Star**

When Buffalo Bill's show played in Seattle September 15–16, 1898, he used the following program (see Denzin, 2011, pp. 204–205). As you can see, he had Anne Oakley, Cossacks, Mexicans, Arabs, gauchos, army veterans, stage coach hold-ups, a re-enactment of the Battle of Little Bighorn with Cody himself playing General Armstrong Custer.

On a drop-down video screen the following program is displayed. The text is read by an off-screen narrator.

Narrator

Good evening folks. Close your eyes. Step back in time with us. You will experience something unique tonight, an authentic Wild West experience. Please welcome Buffalo Bill's Wild West and the Congress of Rough Riders of the World, in the following order:

1. *Miss Annie Oakley, sharp shooter.*
2. *Race of the Races—a race between a cowboy, a Cossack, a Mexican, an Arab, a Gaucho, and an Indian.*
3. *U. S. Artillery Drill by 5th Regiment veterans.*
4. *A cowboy camp is attacked by marauding Indians who are repulsed by Buffalo Bill.*
5. *A Pony Express rider delivers the mail.*
6. *Mexicans do lasso tricks.*
7. *Arab horsemen illustrate their style of horsemanship.*
8. *Indian boys race.*
9. *Indians—Sioux, Arrapahoe, Cheyenne—do war dances.*
10. *Veterans from the 6th U. S. Calvary do military exercises.*
11. *A Deadwood stage is held up.*
12. *The Rough Riders of the world ride.*
13. *Col. W. F. Cody performs sharp-shooting stunts, riding at full speed.*
14. *Buffalo Hunt with real buffalo.*

15. *The Battle of the Little Bighorn*, with Col. W. F. Cody playing Gen. George Armstrong Custer.

16. *The Battle of Warbonnet Creek*, when Col. W. F. Cody takes the first scalp for Custer.

17. *Curtain:* A cowboy in Dodge City, 1882.

Lights dim, then an actor dressed as Buffalo Bill steps forward.

Speaker One: **Buffalo Bill**

I built my show around the Last Stand. The climax is the reenactment of Custer's Last Stand, and then my killing Chief Yellow Hair. Folks said I made this all up. Not true. We just try to give the folks a good show that looks real! I sure had fun playing General Custer.

Speaker Two: **Sherman Alexie**

This idea of the Last Stand is a joke. It should never have been called 'Custer's Last Stand.' Oh, sure, it was his last stand. He died there. But he was easily replaced. Not so for the Indians. Little Bighorn was the last real battle of the Indian Wars. Custer's Last Stand was really the Indians' last stand, but boy, on that day they were crazy good! (Alexie, 2007, p. 70, paraphrase).

CUSTER DIED FOR YOUR SINS

Chapter 6 ⣿ Indian Painters, Patrons, and Wild West Shows

ACT THREE, SCENE THREE
Wendy and Bill

Speaker One: **Seventh Generation Performers**

Wendy, so that was Bill's program. Are you really using his program?

Speaker Two: **Wendy Red Star**

NO! We don't use Cody's program. We just want people to see what his program looked like. My show is the Wild West seen from the Native American standpoint. I'm doing it on behalf of my great grandparents who participated in Buffalo Bill's West shows and my grandparents who participated in the St. Louis World's Fair (1904) and the Chicago World's Fair (1893). This is my version of a Wild West show, in the sense that the participants will be allowed to exercise control concerning how Native American are represented in art and performance.

Speaker One: **Seventh Generation Performers**

Everybody knows Buffalo Bill allowed his Indian performers to bring their special riding skills to their performances, but they never controlled what they were performing. You are taking it to a new level (see McNenly, 2012, p. 6). Now the Native performers have full control of their artistic contributions.

Speaker Two: **Wendy Red Star**

That is the main point. We are giving artists their own performance spaces. Native artists in our show will have a chance to present and distribute their own work. These artists represent a diverse spectrum of Native American identities in the 21st century. They are rough riders who shatter many of the stereotypical notions placed upon Native Americans. Indeed, my show features many of the top Native American and First Nations artists and performers working today—Da-Ka-Xeen Mehner, Amelia Winger-Bearskin, Peter Morin, John Feodorov, Shawennati, Nicholas Glanin, Tanis S'Eltin, Jim

INDIANS IN COLOR

Denonie, Demian Diné Yazhi', Terrance Houle. In addition, because it is a Wild West show, I have 100 horses, buffalo, and longhorn steers. It's time to bring Wild West shows and Native art together.

Speaker One: **Ms. Coyote**

You are turning the Wild West show upside down. No semi-naked Indian warriors on horseback chasing buffalos and attacking white settler cabins.

Speaker Two: **Wendy Red Star**

Exactly! If you walk around the arena, you will see that we have separate stages for different performances. One stage is devoted to a Native American re-enactment of Buffalo Bill's 1898 program. We have Native actors in red face and in costume playing the parts of Anne Oakley, 5th Regiment veterans, Buffalo Bill himself, and General Custer. The use of red face turns the performance into a minstrel show. The tables are turned. Indians have the power. They are doing caricatures. Annie Oakley is riding a mule, not a horse, firing toy pistols. 5th Regiment veterans are dressed in loin clothes, not regulation regiment dress. Buffalo Bill wears a dress. General Custer is dressed as a clown. Indian artists walk back and forth, displaying their paintings and art work.

Speaker One: **Tonto**

Awesome! You are going one step further. You are placing minstrelsy and Native art at the center of your show.

Shouts from off-stage.

Speaker One: **Imaginary Indians**

STOP, STOP! We are the Imaginary Indians from Chapter Two. Back then we were looking for an author to write a new play for us. Listening to Wendy Red Star, we think we have found our lost author. We want to join her Wild West show. We

Chapter 6 ⊞ Indian Painters, Patrons, and Wild West Shows

want to break out of the Buffalo Bill-Disneyland story about Indians and the Old West.

Speaker Two: **Wendy Red Star**

I was hoping you guys would show up.

We have place for you.

Speaker One: **Imaginary Indians**

Just tell us what to do.

Speaker Two: **Wendy Red Star**

Go to stage G. It is next to the stage where Buffalo Bill reenactments are going on. I want you to tear off your nametags, masks, buckskins, and headdresses. Then I want you to invite the audience to take part in a discussion on Wild West shows.

Why should we stop staging Wild West shows? Does the audience agree that these shows:

1. Are racist and perpetuate stereotypes?

2. Make Indians historical re-enactors of a past that never was?

3. Foreclose any possibility that Indians as re-enactors will ever be able to occupy the same historical space as white audiences (Deloria, 2004, p, 67)?

4. Foreclose any possibility that whites will ever stop appropriating Indian culture for white purposes?

Speaker One: **Imaginary Indians**

We're on it. Thanks, Wendy. It is not a happy day when we have to consider doing these Wild West show reenactments; even getting close to them is upsetting. We are not Indian hobbyists! (Kalshoven, 2012). But your show allows us to make fun of Buffalo Bill and his circus—his cowboy clowns, his pretend imaginary Indians bedecked in paint and feathers (see Vizenor, 1994/1999, p. 134).

INDIANS IN COLOR

Speaker Two: **Ms. Coyote**

Hey. Don't forget the fifth reason for terminating these shows. They inspire Indian hobbyists.

ACT THREE, SCENE FOUR
Why Seattle?

Speaker One: **Tonto** (to Wendy)

Why the Seattle Civic Center?

Speaker Two: **Wendy Red Star**

It's all symbolic. The Seattle Center, which is the home of Bumpershoot, was originally built for the 1962 World's Fair. This connection to world fairs is what I am after. It illustrates the complicated history linking art and living exhibits of Indigenous peoples on stages and in cages at world, county and state fairs and in expositions and Wild West shows (see Appendix A for a list of these sites where Native peoples were exhibited, like animals in a zoo). They were a main attraction. They were entertainment for millions of people. They were usually presented in a so-called "natural" or "primitive" state, in dioramas, sometimes in cages. They were presented as being lower on the scale of evolutionary progress. On posters and billboards they were represented as a counterbalance to dominant Western European civilization (see Moses, 1996, pp. 129–168). The original world fairs celebrated manifest destiny and the colonial model of progress.

I want to give Native American contemporary artists the opportunity to insert themselves into history and to take back ownership of Native American representations. White artists and Wild West shows sold out Indians and the West. I want to reclaim that territory.

Speaker One: **Mr. Coyote**

Can you be specific?

Chapter 6   Indian Painters, Patrons, and Wild West Shows

Speaker Two: **Wendy Red Star**
Look at our poster and the following installations.

Stage Right: Spotlight shines on poster listing Artistic Events in Wendy Red Star's 2014 Bumpershoot Wild West Show:

Lights dim, curtain lowers.

Curtain rises, the gallery slowly rotates, revealing seven separate stages. On each, performers are engaged in the activities announced in the poster.

Native Art at Bumpershoot

Stage One. **Skawennati** (Mohawk) exhibits a video game where futuristic characters can revisit historical moments, but they cannot change them. A Mohawk warrior from the future can watch a massacre of Mohawks in the past, but do nothing about it.

Stage Two. **Demian Diné Yazhi'** Exhibit: "Don't trip over Custer"—A life-size sculpture of Custer is lying dead on the gallery floor.

Stage Three. **Peter Morin** (Tahitan) Exhibit: a video compilation, on endless repeat, of all the sequences of Pocahontas's animated hair waving in the Disney wind.

Stage Four. **John Feodorov** (mixed-Native American) Exhibit: a giant warbonnet is positioned in the middle of the gallery.

Stage Five. **Tanis S'eiltin** (Tlingit) Exhibit: uses found photographs of her mother visiting the Seattle World's Fair to stage a re-creation of her mother's art.

Stage Six. **Wendy Red Star** Exhibit: "Four Seasons" series—Wendy poses in Crow regalia in the midst of fake nature with cheesy landscape paintings for backdrops, thrift-store objects for props, including a blow-up deer, and stuffed animals based on drawings a Crow chief made in 1880.

Stage Seven. **Wendy Red Star** Exhibit: Celebrating a message of peace, Wendy and a friend, wearing warbonnet headdresses, restage a photograph taken of John Lennon and Yoko Ono during their 1969 Bed-ins for Peace (Graves, 2014).

Speaker One: **Ms. Coyote**

This is incredible! What happened to Buffalo Bill?

Speaker Two: **Wendy Red Star**

In another show Buffalo Bill is killed by Custer.

It is an accident. Custer is drunk and mistakes Bill for Sitting Bull.

Lights dim, curtain lowers.

ACT THREE, SCENE FIVE
Whose Art, Whose West?

Lights come up, curtain rises.

Supaman joins hands with the San Geronimo Clowns. Together they dance across the stage. Georgia O'Keeffe steps forward.

Speaker One: **Georgia O'Keeffe**

We have come a long way, dear audience and dear readers.

You have been very patient. It is time for closure.

Speaker Two: **Tonto**

You may say we have come a long way. That is easy for you to say. But you did not have to watch bare-chested Johnny Depp in white face acting like he was the new real Tonto. It is the same recycled story of cultural appropriation, another version of white people playing Indian (Aylwin, 2013; Deloria, 1998; Hearne, 2012a).

Chapter 6 Indian Painters, Patrons, and Wild West Shows

Speaker One: Wendy Red Star

> Johnny Depp thought he was turning stereotypes on their heads by giving Tonto a voice he never had. But it is Depp's white voice that is heard (Aylwin, 2013).

Speaker Two: Unidentified Speakers shout from offstage
STOP, STOP! LET US BE HEARD!

Speaker One: Georgia O'Keeffe

> By all means. Come forward and introduce yourselves.

Speaker Two: Children of Native Artists

> We are friends of Wendy Red Star. We are the children, and grandchildren and great grandchildren of the two Alberts, Juan, Fritz, Kevin, and R. C. We are artists, painters, sculptors, filmmakers, poets, writers. Some of us are doctors, nurses, lawyers, carpenters, mechanics, chefs, social workers, and Indian chiefs. We follow in the footsteps of our parents. We are Indian activists. We believe art can make a difference in the world. As you bring this play to a conclusion, we have some ideas for you to consider.

Speaker One: Georgia O'Keeffe

> By all means.

Speaker Two: Children of Native Artists

> We've been studying some of the arguments made by the Radical Indigenous Survivance and Empowerment (R.I.S.E.) group.[7] They are committed to using art, stories, and performances for social justice purposes. Survivance art honors visual reminiscence, native presence, human rights, and tribal sovereignty. It creates an active Native presence, like the art of Fritz or Kevin. With the phrase, "Bury My Art at Wounded Knee," R.I.S.E. invokes the legacies and memories of Wounded Knee (Means, 1995, pp. 257–273; Oberg, 2010, pp. 318–323; Ostler, 2004; Smith and Warrior, 1996).[8]

INDIANS IN COLOR

Stage Right: Spotlight shines on this poster:

Manifesto:
Bury My Art at Wounded Knee[9]

Speaker One: **Demian Dine' Yashi'**

Through visual, written, & speech-based forms of cultural representation, *Bury My Art at Wounded Knee* aims to explore, and thereby challenge, contemporary notions of Native art. The main objective is to acknowledge Indigenous resistance through the origins of the American Indian Movement (A.I.M.), Native north american political art, & present day issues in Native america. It is dedicated to the long legacy of Native north american artists, warriors, activists, writers, & visionaries.[7]

Speaker Two: **Tonto**
What is R.I.S.E.?

Speaker One: **Demian Dine' Yashi'**

R.I.S.E., Radical Indigenous Survivance and Empowerment, was established in 2010, through a heightened awareness of the atrocities that have resulted from patriarchal colonization. The seeds of the collective have been planted firmly in the ground since the onslaught of European madness. At its foundation, R.I.S.E. is invested in the education, perseverance, and dissemination of Native North American art, activism, writing, history, storytelling, and lived experience. R.I.S.E. is a call to action yielding multiple tools, including photographs, paint, wheat paste, clay, beadwork, dancing, words, voices, sounds, ritual, and more.[9]

Chapter 6 Indian Painters, Patrons, and Wild West Shows

R.I.S.E. is about the political use of art for Indigenous peoples everywhere.

❖❖❖

The lights go down. A YouTube video—Honoring Our Great Artists—is projected onto the giant drop-down screen in the center of the stage. In rapid succession the video moves through painting after painting by Fritz Scholder, R. C. Gorman, and Kevin Red Star.

Lights come up.

The San Geronimo Clowns enter stage left, join hands, and bow to the audience. They turn and take the steps leading off the stage, laughing loudly as they leave the theater.

Applause. Scenes from the Unesco website for the Taos Pueblo appear on the drop down screen (whc.unesco.org/en/list/492/video).

The theatre goes dark.

Lights come up. The curtains rise. A huge poster filling the expanse of the stage is slowly lowered. Spotlights shine on the text:

BURY MY ART AT WOUNDED KNEE

BURY OUR ART AT WOUNDED KNEE

Let the Healing Begin

THE END

(in memory of Dee Brown)

CODA
Back to the Future

This book has been about one thing: How Wild West shows and the Taos Society of Artists (and other white artists) sold out Indians in the service of an imaginary Wild West (Taggett and Schwartz, 1990). This narrative required the concept of a unified Indian subject who stood outside time and space. In this imaginary space Indians found their place either on reservations, on the stages of Wild West shows as Indians in color (redface) on the canvases produced by white artists, or in Hollywood film. Same Indian, just different spaces.

Indigenous and Third Chapter painters challenged these representations. Their work repudiated the concept of the romanticized noble savage so central to the 19th- and 20th-century images of the Native American. The Institute of American Indian Arts was a major factor in these battles. The IAIA faculty trained a new generation of Indian artists who had a commitment to an aesthetic that said art could be both a tool of self-expression and an agent for social change. The IAIA trained artists, like the Forgotten Taos Three, became agents of the very change their paintings embodied. They created a new visual

---

Indians in Color: Native Art, Identity, and Performance in the New West by Norman K. Denzin, 181–184. © 2015 Taylor & Francis. All rights reserved.

language, the language of a New Native American. Their story, this book's story about art and Native Americans, started in the Taos Pueblo, and it ends there. These artists carried forward the very essence of the concept of 'survivance'[1] embodied in Taos Pueblo's 1,000 years plus of resistance to colonial domination. This is their lasting legacy and the Pueblo's gift to them.

The Wild West imaginary required consumers who would buy a product, a ticket to a show or a movie, admission to a museum, or the purchase of a Western painting. It required wealthy industrialist patrons, railroad lines, art schools, art teachers, a tourism industry, and little boys and little girls who wanted to own and wear an Indian headdress, a cowboy outfit, a red bandana, buckskins, a fake leather vest, a cowboy hat, toy pistols. It required a consumer who had been taught to embrace, and even perform, white fantasies about Indians, cowboys, and Wild West shows. I am such a consumer. At an early age I fell in love with the Wild West. I was Tonto, Little Beaver, the Lone Ranger, Roy Rogers, Gene Autry. I was Squanto in the fourth grade.

So I end by returning to the beginning; the spaces of memory, an imaginary Wild West, those cowboy and Indians movies from my childhood. Hours spent in darkened theatres. How do I name the feelings, the guilt, the longing, the emptiness? I was taught to be a consumer of these Wild West fantasies, to find solace in them.

Has this book been about my desire to heal? Is it yet another misuse of Native Americans by a privileged white man? Have I written my self into a corner? Even to this day I remember those Saturday mornings and those Saturday nights, those TV shows and those movies at the Strand, and I remember Sonny, hot doughnuts, our cowboy outfits. Now, 60 years later, I wonder if my grandfather and I got the same things out of these movies, out of being in the quietness of that elegant theatre. We seldom talked about a movie on the way home, but it was clear the movies filled a need. They did something really important for us. We did not have to talk. We'd sit in silence in the big old Pontiac Grandpa drove. I'd close my eyes and relive those scenes—Shane, Shane, come back. Often, I'd be asleep before we got home.

Coda ▦ Back to the Future

In the theatre I was safe from life. This was the summer my parents announced in Grandpa and Grandma's TV room that they were getting divorced, and that they were leaving Mark and me to live with Grandpa and Grandma.

I felt safe inside these old westerns. I think Grandpa did, too. Those cowboys knew how to hold their families together, even when they were under attack from robber barons, bloodthirsty Indians, or psychopathic gunslingers. Come back, Shane, come back. We need you.

I'm not saying Grandpa was Shane, but he did hold our family together, with Grandma's help. And maybe I wasn't little Joey, but I wanted a stronger father figure then the one my father was able to gave me.

Today, I want to write my way out of this family history. I want to get beyond cowboy and Indian movies. I want a new story, a new beginning. I've been trapped for too long inside the same old Wild West dime novels turned into Wild West movies turned into personal stories by little lonely white kids living with their grandparents. I need to let a new story find me. But haven't whites always done this? Do I need cowboys and Native Americans to make sense of my life and political leanings. Do I even have the right to tell this story?

I think I'm like the narrator in Guy Maddin's 2007 film, *My Winnipeg*.[2] In the film Maddin returns to his family home and rents the house for a month so he can re-do some things that happened in that house when he was twelve years old.[3] He hires actors to play his mother, father, brother, and sister. He rents a pet dog. When the month is up, there are still issues that have not been resolved.

I could be like Gay Maddin. I'd rent the Iowa farm house for one week, and hire actors to play me, Mark, our mother, our father, Grandpa and Grandma. I'd get a VCR to show films on an old black and white Sylvania TV. Grandma would make her doughnuts. We'd watch cowboy movies from the 1950s. I'd have Dad tell Mother how much he loved her. They would kiss and act as if they loved each other. Mark and I would hug them, and Grandma and Grandma would have big smiles.

But now I'm doing it again, using someone else's past to make sense of my own. And this is just another version of the same story. Sherman Alexie (1993) says to be careful with your story. Waylong Gary White Deer (2013) says let the stories find you. Margaret Kovach (2010) says stories will wait for us until we are ready. How much longer must I wait? Am I really ready to move forward? Am I ready to stop playing Indian? Can I stop playing Indian?

Willie Nelson cautions (paraphrase):

Mamas, don't let your little boys grow up to be cowboys, or Indians,

'Cause if they think they're cowboys, next thing you know

They'll be out there playin' Indian.[4]

White boys playing Indian, white painters painting red Indians. Whites owning Indianness. Whites needing Indians in order to be whole. When will it end?

In the following injunction Ralph Ellison says it will never end. Substitute Native American for Negro:

This society is not likely to become free of racism, thus it is necessary for Native Americans to free themselves by becoming their idea of what a free people should be (Ellison, 1999, p. 356).

And whites should stop telling Native Americans what it means to be a free people.

Sherman Alexie would seem to agree. Consider how he discusses Junior Polatkin's dream (2007, p. 232, paraphrase):

In the dream he sometimes had, Junior Polatkin would be gunfighter. A gunfighter with braids and a ribbon shirt. He wouldn't speak English, just whisper Spokane as he gunned down Wild Bill Hickok, Bat Masterson, even Billy the Kid. Junior dreamed his name would be Sonny Six-Gun, and he dreamed that white and Indian people would sing ballads about him, and he would be a star in his own Wild West show.

Is this the freedom Ellison is seeking?

Appendix A
Time Line
Staging and Marketing American Indians, and Federal Indian Policy

1775	Bureau of Indian Affairs formed.
1795–1822	The Indian Factory System is created to regulate trade with Indians, while hastening their assimilation into White culture.
1819	Indian Civilization Act passed.[1]
1830	Indian Removal Act passed.[2]
1860	Navajo's forced 'Long Walk' to prison camp at Bosque Redondo, New Mexico.
1860–1893	U. S. museums begin to collect and offer public displays of Indian life: Smithsonian ethnological collection (1860); Harvard's Peabody Museum (founded 1866); American Museum of Natural History (founded 1869); Chicago's Field Museum (1893).

Indians in Color: Native Art, Identity, and Performance in the New West by Norman K. Denzin, 185–192. © 2015 Taylor & Francis. All rights reserved.

INDIANS IN COLOR

1876	Battle of Little Big Horn.
1879–1926	Carlisle School, the first Indian boarding school, opens in 1879 and closes in 1926. Assimilation of Indians is official Indian policy.[3]
1878	Fred Harvey's (1835–1901) company (trading posts, hotels, restaurants) signs food service contract with Santa Fe Railroad.
1887	Dawes Act enacted.[4]
1890–1920	Progressive Era; Native Americans challenge federal policies; native anthropologists and artists record aspects of ceremonial life.
1893–1922	Indian Industries League of Boston formed.
1899	Fred Harvey Company commissions Indian art for sale at Harvey Houses located along Santa Fe Rail Line throughout Southwest.
1902	Fred Harvey Indian Department and Indian Museum opens in Albuquerque, commissioning Native arts and crafts for sale. Harvey Indians are hired to perform for tourists. Tours to Santa Fe and Taos Pueblos are organized (Fried, 2010, pp. 185–189).
1905	Francis Ellington Leupp (1849–1918) becomes Indian commissioner and works to re-orient Indian policy away from assimilation.
1906	Burke Act is enacted.[5]
1906	American Antiquities Act is passed, protecting prehistoric Indian ruins and artifacts.
1907	School of America Research and the Museum of New Mexico established in Santa Fe under the leadership of Edgar Hewett (1865–1946) and Mary Austin (1868–1934). The museum becomes the center for the collection and exhibition of regional arts produced by Native and non-Native artists (Meyer, 2001, pp. 194–195).

Appendix A ▦ Time Line

1893–1904 Living Exhibits, Exposition Hall Indians and
Reservation Fairs:

1893	Colombian Exposition, Chicago
1895	Atlanta Exposition
1895	Nashville Exposition
1898	Omaha Exposition
1899	Omaha Exposition
1901	Buffalo Exposition
1904	Louisiana Purchase Expo, St. Louis
1905	Pueblo, Colorado State Fair
1906	Denver, Wild West Show, Elks Club
1909	Alaska-Yukon Pacific Expo, Seattle
1907– 1912	Ute Reservation Fair , Pueblo, Colorado
1909	Crow Reservation Fair
1912	Lower Brule Fair
1915	By 1915, 54 reservations were staging annual fairs and Indian expos (Moses, 1996, p. 212)

1899–1927 Taos Art Society formally created (1915–1927).[6]

1916 "Images from the Taos Society Painters are used extensively by the Santa Fe Railway and the Denver & Rio Grande Railway for advertisement" (Scott, 1998, p. 120), enticing tourists to travel to the Southwest, while dining in Harvey Cars and sleeping in Harvey Hotels.

1917 E. L. Hewett and associates recreate Santa Fe festival, emphasizing Native processions, reenactments, and Indian dances for tourist consumption (Meyer, 2001, p. 195).

INDIANS IN COLOR

1920	Reforms in U. S. Indian assimilation policy are initiated. Leaders and supporters include John Collier (1884–1896, commissioner of Bureau of Indian Affairs, 1933–1945), Mabel Dodge Luhan (1879–1962), Mary Austin, and others, including the Society of Taos artists.
1922	Bursum Act, which took lands away from the Taos Pueblos, is defeated. Opposition to the bill is lead by Austin, Luhan, Collier, the Taos Society of Painters, and a national coalition that included Carl Sandburg, Vachel Lindsey, E. L. Masters, the American Ethnological Society, and the Girl Scouts and Boy Scouts (Goodman and Dawson, 2008, p. 221).
1922	Santa Fe Indian Fair opens. Native artists exhibit and sell 'authentic' art, prizes are given, consumer markets and prices are set.
1924	Indian New Deal program launched by John Collier.
1925	Mary Austin and colleagues establish Indian Arts Fund to collect and preserve America's 'last handicraft culture.' Their focus was on Pueblo pottery, jewelry, weavings, and paintings. A goal was to protect all Indian art from commercialization (Meyer, 2001, p. 198).
1925	The Indian Arts Movement and the Taos Society of painters market romanticized views of "Indians as exotic Others" (Meyers, 2001, p. 206).
1926–1927	John D. Rockefeller, Jr., funds Indian Arts Fund.
1928	Meriam Report reveals the failure of federal Indian policies.
1934	Indian New Deal, under Indian Reorganization Act, emphasizes Indian self-determination and the return of communal tribal lands.
1935	Indian Arts and Crafts Board (and Act) are established (see Schrader, 1983).

Appendix A ⚜ Time Line

1930–1940	Indian Civilian Conservation Corps is created. Indian education is rooted in local communities and the values of Native culture. Boarding schools are abandoned. Indian schools teach Indian history. Bilingual pamphlets appear. Interest in Indian art grows.
1941	Over 7,000 Indians register for the draft, including the 'Navajo Code Talkers' (Oberg, 2010, p. 299).
1942	Delegates from the Six (Seneca) Nations, the New World's oldest democracy, declare war against Germany, Italy, and Japan (Oberg, 2010, p. 300).
1944	National Council of American Indians is formed.
1940–1950	During World War II funding for reservations is cut. Indians are sent to off-reservation boarding schools. The policy of 'de-Indianizing the Indian' returns. Reservations become domestic dependent nations.
1953	Public Law 280 implements a policy of terminating the sovereign status of tribal nations—over 100 tribes are terminated.
1960s	Along with federal guidelines, Native and non-Native associations form to protect native cultures from un-regulated tourism. National Indian Youth Council (NIYC) is created. Vine Deloria is elected executive director (Oberg, 2010, p. 319).
1962	Lloyd Kiva New (Cherokee, 1916–2002) and George Boyce found the Institute of American Indian Arts (IAIA), situated in Santa Fe and created by President Kennedy. New is hired as the first director for the art high school for Native Americans in Santa Fe. It becomes a two-year college in 1975, offering associate degrees in Studio Arts. In 1986 it becomes a chartered college, charged with the preservation and dissemination of traditional and contemporary expressions of Native American language, literature, history, oral

traditions, and the visual and performing arts. A new generation of Native artists are trained. Notable faculty and alumni include Fritz Scholder, Earl Biss, Kevin Red Star, and Charlene Teeters.

1965   National Advisory Council on Indian Education and the Kennedy Report speak of Indian education as a national tragedy. Indian self-determination becomes the new watchword.

1965   National Congress of American Indians launches a campaign to eliminate the use Native American mascots in sports.

1968   Indian Civil Rights Act of 1968; activists fight against forces of assimilation and to protect tribal statuses as sovereign nations. Dennis Banks and Clyde Bellocourt found AIM in the Twin Cities of Minnesota.

1969   Birth of Native American Red Power movement, which re-fashions 1920s "reform efforts ... into a new, more emboldened campaign for Indian self-determination" (Deloria, Jr., 1969; Meyers, 2001, p. 207; Smith and Warrior, 1996).

1969–1971   Occupation of Alcatraz, BIA takeover, and Wounded Knee.

1972   Trail of Broken Treaties.[7]

1972   Museum of Contemporary Native Arts, as part of the IAIA, opens, and in 1990 moves to the downtown Federal Building in Santa Fe. In 2010 it moves to a 7,000-square-foot state-of-the-art building on the IAIA campus.[8] It holds the premier collection of contemporary Native American art.

1973   Occupation of Wounded Knee, South Dakota, site of 1890 massacre of more than 350 Lakota men, women, and children.

Appendix A ⬛ Time Line

1975	Indian Self-Determination and Education Resistance Act of 1975.[9]
1975	Indian gaming casinos begin to appear.
1978	The Longest Walk, led by AIM, in support of tribal sovereignty.
1978	Tribally Controlled Community College Assistance Act.
1978	American Indian Religious Freedom Act.
1980	Indian studies programs open in American colleges and universities.
1988	Congress enacts Indian Gaming Act.
1989	National Museum of the American Indian is authorized. It opens in 2004 in Washington, D. C.
1990	Indian Arts and Crafts Act of 1990 enacted.
1990	Native American Graves Protection and Repatriation Act enacted.
1994	Tribal Governance Act enacted.
1994–2004	First International Decade of the World's Indigenous Peoples.
2000	Indian Arts and Crafts Act of 2000 enacted.
2002	Over 460 Indian gaming establishments, many on reservation with resorts.
2005–2014	Second International Decade of the World's Indigenous Peoples.
2008	The Longest Walk 2, involving representatives from more than 100 American Indian nations, Maori, and other Indigenous persons.[10]
2010	Websites appear listing Native American scenic byways (sites, villages, festivals) by North American region and tribal nation (w.w.w.native tourism.org/ByWays/ScenicByways.htm).

2010	United States becomes last nation to oppose the UN Declaration on the Rights of Indigenous Peoples.

Appendix B
The Taos Society of Artists and Their Descendants

Taos Founders: The Original Six Plus (1915–1927)[1]

1. Joseph Henry Sharp (1859–1953)
2. Ernest L. Blumenschen (1874–1960)
3. W. Herbert Dunton (1878–1936)
4. E. I. Couse (1866–1936)
5. Bert G. Phillips (1868–1956)
6. Oscar E. Berninghaus (1874–1960)
7. Walter Ufer (1876–1936)
8. Victor Higgins (1884–1949)
9. Julius Rolshoven (1858–1930)
10. Catharine Critcher (1868–1964)
11. Kenneth Adams (1897–1966)
12. E. Martin Henning (1886–1956).[2]

Indians in Color: Native Art, Identity, and Performance in the New West by Norman K. Denzin, 193–194. © 2015 Taylor & Francis. All rights reserved.

INDIANS IN COLOR

The Three Forgotten Taos Pueblo Artists (1920–1950)

Albert Looking Elk (Martinez) (1888–1940)
Albert Lujan (1892–1948)
Juan Mirabal (1903–1970)

Taos Moderns (1940–)

Ansel Adams (1902–1984)
Andrew Dasb (1870–1953)
Agnes Martin (1912–2004)
Beatrice Mandelman (1912–1998)
Georgia O'Keeffe (1887–1986)
Nicolai Rechin (1881–1955)
Louis Ribak (1902–1979)
John Sloan (1871–1951)

Chapter III (1960–)

Jim Wagner (1940–)
R. C. Gorman (1931–2005)
Fritz Scholder (1937–2005)
Woody Crumbo (1912–1989)
Kevin Red Star (1937–)

Notes

Dramatis Personae

1. Ferlyn Brass, Kevin Dust, Kevin Mustus, Ernest Rangel, and Carter Yellowbird were all interviewed by McNenly (2012, pp. 140–165) and quoted in her chapter on Euro Disney's Wild West Show. Unless otherwise indicated, the words they speak in my play(s) are words I have given them.

Chapter One: Native Art, Identity and Performance in the Postmodern West

1. One of the largest collections of paintings by the Taos Society of Artists is in the Eiteljorg Museum of American Indians and Western Art in Indianapolis, Indiana (see www.eiteljorg.org/explore/collections). See Appendix B for a list of the TSA painters.
2. Attending a session at the International Congress of Qualitative Inquiry on "Cowboys and Indians," Henhawk asks, "What did I get myself into? I feel like I'm the only Indian in the room" (2013, p. 519).
3. As well as visits to art galleries in Taos and to the Museum of Indian Arts and Culture in Santa Fe.
4. By Indian art I refer to modern Indian painting not the full-range of Native American art, which, in addition to paintings, includes, among other forms, baskets, jewelry, pottery, sculpture, weavings, Zuni fetishes, and Hopi Kachina dolls, etc.
5. I acknowledge the misnomer "Indian" and the cumbersome "Native American" or equally cumbersome "Indigenous person," using wherever possible the name of a specific tribe: Lakota Sioux, Crow, Hopi, Navajo, etc. (see Yellow Bird, 2004).

INDIANS IN COLOR

6   I criticize the marketing concept of Third Chapter in Chapter Five.

7   Hoffman's 1986 discussion of Native American in the context of modern and postmodern art distinguishes three major movements—traditional/archetypal/premodern; modern (impressionism, expressionism, cubism, abstraction, magical realism), and postmodernism. J. J. Brody complicates the situation, outlining five chronological phases of 'modern' Indian painting: (1) Proto-modern (1885–1917): easel paintings; (2) Self-taught (1910–1930): stylistically similar easel painting by self-taught Pueblo artists sold to patrons; (3) Early Institutional (1928–1937): Indian artists trained by white instructors—two distinct styles, one at the University of Oklahoma and another at the Santa Fe Indian School Studio; (4) Later Institutional (1937–1962): Indian artists trained in segregated schools in the Santa Studio Style; (5) Idiosyncratic (1962–present): Indians trained by Indians at the Institute of American Indian Art (Brody, 1971, pp. 57–58).

8   See Brody (1971), Strong (2013), Deloria (1998, 2004), Raheja (2010), Cotter (2014).

9   The Institute of American Indian Arts (IAIA) was established in 1962 under the leadership of Dr. George Boyce and Lloyd Kiva New. It opened on the campus of the Indian School in Santa Fe, New Mexico. It was first a high school formed under the Department of Interior's Bureau of Indian Affairs. In 1975 it became a two-year college offering associate degrees in Studio Arts, Creative Writing, and Museum Studies. It became a congressionally chartered college in 1986 and in 2013 began offering a graduate program, a MFA in creative writing (see www.iaia.edu/about/history). The original faculty included Allan Houser, Fritz Scholder, Charles Loloma, Otelliee Loloma, and James McGrath (Gibson and Leaken, 2014, p. 36). The Institute was for talented Indian high-school art students who were recruited from schools across the country. Kevin Red Star, for example, was recruited in 1962 from Lodge Grass High on the Crow Reservation in Eastern Montana (Gibson and Leaken, 2014, pp. 31–32). This Santa Fe initiative had some parallels with the 1968 federally funded New Communicators program which was designed to train minority filmmakers. UCLA was the primary training ground for the new filmmakers (see Denzin, 2002, pp. 43, 90).

10   'Postindian' is Vizenor's term (1999, p. viii) which replaces the traditional racist term Indian. Indian is a primitive simulation, the product of colonial domination. Postindians embody survivance. They resist colonial domination and perform, paint, and tell stories of the new postmodern postindian.

11   Including Dennis Hopper, Robert Redford, Rod McKuen, and Andy Warhol (see Sims, 2008a, p. 19).

✦ Notes

12 For a montage of Schlder's paintings see centerofthewest.org/explore/ western-art/research/fritz-scholder/

13 Taos Pueblo is an ancient pueblo belonging to the Taos speaking Native American tribe of Pueblo people. It is approximately 1,000 years old and lies about one mile north of the modern city of Taos, New Mexico. It is a UNESCO World Heritage Site (see whc.unesco.org/en/list/492). The Taos Indians and the Pueblo of Taos were the original subject matter of the Taos Society of Artists. More than 4,500 residents live on a reservation of over 95,000 acres. Residents speak Tiwa, English, and Spanish and practice a religion that is a blend of Catholicism and Tanoan. The Taos Pueblo revolted against the Church and Spanish colonizers in 1600, 1680, and 1847, killing priests and burning churches. See Parsons's (1936) anthropological study of the Taos Pueblo and Broder's (1980, pp. 4–6) review of the 19th-century painters who worked as official recorders for the 1846–1847 U. S. Survey expedition into the Taos Valley (also Brody, 1971, pp. 59–75; Eldridge, Schimmel and Truettner, 1986, pp. 17–42; Schimmel and White, 1994, pp. 141–143).

14 This would not be Blumenschein's last interaction with Cody's Wild West show. In June 1905 he married Mary Shepherd Green, an artist, in Paris. "He could not kneel during the wedding ceremony because he was recovering from a knee injury received while playing baseball with Buffalo Bill's Cowboys at the Bois de Boulogne" (Broder,1980, p. 71). On March 29, 1914, and November 8, 1915, he and Mary could have attended Buffalo Bill's Wild West Show in Albuquerque, where it did one-night shows.

15 Money from these assignments funded his first trip to Taos in 1898 (Cunningham, 2008, pp. 31–32).

16 Raheja (2010, p. ix) quotes Sherman Alexie who recalls watching western films on television as a child: "I hated Tonto then and I hate him now."

17 For the purposes of this project he is also known as William Red Cloud. His sister is Alice Red Cloud.

18 See photos of Buffalo Bill's Paris Disneyland at www. disneylandparis.co.uk/dining/disney-village/ buffalo-bills-wild-west-show-with-mickey-and-friends/

19 See pdxcontemporaryart.com/red-star. See Wendy Red Star's Wild West & Congress of Rough Riders of the World, bumbershoot.org/lineup/artist/wendy-red-stars-wild-west-congress-of-rough-riders-of-the-world/. The August 30–September 1, 2014, Bumpershoot event in the Seattle Fisher Pavilion was billed as a journey through the real Wild West. Shantel Martinez directed me to this site. We will meet Wendy again in Chapter Six.

20 A recurring feature of the Wild West show involved Indian attacks on white settler cabins and stage coaches. These attacks framed Indians as threats to white civilization. The inevitable defeat of the Indian, even with white losses, signaled the victory of civilization over barbarism, making the frontier safe for whites (Warren, 2005, p. 94–95). The participation of Native Americans in these performances can be read, in part, as a refusal to accept defeat at the hands of whites; that is, Native Americans steadfastly resisted white domination. Alternative non-violent racial narratives—assimilation, accommodation, separatism—could have been staged and performed but weren't.

21 Dates: Massacre at Wounded Knee: December, 29, 1890; murder of Sitting Bull, December, 15, 1890; and beginning February 27, 1973, American Indian Movement occupies the town of Wounded Knee for 71 days.

22 The SGP are fresh from their closing show in the Paris Disneyland Buffalo Bill Wild West Show with Mickey and Minnie Mouse, aka William and Alice Red Cloud.

23 San Geronimo Feast Day is the feast day for St. Jerome, the patron saint of the Taos Pueblo. The festival begins on day one with a sundown dance and evening vespers, followed, on the second day, by foot races in the morning, and in the afternoon 'clowns' wearing black and white body paint and black and white costumes compete in the pole climb. San Geronimo Feast Day is also a fall trading festival in which neighboring tribes participate in an Indian trade fair, offering Indians crafts and foods for sale. Clowns, dancers, cowboys, art dealers, magicians, showmen, persons selling Western memorabilia and Native American antiques, artists, and native Taos Indians, and Traveling Indian Medicine Show performers all comingle during the festival. The presence of the Traveling Medicine Show lends an air of minstrelsy to the festival (Denzin, 2013, pp. 25–27).

24 Quoting from the museum website, the paintings of the Taos Society of Artists were favorites of the museum's founder, Harrison Eiteljorg, and his collection is a core part of the museum and this gallery. See more at www. eiteljorg.org/explore/collections/western. Native American art is also represented in the Eiteljorg, again from the website: Native American art and artifacts at the Eiteljorg Museum represent all major culture areas of the Western Hemisphere, including tribes in the United States and Canada. The collection began with the personal holdings of founder Harrison Eiteljorg.

25 In 2013 the Denver Art Museum received a major gift of paintings produced by the Taos Society artists (see *New York Times*, August 14, 2013).

26 Beginning in 1948 and continuing through 1969 the College of Fine Arts at the University of Illinois produced "one of the most influential exhibition series in the country" (Witt, 1992, p. 18), privileging the work of 14

⊞ Notes

Taos Modern artists—O'Keeffe, Marin, Sterne, Rothko, and others. It was organized by C. V. Donavan and Allen S. Weller. No Native Taos or Native Santa Fe artists were included in these exhibitions.

27 Like the 1,000-year-old Taos Pueblo itself these artists embodied Vizenor's (2008, p. 11) concept of survivance, the active resistance and repudiation of colonial dominance, the creation of a positive presence that must be heard and witnessed, a formidable presence that is also an absence.

28 Shantel Martinez brought this work to my attention.

29 An obvious play on the title of Dee Brown's *Bury My Heart at Wounded Knee* (1971).

30 Radical Indigenous Survivance & Empowermen, or RISE. Established in 2010 by Demian Dine Yazhi, and drawing on Gerald Vivenor's (2008) aesthetics of survivance, RISE is a call to action yielding multiple tools, including photographs, paint, wheatpaste, clay, beadwork, dancing, words, and more. See www.facebook.com/RISEIndigenous http://burymyart. tumblr.com/. See also the recent art exhibit, "Bury My Art at Wounded Knee: Blood & Guts" which opened in the Stevens Studios of the Portland Northwest College Art School Industrial Complex, May 25, 2014.

31 Seventh Generation: From the great law of the Haudenoaunee people—how will the decisions made today benefit the children seven generations into the future (Benally, 2013). I have created a performance group, the Seventh Generation Performers. The theme of the 2015 Canadian Indigenous/Native Studies Association is "Survivance & Reconciliation: 7 Forward /7 Back" and borrows from the Seven Generations theme (see www.naisa.org/cfp-cinsa-2015-concordia-university-montreal.html).

32 Consider the irony of Johnny Depp, in redface, playing Tonto in Disney's 2013 film, *The Lone Ranger*. The 19th-century minstrel show tradition is alive and well in the Disney Studios.

33 I treat Mr. and Ms. Coyote as tricksters, as disruptive, critical, wise, laughing comic healers, liberators, mythic performers of postindian survivance stories (Vizenor, 1999, p. 89).

34 I introduce musical performances by Taos Pueblo drummers and flute players in Chapters Three, Four, Five, and Six. The music is intended to set a respectful mood, a soft ambience in the scene, and it can heard as Native muzak.

35 The mystory is simultaneously a personal mythology, a public story, a personal narrative, and a performance that critiques.

INDIANS IN COLOR

Chapter Two: Disneyland Indians, circa Paris, 2014

1   I thank Johnny Saldana, Robert Rinehart, Sara Delamont, Paul Atkinson, and especially Mitch Allen for their helpful comments in revising this chapter.

2   Renaud (2010, p. 1).

3   See YouTube video: www.youtube.com/watch?v=OgyRGKzfN4o, also www.google.com/search?q=buffalo+bill+wild+west+show+disneyland+pa ris&sa=X&tbm=isch&tbo=u&source=univ&ei=X6cTUtDOD5OuqQHnh 4DwCw&ved=0CCwQsAQ&biw=1247&bih=1202

4   www.re-member.org/pine_ridge_reservation.aspx

5   Giroux and Pollock (2010, pp. 181–185) discuss the history of the Disneyland Corporation in France and the name change, in 1994, from Euro Disney to Disneyland Paris.

6   Cody's Wild West Show opened in Omaha on May 19, 1883. In the heyday of Wild West performance (1900–1917) there were over 115 Wild West shows, many performing on an international stage (Russell, 1970). McNenly (2012, p. 166) attests to the continuing popularity of these shows, "one could travel across America with the sole purpose of attending these shows."

7   Obviously, I steal Six Indians in Search of an Identity from Pirandello (1998a/1921).

8   See Pirandello, 1921/1998a, pp. 8–9.

9   Recall, the phrase seventh generation is from the Haudenosaunee (Iroquois) people, which holds that tribal actions should be judged by how they will benefit children seven generations from now (Benally, 2013).

10   From the Henry Wadsworth Longfellow 1855 epic poem, "The Song of Hiawatha."

11   Fictional Indian sidekick to Red Ryder, a cowboy, who fought bad guys in popular comic book, radio, film and TV shows (1942–1956).

12   *Hombre* (1967). Paul Newman played the part of John Russell, an Apache-raised white man, caught between white and Native cultures.

13   To repeat: because Disney copyrights the names of its animal characters, I have replaced Mickey and Minnie Mouse with two fictional mice: William and Alice Red Cloud.

14   Howe, Markowitz, and Cummings (2013), Aleiss (2005), Raheja (2010), and Kilpatrick (1999) offer complex readings of Native American performances and participation in traditional cultural forms from Hollywood film (silent era 1888–1924 to the present) to traveling medicine shows, carnivals, county fairs, and ethnographic exhibits at world fairs.

200

⊞ Notes

15   It will soon be revealed that Mickey and Minnie Mouse are brother and sister (William and Alice Red Cloud). They are called Salford Sioux. They were raised on the banks of the River Irwell, Salford, Greater Manchester, England. Their parents (Red Shirt and Madeline), from the Pine Ridge Reservation, performed in Buffalo Bill's 1887 tour of England. They chose to remain in England when Cody returned to America. On the Salford Sioux see Williams (2006), Malik (2012).

16   The term of endearment used by Tonto.

17   Blazing Saddles (1974): Director, Mel Brooks; story by Andrew Bergman; cast—Cleavon Little, Gene Wilder, Harvey Korman, Slim Pickens, Madeline Kahn, Mel Brooks, Dom DeLuise; music—Count Basie Orchestra, "April in Paris"; Warner Brothers.

18   See disney-village.disneylandparis.co.uk/buffalo-bills-wild-west-show/index.xhtml

19   These descriptions of the specifics of the Paris Disneyland Buffalo Bill Wild West Show are taken from McNenly (2012, pp. 142–150).

20   This is not entirely correct. The names of Kicking Bear and Short Bull, identified as the leaders of the Ghost Dance movement, appeared in the 1891 program for Buffalo Bill's European tour (See Denzin, 2013, p. 197; also Moses, 1996, p. 113).

21   Kalshoven (2012, p. 70, n. 23) discusses descendants of Lakota performers still active in show business in France, including Lakota whose great-grandparents performed with Buffalo Bill in Paris in 1905 and remained in France. Performances by the Lakota in Cody's Paris shows created a lasting image which equated the North American Indian with the Lakota Plains Indian (2012, p. 54, paraphrase).

22   The negative Disney representation of Native Americans as violent 'redskins' goes at least back to the 1950s and Frontierland at the original Disney World (see Giroux and Pollock, 2010).

23   This speech is a merger of several voices quoted in McNenly, 2012, pp. 178–181.

24   McNenly (2012) distinguishes performances connected with heritage sites and museums from performances located in entertainment sites like Euro-Disney. In the latter sites the focus is on producing spectacular shows embedded in stereotypical images of the West and the Native past, not the Native present.

25   The fictional Apache warrior in the Karl May Winnetou novels (see May, 1893/2008).

26   Hobby Indians dress in homemade replicas of Indian clothing, create museum-quality Indian artifacts, reenact North American Indian life-worlds (Kalshoven, 2012).

INDIANS IN COLOR

Chapter Three: Copper-colored Primitives

1 (1912–2004): famous abstract expressionist painter (see Broder, 1980, pp. 15–17).

2 A member of the TAS, he often painted Indians doing menial labor, or as servants (Broder, 1980, p. 215). Representative subjects and titles included Indians as auto mechanics (*Bob Abbott and His Assistant*), waiters and waitresses (*Luncheon at Lone Locust*), and poverty (*In the Land of Marana and Hunger*) (Taggett and Schwarz, 1990, p. 180; see reproductions in Broder, 1980, p. 214).

3 See www.denverartmuseum.org/article/press-release/denver-art-museum-announces-landmark-gift-western-american-art-and-creation

4 Eldredge, Schimmel, and Truettner (1986, pp. 87–89) distinguish two generations, or groups, of artists working in Taos. The TSA group, and a second generation, the modernists, arriving after 1917, including Georgia O'Keeffe, John Marin, and John Sloan (see Appendix B).

5 See Appendix A for an expanded timeline.

6 They immediately begin marketing their artwork in exhibits organized by women's clubs in Chicago, Los Angeles, New York, and San Francisco (Bickerstaff, 1955a, p. 137).

7 1903–1997; wealthy industrialist, founder of the Indianapolis Eiteljorg Museum of American Indians and Western Art.

8 Star Road was a self-declared user of peyote. Peyote use, central to the rituals of the Native American Church, was opposed by both the Catholic Church and the Bureau of Indian Affairs (Hassrick, 2008, p. 136; Parsons, 1936, pp. 118–120). The models for this painting were handymen and carpenters—Geronimo Gomez (Star Road) and Juan de Jesus Martinez (White Sun) (Hassrick, 2008, p. 136). A copy of the painting is reproduced on the cover of this book.

9 They were ignored by the mainstream Santa Fe art community, who favored the work of Indian painters trained in the Santa Fe School (see Brody, 1971, pp. 126–132 and Dunn, 1968, pp. 224–229 on the Santa Fe School; also Baca, 2003). They were also ignored by art historians. Their names do not appear in the indexes of the major works discussing Indian art in this time period (e.g., Brody, 1971; Dunn, 1968; Eldridge, Schimmel, and Truettner, 1986; Witt, 2003a, b).

10 The population of Taos in the 1910 census included 1,500 Anglo, Hispanic, Mexican, and Spanish citizens, and 521 Taos Indians.

11 The painting is in The Anschutz Collection Denver. See the reproduction in Broder 1980, p. 81. The painting depicts a crowded plaza winter scene.

♯ Notes

The street is snow covered. Three cowboys stand next to three automobiles in front of McCarthy Merchandise. The right-hand side of the painting depicts Taos Indians—women, men, children—wrapped in colorful blankets standing and seated in horse-drawn wagons. The wagons are in front of the Bargain Clothes store. The Taos Mountains are in the background. Electric power lines cut across the top of the painting.

12 This manifesto continues: We are encouraged by an increased population of tribal members choosing to remain in Taos, as well as by these actions acknowledging Taos's important cultural heritage: Taos declared a National Historic landmark in 1965; Blue Lake returned to Taos in 1970; Taos Pueblo admitted to the World Heritage Society in 1992 as one of the most significant historical cultural landmarks in the world (www.taospueblo.com/about).

13 1922 by Ernest L. Bluemschein, oil on canvas Smithsonian American Art Museum, Bequest of Henry Ward Ranger, No 1975.86.

14 1909, by Eanger Irving Couse, Smithsonian American Art Museum, Gift of William T. Evans, No. 1910.9. 5.

15 1900, by Joseph Henry Sharp, Smithsonian American Art Museum, Museum purchase, No. 1985.66.209, 421.

16 1920, Smithsonian American Art Museum, Bequest of Victor Justice Evans, No. 1985. 66. 362, 160.

17 1926, by Walter Ufer, Smithsonian American Art Museum, Gift of Mr. and Mrs. R. Crosby Kemper, Jr., No 1984. 66.

18 In the 1970s there was a resurgence of interest in the work of the TSA (Eldredge, Schmimel, and Truettner, 1986, p. 8).

19 The painting is reproduced on p. 143 in Hassrick and Cunningham (2008). A second Blumenschein painting, *Idealist Dreamer Realist*, was described (paraphrase) as 'something that might go as an illustration to a whimsically grotesque story, but as an oil painting it holds no interest in any way' (Taggett and Schwartz, 1990, p. 226). Blumenschein destroyed the painting. The painting is reproduced on p. 279 in Hassrick and Cunningham (2008).

20 The School of American Research, founded 1907 (Eldridge, Schimmel, and Teuettner, 1986, pp. 70–71).

21 See Blumenschein's *Feast Day at Ranchos Church, Taos, Church at Ranchos, Ranchos Church with Indians* (pp. 148–150 in Hassrick and Cunningham, 2008).

22 According to John O'Hern (2008), the paintings by many of the Taos Society of Artists are selling at various auctions for hundreds

of thousands of dollars, for example Hennings's *Streamside*, oil on canvas, sold for $1,359,000 on July 26, 2008 (see taospainters.com/TaosFoundersAuctionRecords.html).

23 Paraphrasing one website, collectors should not be discouraged by these prices (taospainters.com/TaosFoundersAuctionRecords.html), "It doesn't take an unlimited budget to begin acquiring original works by these Western painters. In fact, TAS artists like Joseph Sharp, E. Irving Couse, E. Martin Hennings, Gerald Cassidy and Ernest Blumenschein did many small paintings that are available at galleries across the country, well within the price range of even the moderate collector."

24 See note 2.

25 Jung is quoting Ochwiay Biano, a chief of the Taos Pueblo.

Chapter Four: Taos Indians on Canvas

1. Dunn (1968, p. 290) provides an answer. The Santa Fe trained Indian artists painted ceremonials, ceremonial symbols, hunting scenes, antelope, dance, seminaturalistic scenes, with abstract designs, of clouds, rainbows, terraced mountains, trees, shrubs and streams of water.

2 The original exhibit date was January 24–April 20, 2003, at the Harwood Museum of Art in Taos (see Witt, 2003b; also Martinez, Lujan and Mirabal, 2003).

3 These three Taos artists, as well as Jerry and Jim Mirabal, Ben Luhan, Tony and Tonita Luhan, and Little Joe Gomez, worked as models and laborers for many of the Taos Society painters, including Couse, Berninghaus, Ufer, and Sharp (see Brody, 1971; Taylor, 2000; Watson, 1994; Witt, 2003a, b). Parsons lists Kiva and Society chiefs in the Taos Pueblo in 1931 (1936, pp. 80–81). Juan Mirabal was a chief in the Water People Kiva. Albert Martinez was a chief in the Big-Hail Kiva and (at a later date) also governor of the Pueblo of Taos and Society. Albert Lujan was a chief in the Knife People Kiva.

4 The Miriam Report followed on the heels of the protest movement that blocked the Bursam Bill in 1922, which was intended to take land away from the Pueblos. The Miriam Report recommended that the government encourage the training of Native artists using a community-based model (Brody, 1971, p. 127; Schrader 1983, p. 19). Led by Dorothy Dunn, influenced by Mary Austin, Mabel Dodge Luhan, Elizabeth, and John De Huff, the Santa Fe Indian School and Art Colony championed two-dimensional, highly stylized paintings of 'authentic' Indians (see Brody, 1971, pp. 126–127; Hoxie, 2001, p. 18).

5 Millicent Rogers Museum, Taos, New Mexico, Cat. No. 1992–39.

⁂ Notes

6   National Museum of the American Indian, Henry Craig Fleming Collection, Cat. No. 22/8612.

7   Mittler Photography, Santa Fe.

8   Private collection (Witt, 2003b, pp. 14–15).

9   Only infrequently did the TSA painters name the Indian models in their paintings (e.g., Albert Looking Elk Martinez is the named model in Berninghaus's *A Son of the War God.*). As noted in Chapter 3, Note 8, Ernest Blumenschein's *Star Road and White Sun* (1920) was a portrait of his handyman and carpenter, Geronimo Gomez, and an older man, Juan de Jesus Martinez (see Hassrick, 2008, pp. 136–137). I have used the photographs of the Three Taos painters in Witt (2003b) in an effort to match models to Taos Indians in TSA paintings.

10   Watson, 1994, p. 65.

11   National Museum of American Art, Smithsonian Institution.

12   Collection of the Springville Museum of Art, Springville, Utah.

13   In this regard they were not like Crescenio Martinez (1879–1918) who was from a famous family of artists in the San Idefonso Pueblo (see Hoxie, 2001, p. 18; also Dunn, 1968, pp. 198–199).

14   According to Brody, easel painting emerged "at the Rio Grande pueblos shortly after Anglo art colonies had become established in Taos and Santa Fe" (1971, p. 91). It was a "White art medium; it was given to the Indians, and the result for fifty years was meek acceptance. Now, in the last decade (1960–1970) the Indians (e.g., Scholder, Gorman) have taken it ... the result has been a vital, expressive, sometimes unpretty, sometimes polemical, and always stylistically varied art" (Brody, 1971, pp. 205–206).

15   This is called 'synchronicity,' two or more events are meaningfully related, where they are unlikely to be causally related. I thank Katherine E. Ryan for this use of synchronicity in this context.

16   *Hunting Son, Drummer, Three Taos Indians, War Talk, The Bow and Arrow Maker* (see Broder, 1980, pp. 56–57, 61); *The Musicians, Indian Hunter, The Peacemaker, Playing the Game,* in Bickerstaff, 1955a, following page 68).

17   Luis Ribak (1902–1979), social realist and abstractionist painter, immigrated from Russia to New York in 1912, studied at Art Students League, was a founding member of John Reed Club in 1929. In 1933 Ribak assisted Diego Rivera on the mural in the lobby of the Rockefeller Center. He then worked as a muralist for the WPA, and moved to Taos in 1944. In 1947 he founded the Taos Valley Art School, which became a force in the development of the Taos Moderns, a group of artists living in Taos during the 1940s and 50s (www.mandelman-ribak.org/louis_ribak/biography.php).

INDIANS IN COLOR

18   See his *Xmas Eve*, ca. 1932, oil on panel, in Witt, 2003b, p. 15.

19   Eaton studied at The Art Institute of Boston, in Florence, Italy, and at the Art Students League of New York. She was trained in the Stanislavsky method of acting. She participated in the Taos art colony in Taos from 1928 to 1937. She appeared on screen in *Anna and the King of Siam* (1946), *The Time of Their Lives* (1946), *Witness for the Prosecution* (1957), and *Mary Poppins* (1964). She also did voiceover work in Disney feature-length cartoons of the 1950s and 1960s and in television shows from 1953 to 1970, including appearing in the *Lone Ranger* (1950) and *Alfred Hitchcock Presents* (1962). www.rottentomatoes.com/celebrity/marjorie_eaton/biography/;en.wikipedia.org/wiki/Marjorie_Eaton

20   In 1864 military troops under Kit Carson's leadership organized the long walk, which forced Navajos to walk up to thirteen miles a day from their reservation in Arizona to become prisoners at Fort Sumner, New Mexico (see Sides, 2006).

21   The project of the Taos Three—celebrating Taos Pueblo culture and preserving cultural rituals—was continued by Eva Mirabal (Eah-Ha-Wa, 1920–1968), Jonathan Warm Day (Eva's son), and Pop Chalee (Lujan, 2003, p. 6; also Dunn,1968, pp. 319–323). Eah-Ha-Wa served in the Women's Army Corps during WWII and worked as a political cartoonist. Her "G. I. Gertie" series appeared in military publications. Her posters were used to sell war bonds. In one of her posters a warrior fans a fire that reaches upward to a slogan that reads BUY WAR BONDS.

22   See www.fineartsofthesouthwest.com/Fine_Arts_of_the_Southwest/Albert_Lujan_Weasel_Arrow_Taos_Pueblo_Oil_Painting.html

23   *Ethnic art*: art made for, appreciated and used by peoples within their own society to maintain ethnic identity. *Tourist art* or *airport art*: art driven by the profit motive, it may bear little relationship to the traditional arts of the creator culture. *Commercial fine art*: art made for sale, but it adheres to culturally defined Indigenous values and aesthetics. *Assimilated fine art*: the artist takes up the established art form of the colonizer. (Graburn, 1976, pp.5–7)

24   Fritz Scholder was one of the most influential Native American artists of the 20th century (see Sims, 2008a, b). His radical Indian themes, use of color, symbolism, and form established him as the "acknowledged leader of a 'new realism' school of Indian art" (Turk, 1972, quoted in Wasserberger, 2008, p. 37; see also Sims (2008a, b).

25   Called the Picasso of American Indian art by the *New York Times* (www.nytimes.com/2005/11/05/.../05gorman.html; also Fox, 2005). He opened the Navajo Gallery in Taos in 1968. It was the first Native-American owned gallery in Taos (Parks, 1983, p.65).

Notes

26 Artist, flutist, dancer. His paintings are held by the Smithsonian and the Metropolitan Museum of Art. He was director of art at Bacone College, and assistant director and director of the Texas Museum of Art (1960–1968).

27 April 06, 2013, the so-called Third Chapter of the Taos Art Colony— Jim Wagner, R.C. Gorman, Fritz Scholder, and Woody Crumbo—was celebrated at the Harwood Museum of Art Taos, New Mexico. The Third Chapter opened at the Harwood Museum of Art, Saturday, May 18, and remained on view through Sunday, September 8, 2013.

Chapter 5: Postmodern Indians on Canvas

1 Fritz Scholder, advice to his Native American students, in Lowe, 2008, p.151; also, Scholder, in Gover, 2008, p. 10.

2 Aka Christian Parish Takes the Gun, Native American hip hop artist, flute player, drummer and champion powwow dancer from Crow Agency, Montana— voted MTV's New Musician of the Week. His "Prayer Loop Song" was nominated as Best Music Video of 2014 by the Aboriginal People's Choice Awards (see also Baker, 2014; www.youtube.com/ watch?v=_0jq7jIa34Y).

3 I will focus primarily on Scholder and Gorman in this chapter, while also including Kevin Red Star (1943–), who was a student at the Institute of American Indian Arts in Santa Fe (1962–1965), where Scholder, one-quarter Luiseño, taught from 1964 to 1969 (see Brody, 1971, pp, 203–204; Gibson and Leaken, 2014, p. 36). The paintings of T. C. Cannon (Caddo/ Kiowa, 1946–1978) are also very important—see his *Collector # 5* and *Mama and Papa Have the Going Home to Shiprock Blues* (1966), both reproduced in this book.

4 Recall Blumenschein's discussion in Chapter 3, Act One, Scene Four of the first time he saw a Taos Indian, which happened right after his wagon broke down.

5 See www.google.com/?gws_rd=ssl#q=rc+gorman+paintings&tbm=shop; R. C. Gorman: Early Prints (name.si.edu/explore/exhibitions/item/474); si.edu/releases/national-museum-american-indian-presents-early-work-navajo-artist-rc-gorman

6 See Sims, 2008a and b, for reproductions of these paintings; also nmai. si.edu/exhibitions/scholder/biography.html; also centerofthewest.org/ explore/western-art/research/fritz-scholder/

7 See the reproductions in Gibson and Leaken, 2014; also kevinredstar.com

8 See collections.centerofthewest.org/treasures/view/crow_indian_ parade_rider; centerofthewest.org/explore/western-art/research/ fritz-scholder/

INDIANS IN COLOR

9   I served alongside my Navajo brothers, the code talkers (see navajopeople. org/navajo-code-talker.htm; also the 2002 movie, *Windtalkers*).

10   Racial slur toward an Indian. The word 'prairie' is used because many Indians live on reservations that are usually located in the prairie. "Go back to the rez, you prairie nigger," sometimes called "Red Nigger." (See www. urbandictionary.com/define.php?term=red%20nigger)

11   See centerofthewest.org/explore/western-art/research/fritz-scholder/

12   For example, in 1903, needing money, Ernest Blumenschein accepted a commission to provide illustrations for *Indian Fights and Fighters* by Cyrus Townsend Brady. His illustrations showed a valiant Custer surrounded by Indians moving in for the kill (Taggett and Schwartz, 1990, p. 86). However, he later produced "We Circled Around Him," an illustration that honored the sacrifices of the Sioux warriors over Custer's soldiers (Hassrick, 2009a; also www.themagazineantiques.com/articles/ernest-blumenschein-and-the-indians/5/). In 1893, Joseph Henry Sharp, a founding member of TSA, built a cabin-studio on the Little Bighorn battlefield. He specialized in Crow Indian camp and ceremonial scenes as well as portraits of Indians dressed as warriors (see Bickerstaff, 1955a, b).

13   During the 1920s, Native photographers like Horace Poolaw produced a body of work that deconstructed the romantic photos of Native Americans made by Edward S. Curtis and others (Sims, 2008b, p. 97).

14   The following section extends interpretations in Denzin, 2013, pp. 59–64.

15   Henceforth, each speaker comes forward and speaks from behind the podium.

16   Actually the museum does devote considerable space to Native Americans. Continuing Native American exhibitions are located in the second floor galleries. See more at www.eiteljorg.org/explore/exhibitions/native-american-continuing-exhibitions#sthash.PTRpFLYw.dpuf. The museum annually invites Indigenous artists to be visiting fellows in residence; their work is then exhibited during the time of their residency. See Strong's (2013, pp 178–185) reading of exhibit space in the National Museum of the American Indian and the deployment of a postcolonial era of museology which replaces the authoritarian anonymous curatorial voice of the traditional museum.

17   British figurative painter known for his bold imagery.

18   One of the earliest galleries to show Scholder's work was the Tally Richards Galley in Taos (Gilbert, 1980; artlinesarchive.blogspot.com/2012/03/tally-richard-eleven-years-ago-fritz.html).

⬚ Notes

Chapter Six: Indian Painters, Patrons, and Wild West Shows:
A New Imaginary

1 Apologies to J. J. Brody (1971) for using the title of his book.

2 To repeat, by 'Indian art' I refer to modern Indian painting, not the full range of Native American art, which, in addition to paintings, includes baskets, carvings, jewelry, pottery, sculpture, weavings, Zuni fetishes, and Hopi Kachina dolls, etc.

3 The annual festival brings over 175,000 people to Santa Fe, in addition to more than 1,000 Native artists (swaia.org/Events/index.html).

4 Highwater's falsely claimed American Indian ancestry was exposed in 1984 by Hank Adams and Jack Anderson (see Vizenor, 1999/1994, p. 178).

5 This includes the following museums in the Museums West consortium: Amon Carter Museum, Booth Western Art Museum, Buffalo Bill Historical Center, C. M. Russell Museum, Eiteljorg Museum of American Indians and Western Art, Gilcrease Museum, Joslyn Art Museum, National Cowboy & Western Heritage Museum, National Museum of Wildlife Art, Petrie Institute of Western American Art at Denver Art Museum, Rockwell Museum of Western Art, and Stark Museum of Art (see theautry.org/get-involved/membership-levels).

6 Apologies to Taggett and Schwarz (1990) for stealing the title of their book.

7 See www.facebook.com/RISEIndigenous

8 Two memories, two dates: Massacre at Wounded Knee: December 29, 1890. Occupation of Wounded Knee by AIM: February 27–May 8, 1973.

9 "Bury My Art a Wounded Knee": Blood & Guts in the Art School Industrial Complex of the Pacific Northwest College of Art Museum and Contemporary Craft, Portland, Oregon, is a Native North American art exhibition curated by Demian Dine' Yashi' that celebrates contemporary Indigenous art production on and off the imaginary boundaries of modern day Indian reservations. The first exhibition was December 5–23, 2013.

10 www.burymyart.tumblr.com/; www.facebook.com/RISEIndigenous

Coda: Back to the Future

1 Vizenor (2008).

2 Maddin is a well-known Canadian filmmaker. *My Winnipeg* was awarded the prize for Best Canadian Feature Film in 2007. Materials on this page draw from Denzin (2014, pp. 64–65).

3 His pet dog died. His sister had a big fight with his mother. His father may have died.

209

INDIANS IN COLOR

4   Willie Nelson (1975), "Mama Don't Let Your Babies Grow Up to Be Cowboys" lyrics, MetroLyrics.

Appendix A: Time Line, Staging and Marketing American Indians, and Federal Indian Policy

1   Provided "$10,000 annually for the support of missionary schools in Indian country" (Viola, 1976, p. 18). They were precursors to Native American boarding schools.

2   Cherokees and other southern tribes could be removed from their homelands.

3   Students wore uniforms, were given new names, were not allowed to eat traditional foods or speak native languages.

4   Allotted tribal lands for homesteads for Native Americans, in exchange for becoming U. S. citizens and giving up some forms of tribal government.

5   Supposedly corrects defects in the Dawes Act by giving people deemed capable and competent (mixed blood Indians with European ancestry) the power to keep or sell land (see en.wikipedia.org/wiki/Burke_Act).

6   Official dates of the Taos Society of Artists are 1915 to 1927 (Scott, 1998, p. 3). Their work focused on representations of the Taos, New Mexico, landscape as well as on paintings of Native Americans in traditional dress. The first two members (Blumenschein and Phillips) of the original six members of the Taos Society of Artists arrived in Taos together in 1899. See Appendix B for a list of the members.

7   See Deloria (1974) for a discussion of twenty-point position paper drawn up by the Native Americans who participated in *The Trail of Broken Treaties*.

8   The Robert and Barbara Ellis Family gave a generous donation.

9   Made tribal self-determination the focus of government action.

10 The 2008 Walk focused on the protection of sacred sites, tribal sovereignty, and the end to global warming.

Appendix B: Taos Painters

1   Before the Taos Society painters, there were earlier artists who traveled to New Mexico (see Broder, 1980, p. 4): John Mix Stanley (1846–1847), R. H. Kern (1848–1849), Worthington Whittredge (1866), Thomas Moran (early 1880s), Charles Craig (1881, the first dated Taos image), Montgomery Roosevelt (1881), Henry R. Poore (1890, the first painting of Taos to be reproduced), Joseph Henry Sharp (1893, *Harper's Weekly* illustration).

2   There was also a group of associate members, including Robert Henri, John Sloan, and Randall Davey (Scott, 1998, p. 8).

References

Aleiss, Angela. 2005. *Making the Indian White: Native Americans and Hollywood Movies.* Westport, CT: Praeger
Alexie, Sherman. 1993. *The Lone Ranger and Tonto Fistfight in Heaven.* New York: Atlantic Monthly Press.
Alexie, Sherman. 2007. *Flight.* New York: Black Cat.
Allen, Chadwick. 2012. *Trans-Indigenous Methodologies for Global Native Literary Studies.* Minneapolis: University of Minnesota Press.
Aylwin, Nicole, 2013. "Appropriation of the Month Who Is That Masked Man? Johnny Depp's New (and Improved?) Tonto." www.sfu.ca/ipinch/outputs/blog/appropriation-month (Posted by Kristen Dobbin, July 17, 2013.)
Baca, Elmo. 2003. "Taos Pueblo Painters." *New Mexico Magazine, 81,* No. 1 (January): 64–68.
Baker, Alastair. 2014. "SupaMan Flys In and Takes Festival by Storm. Carbon County News, August 7: 1.
Basso, Keith H. 1996. *Wisdom Sits in Places: Landscape and Language Among the Western Apache.* (1st ed). Albuquerque: University of New Mexico Press.
Becker, Howard S. 1982. *Art Worlds.* Berkeley: University of California Press.
Benally, Suzanne. 2013. "Hope Lies in the Seventh Generation." *Cultural Survival Quarterly, 32,* 2 (June): 1.
Benjamin, Walter. 1983. "N Theoretics of Knowledge: Theory of Progress." *The Philosophical Forum,* 15.
Benjamin, Walter. 1969. *Illuminations.* Trans. Harry Zohn. New York: Harcourt, Brace & World.
Bhabha, Homi K. 1994. *The Location of Culture.* New York: Routledge.
Bickerstaff, Laura A. 1955a. *Pioneer Artists of Taos,* with an Introduction by Ernest L. Blumenschein. Denver: Sage Books.
Bickerstaff, Laura A. 1955b. "Ernest L. Blumenschein," pp. 29–50 in Laura A. Bickerstaff, *Pioneer Artists of Taos,* with an Introduction by Ernest L. Blumenschein. Denver: Sage Books.
Bigert, Claus. 1976. *Seit 200 Jahren ohne Verfassung.* Reinbek: rororo Verlag.

Blew, Mary Clearman. 1999. *Bone Deep in Landscape: Writing, Reading and Place*. Norman: University of Oklahoma Press.

Blumenschein, Ernest L. 1898. "Behind the Scenes at a 'Wild West' Show," *Harper's Weekly, 42*, 2158 (April): 422.

Bourdieu, Pierre and Alain Darbel, with Dominique Schnapper, translated by Caroline Beattie. 1997. *The Love of Art: European Art Museums and Their Public*. Cambridge, UK: Polity Press.

Broder, Patricia Janis. 1980. *Taos: A Painter's Dream*, Foreword by Carl Schaefer Dentzel. Boston: New York Graphic Society.

Brody, Jerry J. 1971. *Indian Painters and White Patrons*. Albuquerque: University of New Mexico Press.

Brooks, Van Wyck. 1952. *The Confidence Years, 1885–1915*. New York: E.P. Dutton.

Brown, Michael. 2003. *Who Owns Native Culture?* Cambridge, MA: Harvard University Press.

Brown, Dee. 1971. *Bury My Heat at Wounded Knee: An Indian History of the American West*. New York: Bantam

Bryant, Keith L., Jr. 1978. "The Atchison, Topeka and Santa Fe Railway and the Development of the Taos and Santa Fe Art Colonies." *Western Historical Quarterly, 9*, 4 (October): 437–454.

Carbon County News. 2014. "Festival of Nations," August 1 & 2: 8.

Caven, Febna. 2013. "In Alliance as Native Youth Leaders, as Family." *Cultural Survival Quarterly, 32*, 2 (June): 14–15.

Coke, Van Deren. 1963. *Taos and Santa Fe: The Artist's Environment, 1882–1942*. Albuquerque: University of New Mexico Press.

Conquergood, Dwight. 2013. *Cultural Struggles; Performance, Ethnography, Praxis*, Edited, with an Introduction, by E. Patrick Johnson. Ann Arbor: University of Michigan Press.

Cotter, Holland. 2014. "Material Histories: Artists in Residence 2013–14: Art Review." *New York Times*, Weekend Arts, Friday (August 29): C17, C21.

Cowen, Mary S. 1981. "A Native Art: Timeless, But Still Changing." *Christian Science Monitor,* (June): 1–3. www.csmonitor.com/1981

Cunningham, Elizabeth J. 2008. "Building Color Muscle: The Path to Painting, 1874–1909." Pp. 11–64 in Peter H. Hassrick and Elizabeth J. Cunningham (Eds.), *In Contemporary Rhythm: The Art of Ernest Blumenschein*. Norman: University of Oklahoma Press.

Deloria, Vine, Jr. 1980. "The Indians." Pp. 45–56 in Brooklyn Museum (Ed.), *Buffalo Bill and the Wild West*. Brooklyn: Brooklyn Museum.

Deloria, Vine, Jr. 1974. *Behind the Trail of Broken Treaties: An Indian Declaration of Independence*. New York: Delacorte Press.

Deloria, Vine, Jr. 1969/1988. *Custer Died for Your Sins: An Indian Manifesto*. Norman: University of Oklahoma Press.

Deloria, Philip J. 2004. *Indians in Unexpected Places*. Lawrence: University of Kansas Press.

Deloria, Philip J. 1998. *Playing Indian*. New Haven, CT: Yale University Press.

Denzin, Norman K. 2014. Interpretive Autoethnography, 2nd ed. Thousand Oaks, CA: Sage.

⧉ References

Denzin, Norman K. 2013. *Global Indians: The Commodification of Native America in Performance, Art and Museums.* Walnut Creek, CA: Left Coast Press, Inc.

Denzin, Norman K. 2011. *Custer on Canvas: Representing Indians, Memory, and Violence in the New West.* Walnut Creek, CA: Left Coast Press, Inc.

Denzin, Norman K. 2008. *Searching for Yellowstone: Race, Gender, Family and Memory in the Postmodern West.* Walnut Creek, CA: Left Coast Press, Inc.

Denzin, Norman K. 2002. *Reading Race: Hollywood and the Cinema of Racial Violence.* London: Sage.

Dolan, Jill. 2005. *Utopia in Performance: Finding Hope at the Theatre.* Ann Arbor: University of Michigan Press.

Dorst, John D. 1999. *Looking West.* Philadelphia: University of Pennsylvania Press.

Du Bois, W. E. B. 1926. "Krigwa Players Little Negro Theatre: The Story of a Little Theatre Movement." *Crisis,* July: 134–136.

Dunn, Dorothy. 1968. *American Indian Painting of the Southwest and Plains Areas.* Albuquerque: University of New Mexico Press.

Eastman, Charles A. 1902. *Indian Boyhood,* with Illustrations by E. L. Blumenschein. New York: McClure.

Eldredge, Charles C., Julie Schimmel and William H. Truettner.1986. *Art in New Mexico, 1900–1944, Paths tio Taos and Santa Fe.* National Museum of Art, Smithsonian Institution, Washington, D.C. New York: Abbeville Press.

Ellison, Ralph. 1999. *Juneteenth.* New York: Random House.

Erdrich. Louise. 2010. *Shadow Tag.* New York: HarperCollins.

Fassnacht, Annette. 1936. "Exhibition Shows How Indian Artist Profits by Contact with Ancient, Modern Art." *Santa Fe New Mexican,* May 9: 3.

Faulkner, William. 1950. *Sanctuary* and *Requiem for a Nun,* two novels. New York: New American Library.

Fischer, David Hackett.1970. *Historians' Fallacies: Toward a Logic of Historical Thought.* New York: Harper Torchbooks.

Fox, Margalit. 2005. "R. C. Gorman, Painter of Strong Navajo Women." *New York Times,* November 5: www.nytimes.com/2005/11/05/arts/05gorman.htm

Freire, Paulo. 1992. *Pedagogy of Hope.* New York: Continuum.

Fried, Stephen. 2010. *Appetite for America: How Visionary Businessman Fred Harvey Build a Railroad Hospitality Empire that Civilized the Wild West.* New York: Bantam Books.

Garfield, Donald. 1995. "Interview with J. J. Brody on Museums." *El Palacio,* 100 (Summer): 18–54; archived Spring 2008, 113, 1; www.elpalacio.org/articles/spring08/brody

Gibson, Daniel and Kitty Leaken. 2014. *Kevin Red Star: Crow Indian Artist.* Layton, UT: Gibbs Smith.

Gilbert, Lois. 1980. "Tally Richards: Eleven Years Ago, Fritz Was 32." *ART*lines Archive: artlinesarchive.blogspot.com/2012/03/tally-richard-eleven-years-ago-fritz.html

Giroux, Henry and Grace Pollock. 2010. *The Mouse That Roared: Disney and the End of Innocence.* Updated and Expanded Edition. Boulder, CO: Roman & Littlefield.

Good, Stephen K. 1955. "The Taos Society of Artists: a Critical Overview." Pp. 11–21 in Laura A. Bickerstaff, *Pioneer Artists of Taos,* with an Introduction by Ernest L. Blumenschein. Denver: Sage Books.

Goodman, Susan and Carl Dawson. 2008. *Mary Austin and the American West*. Berkeley: University of California Press.

Gover, Kevin. 2008. "Foreword: A New Kind of Indian Art." Pp. 9–13 in Lowery Stokes Sims, with Truman T. Lowe, and Paul Chaat Smith (Eds.), *Fritz Scholder: Indian not Indian*. National Museum of the American Indian, Smithsonian Institution. London and New York: Prestel.

Graburn, Nelson H. H. 1976. "Introduction: The Arts of the Fourth World." Pp. 1–32 in Nelson H. H. Graburn (Ed.), *Ethnic and Tourist Arts: Cultural Expressions from the Fourth World*. Berkeley: University of California Press.

Graves, Jen. 2014. "Maybe Don't Wear a Warbonnet to the First-Ever All-Native Art Exhibit at Bumbershoot, and Don't Trip Over Custer." *Bumbershoot Guide*, August 27: www.thestranger.com/seattle/maybe-dont-wear-a-warbonnet-to-the-first-ever -all-native-art-exhibit-at-bumbershoot/Content?oid=20410649

Hall, Stuart. 1997. "What Is This 'Black' in Black Popular Culture?" Pp. 123–134 in Valerie Smith (Ed.), *Representing Blackness: Issues in film and video*. New Brunswick, NJ: Rutgers University Press.

Haraway, Donna. 1991. *Simians, Cyborgs, and Women*. New York: Routledge.

Hassrick, 2009a. "Ernest Blumenschein and the Indians." *The Magazine ANTIQUES*, November: www.themagazineantiques.com/articles/ernest-blumenschein-and-the -indians/print/

Hassrick, Peter, 2009b. "Taos Transformations: the Art of Ernest L. Blumenschein." Lecture given to the Taos Traditios, 2nd Annual Western Art Symposium, Denver Art Museum, January 6–25, 2009: taospainters.com/taos-high-road-western-art-collector.html

Hassrick, Peter. 2008. "Chasing Rainbows: Taos in the 1920s." Pp. 129–196 in Peter H. Hassrick and Elizabeth J. Cunningham (Eds.), *In Contemporary Rhythm: The Art of Ernest Blumenschein*. Norman: University of Oklahoma Press.

Hassrick, Peter H. and Elizabeth J. Cunningham (Eds.). 2008. *In Contemporary Rhythm: The Art of Ernest Blumenschein*. Norman: University of Oklahoma Press.

Hearne, Joana, 2012a. *Native Recognition: Indigenous Cinema and the Western*. Albany, NY: SUNY Press.

Hearne, Joana, 2012b. *Smoke Signals: Native Cinema Rising*. Lincoln: University of Nebraska Press.

Henhawk, Daniel A. 2013. "My Critical Awakening: A Process of Struggles and Decolonizing Hope." *International Review of Qualitative Research, 64* (Winter): 510–525.

Henningsen, Charles. 1983. *R. Gorman: A Portrait*. Text by Stephen Parks. Boston: Little, Brown and Company.

Hewett, Edgar L. 1948. *Ancient Life in the American Southwest: With an Introduction on the General History if the American Race*. New York: Tudor.

Highwater, Jamake. 1986. "Controversy in North American Art." Pp. 223–242 in Edwin L. Wade (Ed.), *The Arts of the North American Indian: Native Traditions in Evolution*. New York and Tulsa: Hudson Hills Press in Association with the Philbrook Arts Center.

Hill, Richard W., Sr. 2008. "The Institute of American Indian Arts and Contemporary Native Art." Pp. 121–135 in Lowery Stokes Sims, with Truman T. Lowe and Paul

References

Chaat Smith (Eds.). *Fritz Scholder: Indian not Indian*. National Museum of the American Indian, Smithsonian Institution. London and New York: Prestel.

Hoffman, Gerhard. 1986. "Frames of Reference: Native American Art in the Context of Modern and Postmodern Art." Pp. 283–307 in Edwin L. Wade (Ed.), *The Arts of the North American Indian: Native Traditions in Evolution*. New York and Tulsa: Hudson Hills Press in Association with the Philbrook Arts Center.

Howe, LeAnne. 2013a. *Choctalking on Other Realities*. San Francisco: Aunt Lute Books.

Howe, LeAnne. 2013b. "Review of Smoke Signals." Pp. 113–115 in LeAnne Howe, Harvey Markowitz and Denise K. Cummings (Eds.), *Seeing Red: Hollywood's Pixeled Skins*. East Lansing: Michigan State University Press.

Howe, LeAnne, Harvey Markowitz and Denise K. Cummings (Eds.). 2013. *Seeing Red: Hollywood's Pixeled Skins*. East Lansing: Michigan State University Press.

Hoxie, Frederick E. 2001. "Introduction." Pp. 1–28 in F. E. Hoxie (Ed.), *Talking Back to Civilization: Indian Voices from the Progressive Era*. Boston: Bedford/St. Martin's.

Jung, C. G. 1976. "The Pueblo Indians." Pp. 37–43 in Tony Hillerman (Ed.), *The Spell of New Mexico*. Albuquerque: University of New Mexico Press.

Kalshoven, Petra Tjitske. 2015. *Crafting the Indian: Knowledge, Desire & Play in Indianist Reeactment*. New York: Berghahn.

Kaufman, Moises and the Members of the Tectonic Theatre Project. 2001. *The Laramie Project*. New York: Vintage.

Kaufman, Moises, Leigh Fondakowski, Greg Pierotti, Andy Paris, and Stephen Belber 2014. *The Laramie Project: Ten Years Later*. New York: Vintage.

Kilpatrick, Jacquelyn. 1999. *Celluloid Indians: Native Americans and Film*. Lincoln: University of Nebraska Press.

Kittridge, William. 1996. *Who Owns the West?* San Francisco: Murray House.

Kovach, Margaret. 2010. *Indigenous Methodologies: Characteristics, Conversations, and Contexts*. Toronto: University of Toronto Press.

Laut, Agnes. 1898. "Taos, an Ancient American Capital." *Santa Fe Magazine*, 9, 3 (March): 228–235.

Limerick, Patricia Nelson. 2001. "Seeing and Being Seen: Tourism in the American West." Pp. 39–58 in David M. Wrobel and Patrick T. Long (Eds.), *Seeing and Being Seen: Tourism in the American West*, Foreword by Earl Pomeroy. Lawrence: University of Kansas Press.

Lowe, Truman T. 2008. "Scholder's Legacy: A Roundtable Discussion Moderated by Truman T. Lowe." Pp. 151–178 in Lowery Stokes Sims, with Truman T. Lowe, and Paul Chaat Smith (Eds.), *Fritz Scholder: Indian not Indian*. National Museum of the American Indian Smithsonian Institution. London and New York: Prestel.

Luhan, Mabel Dodge, 1947. *Taos and Its Artists*. New York: Duell, Sloab and Peare.

Lujan, Vernon G. 2003. "Anomalies of the Southwest Indian Painting Movement." Pp. 3–6 in Martinez, Albert Looking Elk, Albert Lujan, and Juan Mirabel, *Three Taos Pueblo Painters*. Taos, NM: Harwood Museum of Art of the University of New Mexico.

MacCannell, Dean. 1976. *The Tourist: A New Theory of the Leisure Class*. New York: Schocken Books.

Madison, D. Soyini. 2012. *Critical Ethnography: Method, Ethics, and Performance* (2nd ed.). Thousand Oaks, CA: Sage.

Madison, D. Soyini. 2010. *Acts of Activism: Human Rights as Radical Performance.* Cambridge, UK: Cambridge University Press.

Malik, Anjun. 2012. *The Lost Salford Sioux.* London: BBC Audiobook.

Martinez, Albert Looking Elk, Albert Lujan, Juan Mirabel. 2003. *Three Taos Pueblo Painters.* Taos: Harwood Museum of Art of the University of New Mexico.

May, Karl. 2008. *Winnetou I.* Translated by Marlies Bugmann. Copping, Australia: English Karl May Books (originally published 1893).

McNenly, Linda Scarangella. 2012. *Native Performers in Wild West Shows: From Buffalo Bill to Euro Disney.* Norman: University of Oklahoma Press.

Means, Russell, with Marvin J. Wold. 1995, *Where Men Fear to Tread: The Autobiography of Russell Means.* New York: St. Martin's Griffin.

Meyer, Carter Jones, 2001. "Saving the Pueblos." Pp. 190–211 in Carter Jones Meyer and Diana Royer (Eds.), *Selling the Indian: Commercializing & Appropriating American Indian Cultures.* Tucson: University of Arizona Press.

Meyer, Carter Jones and Diana Royer. 2001. "Introduction," Pp. xi–xix in Carter Jones Meyer and Diana Royer (Eds.), *Selling the Indian: Commercializing & Appropriating American Indian Cultures.* Tucson: University of Arizona Press.

Moses, L. G. 1996. *Wild West Shows and the Images of American Indians, 1883–1933.* Albuquerque: University of New Mexico Press.

Native Appropriations. July, 2013: "Repost: Why Tonto Matters." nativeappropriations. com/2013/07/repost-why-tonto-matters.html

Nelson, Willie. 1975. "Mama Don't Let Your Babies Grow Up to Be Cowboys." Written by Ed Bryce Bruce and Patsy Bruce, recorded by Ed Bruce, "Ed Bruce," Columbia Records.

New York Times. 2013. "Gift to Denver Museum Bolsters Its Western Art," *The Arts,* August 14: C1.

Nicholas, George. 2013. "Welcome from the IPinCH Director." *IPinCH Newsletter, 4,* 1 (Winter). www.academia.edu/211997/IPinCH_Newsletter_4.1

Oberg, Michael Leroy. 2010. *Native America: A History.* Malden, MA: Wiley-Blackwell.

O'Hern, John. 2008. "Acquiring the Masters: Starting a Collection of Taos Founders at Any Price Range." *Western Art Collector Magazine,* October: 3–5.

Ostler, Jeffrey. 2004. *The Plains Sioux and U. S. Colonialism from Lewis and Clark to Wounded Knee.* New York: Cambridge University Press.

Parks, Stephen. 1983. *R. C. Gorman: A Portrait.* Boston: Little, Brown and Company. Photographs by Chuck Henningsen.

Parsons, Elsie Clews. 1962. *Isleta Paintings.* Bureau of American Ethnology Bulletin 181. Washington, D. C.

Parsons, Elsie Clews. 1936. *Taos Pueblo,* General Series in Anthropology, Number 2. Menasha, WI: George Banta. New York: Johnson Reprint Corporation, 1970.

Pesquera, Yvonna. 2013. "'Third Chapter of Taos Art Colony' Noted by Harwood Museum." *Taos News,* May 17, 2013: m.taosnews.com/entertainment/arts/article_ d9b3c448-bef9-11e2-a846-0019bb2963f4.html?mode=jqm

Peters, Gerald P. III. 1988. "Foreword." P. 1 in Amy Scott, *The Taos Society of Artists: Masters and Masterpieces.* Santa Fe: Gerald Peters Gallery.

⠿ References

Peyer, Bernd C. 1989. "Who Is Afraid of AIM?" Pp. 550–564 in Christian F. Feest (Ed.), *Indians in Europe: An Interdisciplinary Collection of Essays.* Lincoln: University of Nebraska Press.

Phillips, Ruth B. 1998. *Trading Identities: The Souvenir in Native North America Art from the Northeast, 1700–1900.* Seattle: University of Washington Press.

Pirandello, Luigi. 1998a (1921). *Six Characters in Search of an Author.* Middlesex, UK: Penguin. (English Version and Introduction by Eric Bentley.)

Pirandello, Luigi. 1998b (1925). "Author's Preface." Pp. xix–xxx in Luigi Pirandello (1921), *Six Characters in Search of an Author.* Middlesex, UK: Penguin. (English Version and Introduction by Eric Bentley.)

Portalewska, Agnes. 2013. "An Award for a Fearless Woman: 2013 Ellen L. Lutz Indigenous Rights Award." *Cultural Survival Quarterly, 32,* 2 (June): 18–19.

Pratt, Mary Louise. 1992. *Imperial Eyes: Travel Writing and Transculturation.* New York: Routledge.

Raheja, Michelle H. 2010. *Reservation Reelism: Redfacing. Visual Sovereignty, and Representations of Native Americans in Film.* Lincoln: University of Nebraska Press.

Renaud, Rosanna. 2010. "Disneyland Paris Seeks New Recruits for Wild West Show," *Lakota Country Times, 6,* 30 (April 21–27): 1. www.lakotacountrytimes.com/news/2010-04-20/Front_Page/Disneyland_Paris_Seeks_New_Recruits_for_Wild_West_.html

Rudnick, Lois Palken. 1984. *Mabel Dodge Luhan: New Woman, New Worlds.* Albuquerque: University of New Mexico Press.

Russell, Don. 1970. *The Wild West: A History of Wild West Shows.* Fort Worth, TX: Amon Carter Museum.

Said, Edward. 1995. "Secular Interpretation, the Geographical Element, and the Methodology of Imperialism." Pp. 21–39 in Gyan Prakash (Ed.), *After Colonialism: Imperial Histories and Postcolonial Displacements.* Princeton, NJ: Princeton University Press.

Saldana, Johnny. 2011. *Ethnotheatre: Research from Page to Stage.* Walnut Creek, CA: Left Coast Press, Inc.

Saldana, Johnny. 2005. "An Introduction to Ethnodrama." Pp. 1–36 in J. Saldana (Ed.), *Ethnodrama: An Anthology of Reality Theatre.* Walnut Creek, CA: Left Coast Press, Inc.

Scare, Geoffrey and Robin Coningham (Eds.). 2012. *Appropriating the Past: Philosophical Perspectives on the Practice of Archaeology.* Cambridge, UK: Cambridge University Press.

Schimmel, Julie. 1994. "Introduction." Pp. xvii–xxiii in Julie Schimmel and Robert R. White, *Bert Geer Phillips and the Taos Art Colony.* Albuquerque: University of New Mexico Press.

Schimmel, Julie and Robert R. White. 1994. *Bert Geer Phillips and the Taos Art Colony.* Albuquerque: University of New Mexico Press.

Schrader, Robert Fay. 1983. *The Indian Arts & Crafts Board: As Aspect of New Deal Indian Policy.* Albuquerque: University of New Mexico Press.

Scott, Amy. 1998. *The Taos Society of Artists: Masters and Masterpieces.* Santa Fe, NM: Gerald Peters Gallery.

Sherman, Lisa. 1981. "Fritz Scholder: The Figure in Flux (1981)." *ARTlines* Archive, artlinesarchive.blogspot.com/2012/03/fritz-scholder-figure-in-flux-1981.html

Shipley, James R. and Allen S. Weller. 1969. *Contemporary American Painting and Sculpture*, Fourteenth Exhibition, Krannert Art Museum. University of Illinois Press.

Sides, Hampton. 2006. *Blood and Thunder: The Epic Story of Kit Carson and the Conquest of the American West*. New York: Anchor Books.

Sims, Lowery Stokes, 2008a. "Introduction." Pp. 19–24 in Lowery Stokes Sims, with Truman T. Lowe, and Paul Chaat Smith (Ed.), *Fritz Scholder: Indian not Indian*. National Museum of the American Indian Smithsonian Institution. London and New York: Prestel.

Sims, Lowery Stokes, 2008b. "Scholder's Figuration: Art and Culture in American Art." Pp. 77–120 in Lowery Stokes Sims, with Truman T. Lowe and Paul Chaat Smith (Ed.), *Fritz Scholder: Indian not Indian*. National Museum of the American Indian, Smithsonian Institution. London and New York: Prestel.

Sims, Lowery Stokes, with Truman T. Lowe, and Paul Chaat Smith (Ed.). 2008. *Fritz Scholder: Indian not Indian*. National Museum of the American Indian, Smithsonian Institution. London and New York: Prestel.

Skinner, Quentin. 2002. *Visions of Politics: Volume I, Regarding Method*. Cambridge, UK: Cambridge University Press.

Smith, Anna Deavere. 2004. *House Arrest and Piano*. New York: Anchor.

Smith, Anna Deavere. 2000. *Talk to Me: Listening Between the Lines*. New York: Random House.

Smith, Linda Tuhiwai. 2012. *Decolonizing Methodologies: Research and Indigenous Peoples* (2nd ed.). London: Zed Books.

Smith, Paul Chaat, 2008. "Monster Love." Pp. 25–36 in Lowery Stokes Sims, with Truman T. Lowe and Paul Chaat Smith (Ed.), *Fritz Scholder: Indian not Indian*. National Museum of the American Indian, Smithsonian Institution. London and New York: Prestel.

Smith, Paul Chaat, and Robert Warrior. 1996. *Like a Hurricane: The Indian Movement from Alcatraz to Wounded Knee*. New York: New Press.

Smith, Valerie. 1997. "Introduction." Pp. 1–12 in Valerie Smith (Ed.), *Representing Blackness: Issues in Film and Video*. New Brunswick, NJ: Rutgers University Press.

Stegner, Wallace. 1990. "Foreword." Pp. iv–xi in Wallace Stegner, *Collected Stories of Wallace Stegner*. New York: Penguin.

Strong, Pauline Turner. 2013. *American Indians and the American Imaginary*. Boulder, CO: Paradigm.

Taggett, Sherry Clayton, and Ted Schwartz. 1990. *Paintbrushes and Pistols: How the Taos Artists Sold the West*. Sante Fe, NM: John Muir.

Taylor, Bradley F. 2000. "Albert Lujan: Entrepreneurial Pueblo Painter of Tourist Art." *American Indian Art Magazine*, 25, 4 (Autumn): 56–65.

Thomas, W. I, and D. S. Thomas. 1928. *The Child in America: Behavior Problems and Programs*. New York: Knopf.

Trout, Lawana (Ed.). 1998. *Native American Literature: An Anthology*. New York: McGraw Hill.

Turk, Rudy H. 1972. "Commentary." P. 59 in *Fritz Scholder, Scholder/Indians*. Flagstaff, AZ: Northland Press.

Turner, Hannah. 2013. "Appropriation of the Month: Playing Dress-Up—'Cowboys and Indians.'" www.sfu.ca/ipinch/outputs/blog/appropriation-month (Posted by Kristen Dobbin, May 21, 2013.)

⏚ References

Ulmer, Gregory. 1989. *Teletheory: Grammatology in the Age of Video.* New York: Routledge.

Valdez, G., and A. Elsbree. 2005. "Queer Coyotes: Transforming Education to Be More Accepting, Affirming, and Supportive of Queer Individuals." *Journal of Latinos and Education, 4,* 3: 171–192.

Velie, Alan R. (Ed.). 1979/1991. *American Indian Literature: An Anthology.* Norman: University of Oklahoma Press (rev. ed., 1991).

Vizenor, Gerald. 2008. "Aesthetics of Survivance." Pp. 1–24 in Gerald Vizenor (Ed.), *Survivance: Narratives of Native Presence.* Lincoln and London: University of Nebraska Press.

Vizenor, Gerald. 1999. *Manifest Manners: Narratives on Postinindian Survivance.* Lincoln: University of Nebraska Press (original publication date 1994).

Warren, Louis S. 2005. *Buffalo Bill's America: William Cody and the Wild West Show.* New York: Alfred A. Knopf.

Warrior, Robert. 2005. *The People and the Word: Reading Native Nonfiction.* Minneapolis: University of Minnesota Press.

Wasserberger, Leslie. 2008. "An American Expressionist." Pp. 37–76 in Lowery Stokes Sims, with Truman T. Lowe and Paul Chaat Smith (Ed.), *Fritz Scholder: Indian not Indian.* National Museum of the American Indian, Smithsonian Institution. London and New York: Prestel.

Watson, Samuel E. III. 1994. "Stylistic Plurality in the Paintings of Albert Looking Elk: An Examination of Patronage." *American Indian Art Magazine, 20,* 1 (Winter): 62–69.

Waziyatawin and Michael Yellow Bird. 2013. "Introduction: Decolonizing Our Minds and Actions." Pp. 1–5 in Waziyatawin and Michael Yellow Bird (Eds.), *For Indigenous Minds Only: A Decolonization Handbook.* Santa Fe, NM: School of American Research Handbook.

Weller, Allen S., and C. V. Donovan, et al. 1948–1963. *Contemporary American Painting and Sculpture* (catalogs). Urbana: University of Illinois Press.

White, Robert R. 1994. "The Taos Art Colony and the Taos Society of Artists, 1911–1927." Pp. 65–83 in Julie Schimmel and Robert R. White, *Bert Geer Phillips and the Taos Art Colony.* Albuquerque: University of New Mexico Press.

White Deer, Waylon Gary. 2013. *Touched by Thunder.* Walnut Creek, CA: Left Coast Press, Inc.

Williams, Gary. 2006. "The Sioux of Salford." *Mirror News,* February 25: www.mirror. co.uk/news/uk-news/the-sioux-of-salford-580039

Witt, David L. 2003a. "Three Taos Pueblo Painters." *Resource Library Magazine,* March 12: www.tfaoi.com/aa/3aa/3aa495.htm

Witt, David L. 2003b. "Three Taos Pueblo Painters 2003." Pp. 7–15 in Albert Looking Elk Martinez, Albert Lujan, and Juan Mirabel, *Three Taos Pueblo Painters.* Taos: Harwood Museum of Art of the University of New Mexico.

Witt, David L. 1992. *Taos Moderns: Art of the New.* Santa Fe, NM: Red Crane Books.

Yellow Bird, Michael. 2005. "Tribal Critical Thinking Centers." Pp. 9–30 in Waziyatawin Angela Wilson and Michael Yellow Bird (Eds.), *For Indigenous Eyes Only: A Decolonization Handbook.* Santa Fe, NM: School of American Research Handbook.

Yellow Bird, Michael. 2004. "Cowboys and Indians: Toys of Genocide, Icons of American Colonization." *Wicazo Sa Review, 19* (Fall): 33–38.

Filmography: Indians on Film, an Incomplete List
1990–2013

Apocalypto (2006).
Atanarjuat: The Fast Runner (2001).
Black Robe (1991).
Bury My Heart at Wounded Knee (2007).
Cabaza de Vaca (1991).
Clearcut (1991).
Coyote Waits (2003, TV Movie)
Crazy Horse (1996, TV Movie).
Dance Me Outside (1994).
Dances with Wolves (1990).
Frozen River (2008).
Geronimo: American Legend (1993).
Into the West (2005).
Ishi: The Last of His Tribe (1992).
Last of the Dogmen (1995).
Last of the Mohicans (1992).
Lone Ranger (2013).
Meek's Cutoff (2010).
The Missing (2003).
New World (1995).
Pathfinder (2007).
Sioux City (1994).
Skins (2002).
Skinwalkers (2002 TV Movie).
Smoke Signals (1998).
Squanti: A Warrior's Tale (1994).
Tecumseh: The Last Warrior (1995).
Thief of Time (TV Movie) (2004).
Thunderheart (1992).
Windtalkers (2002).
Wind River (2001).

Index

A

abstractionism, 112
activist art, 161, 165
Adams, Kenneth Miller, 72
    airport art, 206n23. *See also* tourist art
Alexie, Sherman, 61, 170, 184
Allen, Mitch, 41
American Antiquities Act, 186
American Indian Movement (AIM), 138, 178, 191
American Indian Religious Freedom Act, 191
American Landscape (Scholder), 139
anti-war movement, 138
art. *See also* Native art/artist
    activist, 161, 165
    airport, 206n23
    authentic, 157–58
    ethnic, 206n23
    Indigenous, 100, 117–19
    lyrical abstract expressionism, 112
    murals, 113–14
    national, 160–62
    political, 141, 153
    post-Indian, 27, 126, 142, 165
    postmodern, 165–67
    radical, 133–36
    railroad, 86, 89, 159–160

    survivance, 154, 177
    tourist, 100, 115, 116–19, 206n23
assimilated fine art, 206n23
Atchison, Topeka and Santa Fe Railroad (ATSF), 25, 69, 86–87
Austin, Mary, 186, 188
authentic art, 157–58
Autry National Center of the American West, 165–66

B

Banks, Dennis, 190
Battle of Little Big Horn, 23, 139, 186
Battle of Wounded Knee, 24–25, 190
Bellocourt, Clyde, 190
Berninghaus, Oscar, 69, 72, 105
Biegert, Claus, 31
Blazing Saddles (film), 47
Blumenschein, Ernest
    commission work, 208n12
    describing Taos, 128
    on national art, 87
    on New Mexico landscape, 80
    on Taos Indians, 71
    as TSA member, 29, 69
    on validity of the primitive, 126
    on Wild West shows, 21–22
Bodmer, Karl, 15
Boyce, George, 70, 189, 196n9

INDIANS IN COLOR

Brady, Mathew, 141
Brenneman, Jina, 126–27
Brindza, Christina C., 130–31, 139–140
Broder, Patricia Janis, 24–25
Brody, J. J., 100, 117–18, 123, 196n7, 205n14
Brooks, Mel, 47
Buffalo Bill Historical Center (BBHC), 18
Buffalo Bill Wild West Show
    Blumenschein on, 21–22
    casting of, 38–40
    Disneyland Paris show, 22–23
    Native Americans as actors in, 23–24
    redfacing and, 22
    white fantasies about Indians, 182
Bumpershoot Wild West Show, 174–76
Bureau of American Ethnology (BAE), 69
Bureau of Indian Affairs, 185
Burke Act, 186
Bursum Act, 188

C

Calla Lilies with Red Anemone (O'Keeffe), 85
Cannon, T. C., 27
capitalism, 98
Carlisle School, 186
Carson, Kit, 113
cartoonists, 136
Catlin, George, 15, 45–46, 123
Chapter Three painters
    background of, 123–24
    challenge to romantic Noble Savage, 19
    Crumbo, Woody, 123
    Gorman, R. C., 19, 20, 123, 129, 143–45
    Harwood Museum of Art celebration of, 27
    interpreting, 130–32
    members, 123, 194
    origins of, 127–28
    Red Star, Kevin (*see* Red Star, Kevin)

Scholder, Fritz (*see* Scholder, Fritz)
    TSA painters vs., 132
    Wagner, Jim, 27, 123
Charging Elk, 42
Chatham, Russell, 137
Cody, William, 31
Cody's Wild West Show, 200n6
"Collector #5 or Osage with Van Gogh" (Cannon), 27
Collier, John, 188
colonial domination, 24, 62–63, 91, 96, 196n10
commercial fine art, 206n23
committed documentation, defined, 31
Couse, Eanger Irving, 71, 73, 89, 102
"Cowboy and Indian" movies, 16–17
Coyote, 33
Crow culture, 138, 155
Crow Indian Parade Rider (Red Star), 131
Crumbo, Woody, 123
cultural appropriation, 176
Curtis, Edward, 141
Custer's Last Stand, 170

D

Dawes Act, 186
de-Indianizing the Indian, 189
de Jesus, Juan, 74, 92
Deloria, Philip, 166
Deloria, Vine, Jr., 29, 111, 189
Denver Art Museum (DAM), 84–85, 198n25
Denzin, Norman K.
    as cultural tourist in postmodern west, 16
    white guilt and family, 18–19, 182
Depp, Johnny, 177
Dine Yazhi, Demian, 199n30
Disneyland Buffalo Bill Wild West Show
    Blumenschein's observations of Native Americans in, 22–23
    Carter Yellowbird as cast member of, 45
    casting of, 38–40
    Colonel Cody's Saloon, 49
    rehearsing for, 45–46

222

⚟ Index

Disneyland West, 90–91
Du Bois, W. E. B., 133
Dunn, Dorothy, 204n1
Dunton, W. Herbert, 26, 68, 70
Durand-Ruel, Auguste, 49–55

E
Early Institutional phase of Indian art, 196n7
Eaton, Marjorie, 113–14, 206n19
economic market conditions, 158
Eiteljorg, Harrison, 71
Eiteljorg Museum of American Indians and Western Art, 18, 25–26, 147–48, 162
Ellison, Ralph, 184
ethnic art, 206n23
ethnography, 107–8
European colonialism, 158

F
fair wages, 92
Fassnacht, Annette, 151
Federal Indian Policy, 185–192
Fred Harvey Company, 186
Fred Harvey Hotels, 90, 186
Fred Harvey Indian Department of Art, 86, 186
Fried, Stephen, 87
"Fritz Scholder: Indian/not Indian" exhibition, 27–28

G
Gomez, Geronimo, 74, 92
Gordon Bronitsky and Associates, 58
Gorman, R. C.
    as member of Chapter Three painters, 19, 123
    paintings of, 129
    as pop artist, 20
    solitude of, 143–45
Gover, Kevin, 140–41
Graburn, Nelson, 120
Green, Mary Shepherd, 197n14

H
Half-Breed (Scholder), 137
Hall, Stuart, 35
Harrison, Carter Henry, 16, 73, 88
The Harvest Dance of the Pueblo Indians of New Mexico, 69
Harvey, Fred, 69, 90, 186
Harvey Houses. *See* Fred Harvey Hotels
Harwood Museum of Art, 26, 94, 114–15
Hassrick, Peter, 71, 80
Heard Museum of Native Cultures and Art, 162
The Heartsong of Charging Elk (Welch), 42
Henhawk, Daniel A., 18, 195n2
Hennings, E. Martin, 72
Hewett, Edgar L., 82, 118, 151, 186, 187
Higgins, W. Victor, 72
Highwater, Jamake, 166–67
historical autoethnography, 33
Hobby Indians, 201n26
Ho-Chunk Nation, 58
Hogue, Alexander, 116
Hombre (film), 200n12

I
Idealist Dreamer Realist (Blumenshein), 203n19
Idiosyncratic phase of Indian art, 196n7
Indian art, defined, 195n4, 209n2
Indian artist. *See* Native art/artist
Indian Arts and Crafts Act, 191
Indian Arts and Crafts Board, 188
Indian Arts Fund, 188
Indian Arts Movement, 188
Indian Civilian Conservation Corps, 189
Indian Civilization Act, 185
Indian Civil Rights Act, 190
Indian Corn—Taos (Ufer), 67
Indian Detours, 90–91
Indian Factory System, 185
Indian Gaming Act, 191
Indian Industries League, 186
"Indian Painters and White Patrons" (play), 152
Indian Removal Act, 185

223

INDIANS IN COLOR

Indians. *See* Native Americans
Indian Self-Determination and Education
    Resistance Act, 191
Indian with a Tomahawk (Scholder), 131
Indian with Beer Can (Scholder), 143
Indigenous images. *See* Native art/artist
Indigenous tourist art, 100, 117–19
Institute of American Indian Art (IAIA)
    activist art, 161
    as agents of change, 181–82
    emergence of, 20, 123, 196n9
    faculty of, 190, 196n9
    founding of, 70, 189–190
    home of, 20–21
    Kevin Red Star at, 137
    radical art, 133–36
International Congress of Qualitative
    Inquiry, 195n2

J

Jung, C. C., 83, 96–97

K

Kalshoven, Petra, 201n21
King, Charles Bird, 15
Kovach, Margaret, 144, 184
Kramer, Kevin, 39, 45–46

L

Landscape with Indian Camp
    (Blumenschein), 80
Later Institutional phase of Indian art,
    196n7
Lawrence, D. H., 91
Leupp, Francis Ellington, 186
The Longest Walk, 191
The Longest Walk 2, 191
Looking Elk, Albert. *See* Martinez, Albert
    Looking Elk
Luhan, Mabel Dodge, 81, 188
Lujan, Albert
    as artist, 70, 92, 101–5, 115
    as TSA model, 26, 73
lyrical abstract expressionism, 112

M

Maddin, Guy, 183
Madison, D. Soyini, 33
marketing Native culture, 41
Martinez, Albert Looking Elk
    as artist, 70, 106–7
    cultural integrity of, 108–9
    on his car, 108–11
    as TSA model, 26, 74, 92, 105
Martinez, Crescenio, 205n13
Massacre at Wounded Knee (Scholder),
    139–140
McBride, Henry, 81
McNenly, Linda, 200n6, 201n24
Miller, Alfred Jacob, 15
Mirabal, Eva, 135–36
Mirabal, Juan
    as artist, 70, 92, 111–14
    Marjorie Eaton and, 113–14
    murals and, 113–14
    as TSA model, 26, 74
Miriam Report, 101–2, 204n4
movies, Cowboy and Indian, 16–17
murals, 113–14
Museum of Contemporary Native Arts,
    190
Museum of New Mexico, 70
My Winnipeg (film), 209n2
My Winnipeg (Maddin), 183

N

National Advisory Council on Indian
    Education, 190
national art, 160–62
National Congress of American Indians,
    190
National Council of American Indians,
    189
National Indian Youth Council (NIYC),
    189
National Museum of American Indian
    Art, 162
Native American Red Power movement,
    138, 190

Index

Native Americans
  artistic representations of, 20
  artists (*see* Native art/artist; Taos Three)
  art of (*see* Native art/artist)
  as authors of Indian stories, 42, 57
  character/emotion of famous, 42–44
  dark side of, 60
  as described by TSA painters, 71–73
  exploiting, 89
  redfacing, 41–42, 51–52, 59
  as re-enactors of a Wild West, 23–24
  religious practices in Taos, 82–83
  in search of an identity, 40–45
  as simulation, 62–63
  as subject of colonial domination, 96
  telling admiring stories about, 61
Native American story, writing of, 48–49
Native art/artist. *See also* Institute of American Indian Art (IAIA); Native Americans; *individual artists names*
  aboriginal roots of, 115
  artistic formations of, 19
  at Bumpershoot, 175–76
  cartoonists, 136
  chronological phases of, 196n7
  for commercial purposes, 41
  cultural integrity of, 108–9
  defined, 195n4, 209n2
  economic market conditions, 166–67
  impact on children, 145–46
  importance of, 120
  major movements of, 196n7
  native nationalism of, 120
  non-Native art vs., 147
  other artists' influences on, 148
  political representation of, 21, 141–42
  post-modern, 20
  role of, 15

  sacred spaces and, 125
  sense of place in, 144
  tourist art, 115, 117
  value of, 115
  versions of, 155
Native culture for white entertainment, 41
Native Spirit Production, 58
Native Taos painters, importance of, 120
Native writers, 42, 57
Navajo Code Talkers, 189
Nelson, Willie, 184
New, Lloyd Kiva, 27, 70, 133–34, 189, 196n9
Newman, Paul, 200n12
noble savage, 19–20, 25, 88, 90, 117, 123, 139, 181
non-Native art, 147

O

Oakley, Annie, 172
O'Hern, John, 203–4n22
O'Keeffe, Georgia, 85

P

"Paintings from the Past" (exhibit), 95, 122
Paris Disney Wild West Show. *See* Disneyland Buffalo Bill Wild West Show
Parks, Steven, 127–29
Parsons, Elsie, 25, 82–83, 108–11
The Patrol (Terpning), 166
persons of color, 20, 56
Petrie Institute of Western American Art (PIWAA), 84
peyote, 202n8
peyote boys, 108
Phillips, Bert, 69, 71, 121, 151
Phillips, Ruth, 100, 119, 120
political art, 141, 153
Poolaw, Horace, 208n13
Postindian, 196n10
post-Indian art/artists, 27, 126, 142, 165. *See also* Chapter Three painters
postmodern art, 165–67

225

Powell, John Wesley, 69
prairie niggers, 138, 208n10
Progressive Era, 186
Proto-modern phase of Indian art, 196n7
Public Law 280, 189
Pueblo culture, 79, 81, 82–83

R
racial identity, 35
racial myth, 35–36
racial stereotyping, 56
racism, 137–38, 196n10
radical art, 133–36
Radical Indigenous Survivance and
    Empowerment (R.I.S.E.), 177–79,
    199n30
Raheja, Michelle H., 20, 63
railroad art, 86, 89, 159–160
Rain in the Face (Red Star), 139
Red Cloud, Alice, 55–56
Red Cloud, William, 55–56
redfacing
    ending the practice of, 153
    Raheja's arguments concerning, 22
    for white entertainment, 41–42,
        51–52, 59
Red Nigger. *See* prairie niggers
Red Power movements, 138, 190
Red Star, Kevin
    anti-Custer paintings, 139
    Crow Indian Parade Rider, 131
    on Institute of American Indian
        Art, 134–35, 137–38, 196n9
    as member of Chapter Three paint-
        ers, 19
    paintings of, 130
    postindian art of, 27
    Rain in the Face, 139
Red Star, Wendy, 23, 30, 168–69
Reeves, Tom, 38, 39
religious practices in Taos, 82–83
Ribak, Luis, 112, 205n17
Rivera, Diego, 112, 113
Roath, Henry, 84
Rockefeller, John D., Jr., 188

Rockefeller Indian Art Project, 142
Rolshoven, Julius, 68
rough riders, 171–72
Russell, Charlie, 137

S
sacred rituals
    practice of, 20–21
    protection of, 20–21
    secretness of, 82–83
sacred spaces, 125, 144
Said, Edward, 120
San Geronimo Feast Day, 66, 92–93,
    198n23
Santa Fe festival, 187
Santa Fe Indian Fair, 188
Santa Fe Indian School, 102, 107, 140
Santa Fe-Taos Art movement, 74
Schimmel, Julie, 77, 79
Scholder, Fritz
    American Landscape, 139
    as Chapter Three painter, 19, 123
    description of, 206n24
    Half-Breed, 137
    as IAIA member, 135
    Indian with a Tomahawk, 131
    Indian with Beer Can, 143
    inspirations for, 148
    Massacre at Wounded Knee,
        139–140
    paintings of, 129–130
    painting subjects for, 136–37
    as pop artist, 20
    postindian art of, 27, 142
    rejecting image of noble savage, 139
    at Rockefeller Indian Art Project,
        142
    self-portraits, 137
School of American Research, 70, 186
self-portraits, 137
Self-taught phase of Indian art, 196n7
Seventh Generation Performers (SGP), 33
Sharp, Joseph Henry, 69, 85, 89, 102, 112
Silverheels, Mark, 46
Simpson, William H., 86–87

⊞ Index

simulation, discourses of, 62–63
Sitting Bull, 24–25, 45–46, 58
Smith, Anna Deavere, 33
Smith, Paul Chaat, 143, 152, 167
Smith, Valerie, 35
A Son of the War Chief (Berninghaus), 105
Spanish colonizers, 197n13
Squaw Winter (Sharp), 85
Stanley, John Mix, 15, 210n1
stereotypes, 35–36, 56, 57
Strand Theatre, 16
Supaman, 28, 131
Superstition (Blumenschein), 80
survivance, 154, 177, 196n10, 199n27
synchronicity, 205n15

T
Taos Chamber of Commerce, 76
Taos culture, Western capitalism destroying, 89
Taos Founders. *See also* Taos Society of
    Artists (TSA)
    Adams, Kenneth Miller, 72
    Berninghaus, Oscar, 69, 72, 105
    Blumenschein, Ernest (*see*
        Blumenschein, Ernest)
    Couse, Eanger Irving, 71, 73, 89,
        102
    Dunton, W. Herbert, 26, 68, 70
    Hennings, E. Martin, 72
    Higgins, W. Victor, 72
    Phillips, Bert, 69, 71, 121, 151
    Rolshoven, Julius, 68
    Sharp, Joseph Henry, 69, 85, 89,
        102, 112
    Ufer, Walter, 16, 25, 67, 72, 88–89
Taos Indians
    as described by TSA painters,
        71–73
    as marketable commodity, 81
    as our primitive, 126
Taos landscape, 156–57
Taos models, 73–75, 92–94
Taos Moderns, 125–27, 194
Taos painters. *See* Taos Society of Artists
    (TSA); Taos Three

Taos paintings. *See also* Taos Society of
    Artists (TSA)
    in Smithsonian, 78–80
    titles of, 78
    value of, 84–85
"Taos Plaza, Winter" (Hennings),
    202–3n11
Taos Pueblo. *See also* Pueblo culture
    admitted to World Heritage
        Society, 203n12
    anthropologists in, 82–83
    building of, 69
    description of, 75–76, 197n13
    as Disneyland, 149
    history of art in, 26
    outside influences on, 110
    revolt against Spanish colonizers,
        197n13
    as sovereign nation, 77
Taos Pueblo Culture Center, 95
A Taos Pueblo Painting of a Group of Taos
    Indians at Taos Pueblo (Lujan), 115
Taos Society of Artists (TSA). *See also*
    Taos Founders
    19th century artist's influence on,
        15
    activism of, 95
    Chapter Three painters vs., 132
    commercial endeavor of, 70–71
    description of, 159–160
    dissolution of, 70
    Eiteljorg paintings by, 26
    founding artists, 68, 70
    founding members, 193
    founding of, 68, 187
    idealized version of Taos and Taos
        Indian, 75
    models for, 26, 73–75
    painting Indians on demand, 98
    painting primitives, 87–89
    paintings as representations of
        dying culture, 24, 66
    paintings prices of, 74
    railroad art, 86, 89, 159–160
    Roath collection, 84

227

romanticizing the Taos Indian, 24–25, 188

Taos paintings, 78–80

Taos Three. *See also* Lujan, Albert; Martinez, Albert Looking Elk; Mirabal, Juan
  2003 exhibition, 162–63
  as agents of change, 181–82
  description of, 100–101
  founding members, 194
  Harwood Museum exhibit, 114–15
  importance of, 120
  museums' treatment of, 116
  Painting from the Past exhibit, 122
  paintings as authentic Indigenous art, 119
  rejection of, 163–64
  tourist art of, 116
  training of, 101–2
  views of, 162–64

Taos Trading Post (newspaper), 76

Taylor, Bradley F., 105

Terpning, Howard, 166

Third Chapter of Taos Art Colony. *See* Chapter Three painters

Thomas Theorem, 60

Three Forgotten Taos Pueblo Artists. *See* Taos Three

Tonto, 177

tourism, as form of cultural consumption, 86–87

tourist art, 100, 115, 116–19, 206n23

Tribal Governance Act, 191

Tribally Controlled Community College Assistance Act, 191

TSA painters. *See* Taos Society of Artists (TSA)

U

Ufer, Walter, 16, 25, 67, 72, 88–89

UN Declaration on the Rights of Indigenous Peoples, 192

UNESCO World Heritage Site, 197n13

"Untitled oil" (Looking Elk), 106

U.S. Geological Survey, 69

utopian performatives, 33–34

V

Vizenor, Gerald, 27, 62, 81, 91, 126, 154, 196n10

W

Wagner, Jim, 27, 123

Wal-si-see (Couse), 89

Watson, Samuel W., III, 115, 121

Welch, Jim, 42

Wendy Star's Wild West & Congress of Rough Riders of the World, 23, 168–174

Western art, 166

Western capitalism, 89

Wheelwright, Mary Cabot, 107

white culture, 141, 153, 156–57, 198n20

White Deer, Waylong Gary, 60–61, 184

Whitney Gallery of Western Art, 18, 130

Wild West Show. *See* Buffalo Bill Wild West Show; Bumpershoot Wild West Show; Cody's Wild West Show; Wendy Star's Wild West & Congress of Rough Riders of the World

Witt, David, 164

World Heritage Society, 203n12

Y

Yellowbird, Carter, 45, 57–58

About the Author

Norman K. Denzin is Distinguished Professor of Communications, College of Communications Scholar, and Research Professor of Communications, Sociology, and Humanities at the University of Illinois, Urbana-Champaign. One of the world's foremost authorities on qualitative research and cultural criticism, Denzin is the author or editor of more than four dozen books, three journals, and several book series on these topics.

This is the fourth volume in a series of Denzin studies that reconceptualizes the postmodern American West through a critical, racially sensitive, performative lens. Besides this volume, the series includes *Searching for Yellowstone* (2008), *Custer on Canvas* (2011), and *Indians on Display* (2013).

Denzin also serves as founding director of the International Congress of Qualitative Inquiry.